Labor and an Integrated Europe

Lloyd Ulman
Barry Eichengreen
William T. Dickens
editors

The Brookings Institution
Washington, D.C.

About Brookings

The Brookings Institution is a private nonprofit organization devoted to research, education, and publication on important issues of domestic and foreign policy. Its principal purpose is to bring knowledge to bear on current and emerging policy problems.

The Institution was founded on December 8, 1927, to merge the activities of the Institute for Government Research, founded in 1916, the Institute of Economics, founded in 1922, and the Robert Brookings Graduate School of Economics, founded in 1924.

The Institution maintains a position of neutrality on issues of public policy. Interpretations or conclusions in Brookings publications should be understood to be solely those of the authors.

Copyright © 1993

THE BROOKINGS INSTITUTION

1775 Massachusetts Avenue, N.W., Washington, D.C. 20036

Library of Congress Cataloging-in-Publication data:
Labor and an Integrated Europe
[edited by] Lloyd Ulman, Barry Eichengreen, William T. Dickens.
    p. cm.
    Includes bibliographical references and index.
    ISBN 0-8157-8682-4 (alk. paper)
    ISBN 0-8157-8681-6
    (pbk. : alk. paper)
    1. Industrial relations—European Economic Community countries.   2. Labor mobility—European Economic Community countries. 3. Labor market—European Economic Community countries. 4. Europe—Economic integration. I. Ulman, Lloyd.   II. Eichengreen, Barry J.
    III. Dickens, William T.
    HD8380.5.L33   1993
    331'.094—dc20   92–40273
                                                    CIP

9 8 7 6 5 4 3 2 1

The paper used in this publication meets the minimum requirements of the American National Standard for Information Sciences—Permanence of paper for Printed Library Materials, ANSI Z39.48–1984

Acknowledgments

THE EDITORS wish to acknowledge the financial support for the project provided by the Center for German and European Studies of the University of California, and for the assistance and support of its director, Professor Richard Buxbaum. They also thank the Institute of Industrial Relations at Berkeley for providing a venue for the series of authors' meetings where successive drafts of the chapters were discussed. The support of the National Commission for Employment Policy is also gratefully acknowledged. The authors thank Rebecca Krafft and Patricia Dewey who edited the manuscript, and Julia Petrarkis who provided the index. Finally, they thank Barbara Porter of the Institute of Industrial Relations for organizational assistance in the early stages of the project, Pamela Fox of U.C. Berkeley's Department of Economics for helping to assemble the final version of the manuscript, and Bobbie Figy of the same department for secretarial initiative throughout.

Contents

Tables

Figures

CHAPTER ONE

Labor and an Integrated Europe

Lloyd Ulman, Barry Eichengreen, and William T. Dickens

B y the end of the 1990s the European economy may be fundamentally transformed. In all likelihood, remaining barriers to the movement of commodities between member countries of the European Community will have been removed. Exchange controls will have been abolished, allowing capital to flow as freely between EC countries as it does between states of the United States. If the treaty negotiated at Maastricht in December 1991 is ratified and its provisions come into effect, existing European currencies will be abolished in favor of the ecu and existing central banks superseded by a European central bank.[1] The treaty's defeat in Denmark's June 1992 referendum, its ratification by an extremely narrow margin in France in September, the postponement of its consideration in Britain, the financial turbulence of the intervening period, and the internal strains that were intensified during the GATT negotiations leave us less than certain that these events will ultimately obtain. But some, if not all of them, could still come to pass. Thus currency unification (rather than a return to exchange rate flexibility) has been regarded as a preferred alternative to the fractured system of fixed exchange rates; the movements to reduce barriers to the mobility of goods and labor within the Community were initiated by the Treaty of Rome in 1957 and the Single European Act of 1987, both of which remain in place; and a more modest approach to political unification (featuring a less intrusive bureaucracy and a stricter construction of the doctrine of "subsidiarity") could yet prove both feasible and sufficient for essential policy purposes. And if such changes do come about, they will render the European economy virtually unrecognizable.

---

1. Although the Maastricht Treaty is concerned mainly with monetary unification, it touches on many other issues as well. For the text of the treaty, see Maastricht Treaty (1992).

Among the most far-reaching changes would be the transformation of Europe's labor market. Separate national labor markets would increasingly become a thing of the past. Mutual recognition of technical qualifications would be extended by all EC countries. It would become possible to transfer pension rights across frontiers. Migrants would have the same social security rights as natives, along with free access to job agencies. For the first time workers would be free to seek employment anywhere in the Community, and they may have powerful incentives to do so.

These changes pose profound challenges for workers, employers, and their collective representatives. The purpose of this volume is to identify these challenges and to analyze labor's likely response. The contributions distinguish three aspects of the problem. The first concerns the implications of economic integration for European industrial relations. Wage bargaining, work rules, training programs, and benefits—to mention only a few dimensions of industrial relations—are organized differently across European countries. So too are public welfare programs. Economic integration will bring increasing competition among these national systems and pressure for Community-wide harmonization of industrial relations and social welfare. How this process plays out—in particular whether competition among national systems is allowed simply to prevail, or more uniform systems of industrial relations and social welfare are imposed through consultation, legislation, and directives emanating from Brussels—is the first challenge the integration process poses for labor markets. Conversely, the success of the wider integration process itself will depend on how well the major institutional actors in Europe's national labor markets—politicians, business managers, and unionists—are able to reconcile their differing interests and, in some cases, ideological approaches.

A second, related challenge flows from the prospects for and constraints on labor mobility. True economic integration will entail a comprehensive sectoral and regional reorganization of Europe's national economies. The long-standing segmentation of Europe's internal market has traditionally sustained lower levels of sectoral specialization in member countries than is characteristic of regions in integrated continental economies such as the United States.[2] As the importance of proximity for market access declines, firms engaged in related activities are likely to cluster in order to exploit economies of scale and scope and to make use of local concentrations of the resources that they particularly require.

2. So it is argued, for example, in Krugman (1991). A more extensive analysis of data on the regional specialization of manufacturing in the United States and Europe which reaches the same conclusion is Bini-Smaghi and Vori (1992).

These changes in the location and composition of production will require accompanying changes in employment. Yet European workers have been notoriously hesitant to change occupations and to migrate between regions, even within European countries. Whether mobility will rise sufficiently to accommodate the restructuring of the economy implied by the integration process is the second challenge for European labor markets.

The third dimension of the problem is the challenge posed by European integration to labor markets in other parts of the world. The Cecchini Report, the document providing intellectual justification for the Single Market Program, forecasted a significant boost to European productivity from industrial restructuring and market integration.[3] For other industrial countries, including the United States, this implies an intensification of European competition as EC-based producers penetrate markets previously dominated by other firms. And if economic integration within Europe is accompanied by initiatives to limit the market access of competitors based outside the Community—the scenario popularly known as Fortress Europe—the challenge to the international competitive position of U.S. industry would be more serious still. How U.S. labor markets and institutions respond to this test is one external dimension of the problem. External repercussions will also be prominent in less developed parts of the world. Among the areas where they are likely to be most powerful is eastern Europe, for which the EC constitutes the leading prospective export market.[4] Although market access is paramount, the Community's policies toward guest workers from outside the EC will also have immediate implications for the transition to market-based economies in eastern Europe and the former Soviet republics, all of which wish to keep their skilled labor at home but also regard remittances as an important source of hard-currency earnings.

The challenges of the Single Market Program for European industrial relations, for European labor mobility, and for economies and labor markets in the rest of the world thus provide the focus for this volume.

Recent History and the Dynamics of Integration

To appreciate the nature of the problem, it is essential to understand the dynamics of European economic integration. The Treaty of Rome, initialed in 1957 by Belgium, France, Italy, Luxembourg, the Netherlands,

3. Tommaso Padoa-Schioppa and others (1987).
4. For an optimistic forecast of the prospects for trade between eastern Europe and the EC, see Collins and Rodrik (1990).

and West Germany, committed the signatories to moving toward a customs union free of import duties and quota restrictions on trade between member states. By the end of the 1960s, most overt tariffs on intra-European trade in goods had been removed. However, nontariff barriers, ranging from domestic procurement to technical standards, continued to balkanize European commodity markets. And little progress was made toward integrating markets for services, capital, and labor.

The 1970s saw a pause in the drive toward integration. Europe opted for a wider rather than deeper Community with the entry of Britain, Denmark, and Ireland in 1973. The collapse of the Bretton Woods System of fixed exchange rates complicated trade and financial relations within the EC, and efforts to stabilize European exchange rates proved less than satisfactory until the European Monetary System was established in 1979. The oil shocks of 1973 and 1979 and the unusually severe business cycle fluctuations that followed them encouraged governments to concentrate on domestic problems.

Associated with these difficulties were persistently high unemployment and disappointing economic growth. Newly elected conservative governments concluded in the early 1980s that both problems reflected the effects of excessive regulation. Domestic companies, shut out of markets in other Community countries as well as overseas, complained of their inability to compete with U.S. firms enjoying economies of scale as a result of their access to America's continental market. This diagnosis reinvigorated the process of European integration. Opening up European nations to competition from their neighbors within the Community was seen as a way of forcing them to reduce domestic regulation so that domestic firms might compete successfully with U.S. and Japanese rivals. European integration provided a way of creating a continental economy comparable in magnitude to North America, allowing European producers to reap economies of scale and scope.

The Single European Act, which came into effect in 1987, aimed at creating a unified market in commodities, capital, and labor by the end of 1992. Not only physical barriers but technical obstacles to competition and the free movement of goods throughout the Community were to be removed. The act moved significantly beyond the Treaty of Rome by forcing member countries not simply to remove trade barriers but also to eliminate domestic policies that significantly inhibited intra-European competition. It transcended the treaty by committing the signatories to creating a truly integrated market not just in goods but in capital and labor as well.

This strategy was controversial. Some countries, notably the United Kingdom, insisted that the benefits of integration could be reaped by the creation of a common market in goods and services alone; admitting the chill winds of competition did not also require forging a single market for European labor or creating a single European currency. But most officials adhered to the opposing position. Pressure to eliminate competitive barriers could be resisted, they insisted, so long as capital and labor markets remained segmented. Scale economies could not be reaped, they argued, unless factors of production as well as final products were free to move. The gains from regional specialization would remain incompletely exploited so long as distinct national currencies elevated transactions costs.

Others objected not that deeper economic integration was required to promote deregulation and intensify competition but that the end product was itself undesirable. They viewed the Single Market Program as an opportunity to harmonize European regulatory standards at high levels. This current can be traced all the way back to the Treaty of Rome (Articles 118–22), which had emphasized the need to address social and economic problems at the Community level. But the Single European Act lent new urgency to the issue. Initiatives designed to increase the mobility of capital and labor within the Community raised the specter of competitive deregulation, or "social dumping." Creation of a truly integrated European Community encompassing the Netherlands and Greece, two countries whose levels of wages and productivity differed markedly, raised the possibility that the wages and protection enjoyed by Dutch labor might be eroded by Greek competition. Dutch firms might be tempted to seek out cheaper labor abroad, saddling Holland with high unemployment unless its labor costs declined significantly. To enlist labor's support for the integration process, EC leaders therefore proposed in 1989 a Social Charter guaranteeing the establishment of minimum standards of compensation and welfare throughout the Community. To prevent the erosion of health and safety standards, the charter aimed to harmonize them at the EC level.

However, harmonization proposals like the Social Charter and the establishment of strong Community-wide labor and management institutions have aroused strong opposition (especially in the United Kingdom but elsewhere as well). Moreover, they do bespeak a considerable degree of political unification, so that the mauling of Maastricht has probably tended to dim their prospects somewhat. In any event, the controversy underscores the fact that the future of Europe's labor market looms large even in the debate over such seemingly remote issues as monetary unification.

Scope of the Book

The four chapters that make up part 1 of this volume address the future of industrial relations in an integrated European economy. Melvin Reder and Lloyd Ulman assess the impact of economic unification on European trade unions. They draw on U.S. experience to suggest that market integration gives rise to both centralizing and decentralizing tendencies. In the late nineteenth century, creation of an integrated U.S. market caused an increase in centralized bargaining as unions sought to eliminate geographic differences in wages and labor costs. A century later, intensified international competition has contributed to institutional decentralization and accelerated loss of membership among U.S. unions. Both tendencies are currently evident in Europe. The elimination of barriers to trade between eastern and western Germany has resulted in interregional unionism similar to that in the early United States. Whether this model of increasing centralization is applicable to the EC as a whole is questionable, however, given the relatively high levels of cultural and linguistic homogeneity characteristic of Germany. Other countries have witnessed some decentralization of industrial relations and weakening of industrywide mechanisms, echoing faintly the more pronounced U.S. trend in this direction. Reder and Ulman explain the absence of an equally dramatic decentralization of European labor relations in terms of the resilience of legal and private institutions found in Europe but largely absent in the United States: strong employers' associations, mandatory works council elections, effective deterrents to strikebreaking, extension of contracts to nonsignatory firms, representation of unions in public administration and on labor tribunals, and the legal restriction of certain benefits to union members.

However, to the extent that the dismantling of nontariff barriers to trade provokes radical industrial restructuring within the EC, decentralizing tendencies could be reinforced. Industrywide mechanisms would be weakened if unions were to come under pressure to preside over wage differentiation or if wage bargaining were subordinated to the settlement of issues at the local level through worker participation or codetermination.

Worker participation in management (WPM), one of the most controversial elements of the Social Charter, is the focus of Lowell Turner's chapter. Turner distinguishes negotiated from employer-led WPM. The negotiated variant, found in Germany, Denmark, Sweden, Belgium, and the Netherlands, rests on legal rights. It buttresses the strength of unions and employer associations. The employer-led version, found in countries where unions are not as strong, plays a much less integral role in the organization of work. It has even served as a device for excluding unions or keeping them weak, as, for example, in the United States.

Turner argues that the distinction between the two forms of worker participation lies at the heart of the Single Market debate and the Social Charter controversy. Business interests, which furnished much of the initiative behind the drive to deregulate markets, have resisted the spread of negotiated WPM as part of their opposition to reregulation of labor markets at the Community level. However, many employers in countries where high standards already prevail appreciate the value of raising standards elsewhere in the unified market to protect their competitive position. Within the ranks of labor there has also been division over the issue. French labor (especially the Communist-led union, the CGT) has not been enthusiastic. In contrast, German, Belgian, Dutch, and Danish workers share their employers' desire to export high standards to low-standard countries; they have therefore supported the employee information, consultation, and participation rights provided for by the Social Charter. Britain's traditionally insular Trades Union Council embraced the Social Charter to get out from under the heel of Mrs. Thatcher. For it as for other weakened labor movements, negotiated WPM as part of a supranational Social Charter offers a chance to regain political influence and organizational vitality.

Where Turner differentiates negotiated and employer-led worker participation in management, Wolfgang Streeck distinguishes between mandatory and voluntary cooperation between labor and management. Streeck argues that company-level codetermination combined with industry-level collective bargaining has compelled managers to act more efficiently and enabled them to secure the cooperation of their employees, thereby contributing substantially to Germany's industrial success as a high-wage, high-quality producer and exporter. Like Turner, Streeck therefore recommends for the Single Market industrial relations systems in which the extent of worker participation and labor-management cooperation is not limited by employers' perceptions of their self-interest. Like Reder and Ulman, Streeck also recognizes that multiple systems of industrial relations will likely prevail; all conclude that the centralizing influence of economic integration ultimately is unlikely to overwhelm deep national differences in industrial relations traditions and institutions, in union organizational strength, and in union opinion concerning the desirability of uniform Community-wide labor standards.

David Soskice and Ronald Schettkat present a case study of the German industrial relations system during the period when the integration of western and eastern German labor markets was begun. Like Streeck and other authors in this volume, Soskice and Schettkat argue that German labor market institutions are conducive to economic efficiency and growth in a modern technological order that places a premium on flexible adjustment and external competitiveness. A basic condition for competitiveness, in their view, is long-term employment relationships that encourage investments in training skilled and versatile workers. The system of codetermination, which underwrites the firm's commitment to long-term employment security and equitable treatment for workers, elicits and rewards employee trust and cooperation. In return, employee-elected works councils are forbidden by law to strike or engage in collective bargaining. Works councils enjoy a legal mandate but, according to Soskice and Schettkat, this is not a binding constraint on employers, for whom the councils serve as economically efficient instruments for producing high value-added goods. By implication, this German system should be eminently exportable and could serve as the basis of industrial relations for much of a unified Europe.[5]

The three chapters that make up part 2 consider the effects of European integration on labor mobility and the implications of probable future levels of mobility for the transformation of the European economy. Daniel Mitchell and Jacques Rojot analyze whether pension and health insurance arrangements are likely to constrain worker mobility. In the United States, where health coverage is provided by employers, insurers exclude preexisting conditions from coverage in order to discourage sick workers from shopping for jobs that offer good health coverage; workers with health problems consequently find it difficult to change jobs. By contrast, in Europe, nationally mandated health coverage removes this barrier to mobility. Although there is considerable variation across European countries in the form in which retirement income is delivered, Mitchell and Rojot argue that all of these arrangements are in fact con-

5. This contrasts with Streeck's position; he assigns greater importance to legal mandate and union economic pressure in ultimately forcing the employer's choice in favor of high value-added product lines, with considerably less sanguine implications for the future of labor market institutions.

ducive to worker mobility. In Germany state provision of social security promotes mobility. In France the existence of large negotiated pension schemes encourages it. In Britain it is enhanced by legislation requiring private pensions to be designed to allow portability. Thus Mitchell and Rojot conclude that compared with U.S. pension and health schemes European arrangements do little to penalize workers changing jobs. To the extent that labor mobility remains lower in Europe, it must be for other reasons.

Robert Flanagan examines the question of whether cross-country wage differences within the EC should be expected to narrow significantly as a result of the Single Market Program. Drawing evidence from the effects of earlier stages in the integration process, he finds that the thirty years that have passed since the Treaty of Rome have been marked by relatively little wage equalization across European countries. This contrasts with the experience of the United States, where the perfection of a national market has greatly narrowed regional differentials. Flanagan attributes the contrast to higher levels of geographic labor mobility in the United States, leading him to conclude that the post-1992 narrowing of European wage differentials will be small because cross-country labor mobility will be limited. He considers the possibility of Community-wide regulation of labor compensation but quickly dismisses it.

Barry Eichengreen explores the links between labor markets and European monetary unification. He asks whether individual European countries' inability to alter their exchange rates following monetary unification will exacerbate unemployment problems in regions containing high concentrations of industries sensitive to variations in exchange rates. He considers the variety of regional labor market responses to exchange rate changes in Britain and Italy, two of the countries that have experienced the most difficulty in keeping pace with the process of monetary unification, as well as in the United States, already a fully functioning monetary and economic union. Since geographic labor mobility is lower in both Britain and Italy than in the United States, removal of the exchange rate as an instrument to facilitate adjustment by trade-sensitive industries may be thought to give rise to more serious regional unemployment problems in Britain, Italy, and other European countries.[6] Eichengreen finds little support for this view. While there is considerable

6. On geographic labor mobility within European and North American countries, see OECD (1986).

variation in the response of unemployment to exchange rate changes across Italian and British regions, the range of responses is no greater than in the United States, a finding which Eichengreen explains in terms of the lower levels of regional specialization in Europe than in the United States. Thus, although monetary unification implies a loss of insulation from shocks emanating from neighboring countries or regions, in the short run Britain and Italy appear no more vulnerable than the United States to regional unemployment problems arising from this source. To the extent that regional specialization increases with market integration and deregulation, however, this conclusion is subject to change.

The final three chapters, part 3, analyze external dimensions of the Single Market Program. Bent Hansen notes that the removal of all remaining statutory obstacles to labor mobility within the Community will require the adoption of a common policy toward immigration from outside the EC. He observes that European immigration policies have traditionally taken two very different forms: rotation, typified by the policies of Germany and Switzerland; and permanent immigration restrictions of the sort applied by Sweden and the United Kingdom. In the future there will be strong pressure to harmonize these policies at the Community level. Drawing on Sweden's historical experience, he warns that permanent immigration policies would ultimately prove highly restrictive. Hansen therefore favors the rotation approach. In addition, he warns that the imposition of highly restrictive immigration policies may exacerbate mismatches in European labor markets, worsening the unemployment problem. He marshals historical evidence showing that outward shifts in the Beveridge curve (the relationship between job vacancy and unemployment rates) for various European countries have been associated with tightened immigration policies.

William Dickens considers a variety of possible routes whereby U.S. labor markets may be affected by European integration, emphasizing immigration, capital markets and trade. Immigration effects can essentially be dismissed, Dickens argues, since events in Europe are not of sufficient magnitude to provoke substantial immigration into the United States. The effect on capital markets is harder to predict. Several studies suggest that higher profitability in the EC will increase the demand for investment, raising global interest rates and crowding out capital formation in the United States. Forecasts of increased incomes also suggest, however, an increase in European savings. Dickens considers the potential size of these effects and concludes that even in the most pessimistic scenario this channel will have minimal impact on U.S. labor incomes.

The effects of integration on trade are also difficult to specify. Standard economic theory suggests that a preferential trading arrangement like the EC will have both trade-creating and trade-diverting effects. Dickens draws on evidence from earlier stages of European integration to conclude that the two sets of effects are likely to offset each other, leaving only a negligible impact on U.S. terms of trade and employment. One caveat concerns the possibility of a major trade war between the United States and the European Community, which could have major effects on employment in the United States. Dickens identifies several possible sources of tension that could lead to such a confrontation, the most of important of which is conflict over the EC's Common Agricultural Policy.

In the final chapter, Jasminka Sohinger and Daniel Rubinfeld explore the implications of western European integration for eastern Europe and its labor markets. The countries to the Community's east that are undergoing the transition to market economies are more likely to look to the Community than to the United States or Japan for a model for restructuring their own labor markets. Seeking EC membership, they will be inclined to design their labor market institutions to ensure compatibility with those of Community countries. More than other countries, they would suffer from a Fortress Europe that blocked access to western European export markets. More than any other region (with the possible exception of North Africa) eastern Europe would suffer ill effects from restrictive immigration policies. In the short run, the dislocations created in western Europe by the Single Market Program, especially if they give rise to regional concentrations of unemployment, may elicit protectionist trade and immigration policy responses. Sohinger and Rubinfeld convincingly argue that these policies would be damaging for eastern Europe and are therefore counterproductive for western Europe in the long run.

References

Bini-Smaghi, Lorenzo, and Silvia Vori. 1992. "Rating the EC as an Optimum Currency Area: Is It Worse than the U.S.?" Bank of Italy.

Collins, Susan M., and Dani Rodrik. 1991. *Eastern Europe and the Soviet Union in the World Economy.* Washington: Institute for International Economics.

Krugman, Paul. 1991. *Geography and Trade.* MIT Press.

Maastricht Treaty. 1992. *Treaty on European Union.* Brussels: Office for Official Publications of the European Communities.

OECD. 1986. *Flexibility in the Labour Market: The Current Debate.* Paris.

Padoa-Schioppa, Tommaso, and others. 1987. *Efficiency, Stability, and Equity: A Strategy for the Evolution of the Economic System of the European Community.* Oxford University Press.

CHAPTER TWO

Unionism and Unification

Melvin Reder and Lloyd Ulman

THE COMPLETION OF the European internal market finds labor movements on the defensive in most of the Western world. Regardless of how unions feel about an economically unified western Europe, they have been powerless to resist it and have been compelled to adjust as best they can. This paper outlines the adjustment opportunities available to European unions and the forces that weigh upon their choices. Although differences in societal and institutional terrains will produce perceptible differences in outcomes, it is our view that the forces bearing upon union institutional developments in post-1992 Europe will roughly parallel those that have operated in the United States over the past hundred years.

Conceptual Structure

The conceptual structure utilized here makes five behavioral assumptions about an individual's decision to join a union or to refrain from so doing. First, for most people, the decision regarding union affiliation is determined by the prevailing attitude among fellow workers and the employer. In effect, individuals' choices about unionism are determined by

The authors are most grateful to Lee Badgett and Caroline van Rijckeghem for their research assistance. We also wish to thank the following people for providing information and advice: Uschi Backes-Gellner, Paul Bailey, Christiana Breedz, Karl Casarini, Francois Eyraud, David Foden, Paulo Garonna, Alan Gladstone, David Henderson, Geir Hogsnes, Berndt Keller, Donald MacBain, John Martin, Bjorn Nilssen, Wilhelm Nolling, Muneto Ozaki, Alfred Pankert, Stephen Pursey, Berndt Reissert, Dieter Sadowski, Peter Scherer, Werner Sengenberger, Peter Schwanse, George Strauss, Peter Tergeist, Victor Thorp, Zygmunt Tyskieweiz, Michel Voirin, and Edward Yemen.

choice of workplace. Explicitly, we abstract from the complex issues involved in explaining group attitudes: these matters are considered to be a black box that transmits changes in the environment to individual attitudes and beliefs. At any given time, the members of a workplace group are assumed to weigh the advantages a union is perceived as bringing against the cost they perceive it to entail and to choose the more advantageous option. (When already unionized, they are assumed to choose among alternative courses of action in a similar manner.)

Although most people are conceived of as pursuing their own material advantage unhampered by commitments to institutions or ideologies, important exceptions exist. There are individuals to whom ideology or institutional identification is important, most significantly, full-time professional union officers. This group's relatively great concern with union affairs may at times give its members a disproportionate influence over organizational behavior and the formation of the larger group's attitudes.

Second, under normal circumstances, unions are assumed to act as though seeking the advantage of the typical member—as perceived by the member—subject to preservation of the organization and any ideological objectives the union's leaders may entertain. Normally, the potentially divergent objectives of the various participants in union decision-making are sufficiently harmonized to allow union behavior to be treated as reflecting a consensus.

Third, workers are assumed to expect that under unionism their wages and benefits will exceed what could be obtained otherwise. Failure to obtain the necessary minimum advantage will sooner or later provoke withdrawal from the union or disaffection with its present officers. Also, it is assumed that workers expect their union to deliver employment terms that, at a minimum, satisfy all relevant orbits of coercive comparison. Thus union behavior is constrained by the need to satisfy these expectations.

Fourth, both individuals and union organizations are considered as responding to external (exogenous) forces, and not as initiators of change. Although this perspective is not appropriate to every context, it is useful here.

Fifth, private sector employers are considered to be profit seekers whose behavior toward unions derives from the effect on long-term profits they perceive such behavior as exerting. One particular implication of profit maximizing behavior is applied here: employers weigh the gains from being free of unions against the cost of fending off union attempts at enrolling their employees. Any exogenous increase in the cost of repelling unionization will reduce such efforts and increase the probability of union success at organizing.

Our conceptual framework also relies on certain simplifications of economic history. First, in analyzing private sector behavior, we make one specific departure from conventional static equilibrium frameworks: we assume the existence of a region (such as the United States or the EC) made up of two or more sectors one of which provides real wages and benefits distinctly higher than the other(s). The high-wage sector is analogous to the developed or advanced sector in dual-economy models and the low-wage sector to the traditional or underdeveloped sector.

The high-wage sector is assumed to be strongly unionized, while the low-wage sector is either nonunion or weakly unionized. Although prior assumptions suggest that unionism contributes to the unionized sector's high wages, our argument would be unaffected if the high-wage characteristic of the unionized sector were due entirely to other factors. Whatever the cause of the correlation, however, unions are assumed to be concerned with preventing intersectoral wage differentials from causing loss of member employment, either through imports or labor migration (whether interregional or international).

Second, to satisfy member demands for higher wages or benefits, the union organization or its span of control must be at least as broad as the product market. Otherwise, nonunionized firms would be able to sell goods for lower prices than unionized firms, resulting in loss of union jobs and declining membership.[1] Furthermore, within a given union organization, coordination of wage and employment policy must be coextensive with the area of market competition. As far as the product market is concerned, such coordination is needed to prevent firms with lower unit-labor costs from gaining market share and employment at the expense of higher-cost competitors. In labor markets, freedom to migrate interweaves employment terms and labor supply within the area of free migration such that coordination of rules and contract terms becomes essential to protect local standards. Centralization of rulemaking authority within unions has been an indispensable means of effecting the necessary coordination among local union branches.

---

1. That is, assuming that hourly labor productivity is uniform across firms. Often this does not hold; in particular, higher union wages may parallel higher productivity of union workers. For our purposes, it is assumed that the relevant union-nonunion wage differentials are not completely offset by differences in labor productivity, so that higher wages imply higher unit-labor costs.

Therefore, organizational decline may occur under either of two conditions.

—When product markets become spatially extended or further integrated, *unless* union organization expands with the market, or union decisionmaking becomes more centralized.

—When union organization shrinks within existing market boundaries, *unless* negotiated wage increases cause nonunion workers to join unions or regulations or other arrangements bar nonunion entry or operation.

Two U.S. Episodes

This conceptual structure is useful in discussing and interpreting two episodes in the history of U.S. labor relations that have a bearing on European prospects. Both episodes involved organizational responses to extended or intensified competition in product or labor markets.

Certain behavioral traits of U.S. unionists and employers have long been regarded as "exceptional" by students of comparative industrial relations. U.S. unionists as a whole have displayed a strong preference for aggressive collective bargaining over political action (or any alternative instrumentality). U.S. employers tend to prefer individual bargaining over collective bargaining; short of that, large-scale employers as a whole prefer to bargain collectively at the company rather than the industry level. As a result, most American unions' bargaining power has ordinarily exceeded their "organizing power" because unions could not succeed in "organizing plants of nonunion employers as fast as they took business from union employers."[2] Organizing costs were effectively reduced by the passage of the National Labor Relations Act in the 1930s, which obliged employers to bargain in good faith with unions if a majority of their employees had voted for them. But this landmark legislation did nothing to prevent nonunion employers from entering the field, gaining market share, and undermining unions in the process. (In short, one of the conditions averting organizational shrinkage failed to obtain.)

Single-mindedness on the part of both unionists and employers has also been reflected in organizational responsiveness to changes in market structures. In the first U.S. episode, unionists responded to the expansion of product and labor markets in the late nineteenth and early twentieth

2. Slichter (1941, p. 347).

centuries by forming or strengthening national unions. National unions proliferated, pursuing a number of interrelated objectives: to raise wages in low-wage areas, protecting jobs in high-wage areas; to resist competitive wage-cutting in bad times, maintaining control of the industrywide wage level; to deny a whipsaw advantage to multiplant firms by bargaining on a companywide basis;[3] to keep migrant members unionized by issuing national "traveling cards," thereby protecting local closed-shop arrangements and discouraging the use of migrants as strikebreakers; and to organize nonunion firms. In pursuit of these objectives—especially the first three—the national unions sought to acquire extensive control over bargaining and striking. To this end they built up treasuries, developed expert staff, and evolved bureaucratic organizations. By the end of the nineteenth century, national unionism became the dominant structural form in the U.S. union movement, with control over local unions and autonomy from the central federations (which have had no power over collective bargaining).

As they organized large-scale manufacturing firms in the late 1930s and the wartime forties, national unions in the United States developed two characteristics that increased the scope of their bargaining power as well as their authority. (These also came to distinguish them from most European unions.) First was their involvement in determining conditions of employment on the shop floor (nonpecuniary and monetary). This arose from the national unions' participation in the negotiation of local supplemental agreements and in the administration and interpretation of collective agreements through their representatives on union-management grievance committees. A second characteristic was the tendency for national unions to deal on a company-by-company basis with firms in highly concentrated industries rather than with industry associations, as is customary in Europe.[4] Although the objective generally has been to achieve a pattern of similar settlements, the process of sequential bargaining—or striking—can give the national union a whipsaw advantage. Sequential bargaining also permits the national union to discriminate in favor of firms with distinctly lower levels of profitability. Single-employer bargaining, moreover, has been congenial to large-scale employers willing to forgo the benefits of united resistance in order to keep wage and other policies in their own hands. Multiemployer bargaining, on the other hand, has been most common in highly competitive indus-

3. A whipsaw occurs when a firm (or union) that can deal separately with unions (or firms) in its plants can threaten to shut each one in turn while allowing others to work.
4. Greenberg (1966); Hendricks and Kahn (1982); Mishel (1986).

tries with many small firms, where neither whipsawing nor discrimina-tory wage setting is a viable option for national unions and where em-ployers place a high premium on unified resistance and removing wages from competition.

The second key episode involved the increased internationalization of manufacturing markets in the 1970s and 1980s and the movement to deregulate key sheltered sectors of the economy. (This latter eliminated government controls on price and market entry that had protected many unions quite comfortably.) Union organization relative to the labor force actually began to decline in the mid-1950s as a number of develop-ments—including more restrictive federal and state legislation and the refinement of high-wage human relations personnel policies—enhanced nonunion firms' capacity to resist organization. In the 1970s and 1980s, unions found it particularly difficult to organize nonunion firms in the face of pressures imposed by the presence of foreign competitors. U.S. unions were clearly unable to organize foreign workers (many of whom were union members in their own countries). Nothing short of interna-tional unionism could have coped with international competition, but barriers created by distance, language, and culture ruled it out. Many U.S. national unions were left at the water's edge.

International competition and domestic deregulation placed central-ized institutional arrangements and structures—pattern bargaining, multiemployer bargaining, and even national unions themselves—under great strain. Some of the largest and strongest industrial unions (in au-tomobile, steel, and tire manufacturing, for instance) found themselves to be potential whipsaw victims under intensified competition after hav-ing enjoyed such an advantage for years in company-by-company bar-gaining under oligopolistic conditions. Large-scale employers, whether confronted with the necessity of reducing overall capacity or simply ca-pable of replacing domestic with foreign capacity, demanded that local unions eliminate restrictive work practices and pitted them against each other in rounds of "concessionary" wage bargaining. In addition, some of the leading industrywide bargaining structures broke down (in bitu-minous coal, trucking, construction, basic steel, and other areas) or were abandoned under pressure from nonunion and import competition. As a result, many firms broke away from employer associations.

Any comparison of these two episodes—widely separated in time, economic circumstances, and institutional conditions—must be suspect. Should such a comparison be ventured, however, it might tentatively yield a dichotomous conclusion, that is, if a significant increase in the

scope or intensity of competition fails to result in structural centralization (and possibly an extension of organization) under pressure from
trade unionists strongly oriented toward bargaining, it will instead provide decentralization and a possible decline in union membership under
pressure from strongly individualistic employers.

The Recent European Experience

Will the completion of the European internal market in the 1990s result
in competitive pressures on organized labor markets of the kind that
required and ultimately elicited the increased centralization of bargaining structures in the United States a century ago? Or will the removal of
nontariff barriers in western Europe contribute instead to decentralization and disorganization, as domestic deregulation and import penetra-
tion have tended to do in the United States in the recent past?

Wage Differences and Resource Allocation within the EC

The elimination of nontariff barriers to trade (via the removal of bor-
der controls and the harmonization of technical standards of product
acceptability) within the Economic Community will tend to reduce
the selling costs of intracommunity exports, just as innovations in transportation tended to reduce the costs of intracontinental shipping in the
nineteenth-century United States. On the other hand, hourly wage differentials among the northern countries (excluding the United Kingdom)
are already quite small, as table 2-1 indicates.[5] Therefore these wage
differentials should not furnish a compelling incentive for marketwide
centralization of existing union organizations after completion of the internal market.[6]

North-south wage differentials, however, are still pronounced. Wages
within the European south (Greece, Spain, and Portugal) are markedly
lower than elsewhere in the EC (table 2-1). Unionists and others claim
that these geographic wage differences are offset by differences in labor
quality (as determined by educational and skill levels) and, further, that

5. See also Flanagan in this volume.
6. Neven (1990) shows that within northern Europe, the dispersion of percentage differences in monthly labor costs across countries is not much greater than the analogous
dispersions within (across regions of) the individual countries.

Table 2-1. *European North-South Wage Differentials and U.S.-European Labor Costs, by Wage Component, 1984, 1989*

Compensation components	Dispersion of wages and benefits in Western Europe (coefficient of variation)		Hourly labor costs in manufacturing (percent)		
	Europe[a]	Europe excluding Greece and Portugal	Europe	Europe excluding Greece and Portugal	United States (1989)
Direct[b]	0.36	0.15	78.6	78.7	72.0
Customary[c]	0.78	0.61	4.2	4.7	19.4
Statutory[d]	0.63	0.53	16.0	15.8	8.5
Other[e]	7.78	8.36	1.3	0.7	...
Total[f]	0.36	0.16	100.0	100.0	100.0

Sources: Eurostat, *National Accounts ESA Aggregates, 1970–1987* (Luxembourg). Eurostat, *Labour Costs Survey 1984* (Luxembourg), table 17; *Statistical Abstract of the United States: 1990*.

a. Europe includes Belgium, Denmark, France, West Germany, Greece, Ireland, Italy, Luxembourg, the Netherlands, Portugal, and the United Kingdom. (Data lacking for Spain.)

b. Direct costs for Europe consist of direct earnings for bonuses and premiums, payments for days not worked, and payments in kind. U.S. direct costs are wages, salaries, and supplemental pay (premiums, nonproduction bonuses, and shift pay).

c. European customary, contractual, or voluntary payments include insurance plans operated by the enterprise or the sector, supplementary retirement pension plans, contractual or voluntary guaranteed sick or accident pay, supplementary unemployment insurance, contractual family allowances and other family benefits, and other payments. U.S. customary compensation includes paid leave (vacation, holiday, sick pay, and other), insurance, pensions, and savings plans.

d. European statutory expenditures on social security include sickness and retirement, unemployment insurance, guaranteed sick pay, insurance against industrial accidents and occupational diseases, family allowances, and other. U.S. statutory compensation is social security, federal and state unemployment, and workers' compensation.

e. Other European costs are other expenditures (transport, cultural, and medical facilities), vocational training costs, and taxes minus statutory social subsidies.

f. Columns may not add because of rounding.

modern industry requires more highly skilled and less unskilled labor.[7] However, wages for semiskilled and unskilled labor tend to be depressed in regions that are still heavily agricultural. This tends to make those workers competitive with labor in countries to the north; and further liberalization of capital flows and of government procurement could make them more competitive after 1992.

Elimination of barriers to trade and factor mobility between eastern and western Germany has resulted in a contemporary European demonstration of interregional unionism on the early U.S. model. German unification revealed extreme wage disparities between the two regions and aroused fears among west German unions of large-scale migration of labor from east to west and of jobs in the opposite direction. Their apprehensions were sufficiently strong to lead the DGB (the west German labor confederation) to organize afresh or take over preexisting com-

7. German unionists sometimes argue that their best defense against competition from low-wage foreign labor lies in utilizing their existing national systems of collective bargaining to secure sufficient employer investment in the human capital of their members to maintain or improve their qualitative edge in technical sophistication and versatility.

munist unions, to establish centralized control over the newly unified organizations, and to bargain vigorously to reduce geographic pay differentials. The effectiveness of these organizing and bargaining activities owes in large part to the relatively high degree of cultural and linguistic homogeneity. It also reflects thoroughgoing political unification and, as a result, uniformity of labor market regulations and social welfare standards. In these respects, contemporary Germany resembles the earlier (and present) U.S. setting and differs from the heterogenous environmental conditions prevailing in the EC.

Nonwage Differences and Social Dumping

Compared with their American precursors, contemporary European unions have been less concerned with controlling wage differentials and maintaining centralized collective bargaining institutions than with differentials in a wide variety of nonwage categories. These have been established by various statutory authorities and from a union viewpoint suggest a correlative need for supranational political institutions. In the nineteenth-century United States, of course, nonwage elements constituted a very small component of labor costs. Yet even today statutorily mandated nonwage components constitute a considerably more important part of labor incomes and employer costs in Europe than in the United States. This is reflected in table 2-1, where the U.S. hourly and customary (privately compensated benefit) components of total labor cost are lower than in Europe, although the statutory social security components are higher. Table 2-1 also reveals that among European countries the dispersion of statutory nonwage costs has been much greater than the dispersion of direct labor costs, even when Greece and Portugal are omitted.

Hence, the conditions exist for social dumping to occur within the Community. That is, countries in the south stand to gain a competitive advantage by tolerating lower standards of social welfare, job safety, and health care among the work force; permitting greater environmental damage in the course of production; and generally exploiting their lower total hourly labor costs to expand their share of EC manufacturing employment. The European Commission has taken the lead in proposing that minimum standards be established for parental leave, length of the work week, paid vacations, and other aspects of family labor supply. These concerns are summed up in the call for a Social Charter, the focal point of labor union and social democratic demands for Community legislation.

In pressing for the Social Charter, however, unions are confronted by the principle of subsidiarity, which directs the Community to allow every governmental function to be performed at the lowest level at which it can be effectively performed. However vague, this precept has been emphasized by opponents of government intervention and also by various employer groups.

Contemporary European unions must also contend with member governments whose national interests in maintaining international competitiveness as well as high levels of employment and social welfare lead them to take an active part in a fairly complex international game. This game involves a three-way trade-off among Community-wide minimum standards with their associated labor costs, levels of subsidies by the richer countries to poorer ones via EC regional welfare funds, and the degree of compliance and enforcement actually practiced within each member country.

The effect of economic regulations depends not only on statutory provisions but also on the manner of their administration. Any regulation of working conditions that the Community adopts in the foreseeable future will be administered by national and even local authorities. International enforcement may ultimately occur, primarily through decisions of the European Court, but as yet a European bureaucracy of workplace inspectors has not been seriously proposed. However, if the International Labor Organization practice is a model, the European Commission could subject noncomplying national authorities to public pressure.[8]

Countries that stand to make export gains because of substandard domestic working conditions would benefit from lax enforcement of Community standards. The employment opportunities of workers in those countries would be enhanced. Unions in those countries would face conflicting options: they could demand that community standards for hours and working conditions be maintained and blow the whistle on violators; or they could turn a blind eye to employers and local inspectors who breach standards in order to lower labor costs and increase employment.

Such unions may vacillate between demanding enforcement when employment is high and acquiescing to lax enforcement when job opportunities are scarce. In either situation, the existence of Community regulations will constitute a bargaining chip useful in wage negotiations with

8. Bohning (1987).

employers. In the developed countries unions would welcome such regulations because their own members would be ready to subject them to even higher standards—and anything that raised the costs of low-wage competitors would help protect their jobs and wages. It is worth noting that it is the union movements in countries with the most advanced systems of social welfare and labor standards that have exercised the initiative in pressing for the Social Charter, just as in the United States it was the high-wage local unions that pressed for strong national unions.

Differences in Organizational Experience

Union membership decline and organizational deterioration on the scale experienced in the United States has not occurred in most European countries. The behavior of union density in the United States is shown in the first column of table 2-2. Between 1970 and 1988, the unionized portion of the U.S. labor force declined by more than one-third—from 25 percent to 16 percent. Two-thirds of this total was concentrated in the 1980s.

In the 1980s, however, unionized labor forces also declined in Austria, France, Germany, Italy, the Netherlands, Switzerland, and the United Kingdom. In Sweden and Denmark the rates of membership gain were markedly lower than in the previous decade (although membership densities in those countries left little room for increase). Recent declines in density have raised concerns that deterioration in the United States may presage European developments, with or without unification. For instance, Leo Troy attributes transatlantic differences in organizational experiences to two primary differences in labor market structure:[9] the late growth of union-resistant service sectors in Europe and the early growth of union-prone public sectors in Europe. Hence, he sees sectoral shifts as a major factor in explaining international differences in union density or organizational strength, as opposed to, for instance, differences in employers' responses to unions or in laws or social welfare institutions.[10] Troy proceeds by comparing union densities in market sectors (including employment in enterprises in the public sector), which declined in almost all European countries during the 1980s, though to a smaller degree than in the United States.[11]

9. Troy (1990).
10. Freeman (1988).
11. Column 3 of table 2-2 gives measures of manufacturing density by sector. By excluding services, however, it excludes one of the structural shifts featured in Troy's analysis. Column 2 shows fewer actual declines in density than do Troy's data, and it shows smaller

Table 2-2. *Union Membership Density by Country, Market Sector, and Manufacturing Sector, Selected Years, 1970–88*[a]
Percent

	Austria			Belgium			Denmark		
Year	Economy	Market	Mfg.	Economy	Market	Mfg.	Economy	Market	Mfg.[b,c]
1970	59.8	54.6	68	46.0	n.a.	60	60.0	56.7	80
1975	56.1	50.9	n.a.	55.3	n.a.	n.a.	67.4	67.4	n.a.
1980	53.8	48.9	63	56.5	n.a.	88	76.5	69.3	98
1985	48.6	43.9	56	54.3	n.a.	90	78.3	77.1	100
1988	45.7	41.2	53	53.0	n.a.	95	73.2	72.0	100
Percentage point change									
1970–88	− 14.1	− 13.4	− 15	7.0	n.a.	35	13.2	15.3	20
1970–85	− 11.2	− 10.7	− 12	8.3	n.a.	30	18.3	20.4	20
1970–80	− 6.0	− 5.7	− 5	10.5	n.a.	28	16.5	12.6	18
1980–85	− 5.2	− 5.0	− 7	− 2.2	n.a.	2	1.8	7.8	2
1985–88	− 2.9	− 2.7	− 3	− 1.3	n.a.	5	− 5.1	− 5.1	0

	Netherlands			Norway			Sweden		
	Economy	Market	Mfg.[b]	Economy	Market	Mfg.[c]	Economy	Market	Mfg.
1970	37.0	29.4	41	50.6	43.2	67	67.7	n.a.	84
1975	38.4	19.9	n.a.	52.7	44.8	n.a.	74.5	n.a.	n.a.
1980	35.3	26.2	42	56.9	46.8	81	80.0	79.7	95
1985	28.7	20.3	34	55.7	43.3	85	84.0	82.1	100
1988	25.0	n.a.	25	57.1	41.3	87	85.3	81.3	100
Percentage point change									
1970–88	− 12.0	n.a.	− 16	6.5	− 1.9	20	17.6	n.a.	16
1970–85	− 8.3	− 9.1	− 7	5.1	0.1	18	16.3	n.a.	16
1970–80	− 1.7	− 3.2	1	6.3	3.6	14	12.3	n.a.	11
1980–85	− 6.6	− 5.9	− 8	− 1.2	− 3.5	4	4.0	2.4	5
1985–88	− 3.7	n.a.	− 9	1.4	− 2.0	2	1.3	− 0.8	0

Source: Visser (1991).
n.a. Not available.
a. Based on total employment figures adjusted to exclude retired, unemployed, and self-employed persons.
b. Mining is included in manufacturing.
c. Electricity, gas, and water are included in manufacturing.

Nevertheless, whether unionism in the private (or market) sector remains more robust in Europe than in the United States also depends in large part on how much support and protection each union movement receives from the framework of national legal, social, and political institutions in which it is embedded.

declines or greater increases than the densities based on labor force (in column 1). However, it also shows that all European countries experienced smaller increases or greater decreases in industrial employment density in the 1980s than in the previous decade. The density data in table 2-2 are not inconsistent with Troy's hypothesis; neither do they suggest that structural differences tell the whole story.

France			Germany			Italy		
Economy	*Market*	*Mfg.*	*Economy*	*Market*	*Mfg.*	*Economy*	*Market*	*Mfg.*ᶜ
22.3	n.a.	>15	33.0	26.9	36	36.3	33.7	40
22.8	n.a.	n.a.	36.6	31.2	n.a.	47.2	43.3	n.a.
19.0	18.0	n.a.	37.0	32.5	48	49.3	42.8	57
16.3	n.a.	n.a.	37.4	33.9	50	42.0	34.6	49
12.0	8.0	<5	33.8	29.9	48	39.6	32.2	47
− 10.3	n.a.	n.a.	0.8	3.0	12	3.3	− 1.5	7
− 6.0	n.a.	n.a.	4.4	7.0	14	5.7	0.9	9
− 3.3	n.a.	n.a.	4.0	5.6	12	13.0	9.1	17
− 2.7	n.a.	n.a.	0.4	1.4	2	− 7.3	− 8.2	− 8
− 4.3	n.a.	n.a.	− 3.6	− 4.0	− 2	− 2.4	− 2.4	− 2

Switzerland			United Kingdom			United States		
Economy	*Market*	*Mfg.*ᵇ	*Economy*	*Market*	*Mfg.*	*Economy*	*Market*	*Mfg.*
30.7	24.0	27	44.8	40.1	52	25.4	n.a.	41
32.9	n.a.	n.a.	48.3	40.1	n.a.	22.8	23.7	n.a.
30.7	23.8	34	50.7	44.7	64	23.0	16.8	35
28.8	22.4	33	45.5	39.3	58	18.0	14.6	25
26.0	n.a.	34	41.5	37.8	41	16.4	12.9	22
− 4.7	n.a.	7	− 3.3	− 2.3	− 11	− 9.0	n.a.	− 19
− 1.9	− 1.6	6	0.7	− 0.8	6	− 7.4	14.6	− 16
0.0	− 0.2	7	5.9	4.6	12	− 2.4	16.8	− 6
− 1.9	− 1.4	− 1	− 5.2	− 5.4	− 6	− 5.0	− 2.2	− 10
− 2.8	n.a.	1	− 4.0	− 1.5	− 17	− 1.6	− 1.7	− 3

European Exceptionalism: Potential Deterrents to Nonunion Operation

Contemporary U.S. scholarship has stressed the contribution made to differences in organizational strength and structural stability by certain distinctively American institutions, notably the Taft-Hartley legislation, which served to inhibit union organization and hence to weaken union responsiveness to increases in union-nonunion wage differentials. This approach can be complemented by a search for institutional arrangements which might serve as barriers to nonunion operation by employers in various European countries. Table 2-3 is a checklist of such potential barriers to nonunion operation.

EMPLOYER ASSOCIATIONS. Collective bargaining between national unions and employer associations tends to be more pervasive in

Table 2-3. *Provisional Checklist of Potential Deterrents to Nonunion Operation*

Country	Strong employer associations[a]	Mandatory works council elections[b]	Protection from dismissal for legal striking	Contract extension to nonsignatory firms[c]	Bargained legislation[d]	Union representation on public bodies	Members-only features[e]	Union representation on labor courts
Austria	x	x		x	x	x		x
Belgium		x		x	x	x	x	x
Denmark	x	x	x	x		x	x	x
France		x	x	x	x	x		x
Germany	x	x	x	x	x	x		x
Italy		x	x		x	x		
Netherlands		x	x	x		x		x
Norway	x	x	x	x		x		x
Spain		x	x	x		x		
Sweden	x	x	x	x		x	x	x
Switzerland	x		x	x	(x)	x	x	x
United Kingdom								x

Sources: Blanpain (1987), relevant country references; ILO (1984).
a. Ability to order and financially support lockouts and resist strikes; or membership compulsory; or equivalent authority.
b. Elections mandatory or at the request of specified portion of work force.
c. Extension of contract terms to nonsignatory firms legally possible on order of ministry or court.
d. Agreements between union federations and employer associations become basis of legislation.
e. Collective bargaining or social security systems benefit union members differentially.

Europe than in the United States. Historically, this may reflect the greater emphasis European employers have placed on taking wages out of competition, a result of their relatively strong tradition of cartelism. It may also reflect a greater willingness on the part of European employers to deal with unions, and a correlative support for strong employer associations to implement a unified response to union demands.

The actual bargaining power of an employers' association, however, is, among other things, a function of its ability to order member firms to undergo (or terminate) strikes, to support struck firms by ordering sympathetic lockouts by other firms, to subsidize struck or locked-out firms by raising war chests, and to fine or even expel members for refusing to comply with their directives. In these respects, German employer associations have been exceptionally strong; they can even protect the normal market shares of member firms during authorized stoppages by prohibiting other firms from taking business (or employees) away from them. In fact, industrywide bargaining with lockouts has been both encouraged and regulated by law in the Federal Republic: to qualify as legal bargaining agents, employer associations must be empowered to order lockouts.[12] The Scandinavian employer groups also possess the powers listed above and therefore qualify to varying degrees as strong associations. Sweden's are particularly powerful. The Confederation of Swedish Employers' (SAF) tradition of threatening lockouts and pooling strike risks dates to the beginning of the century and has continued into the postwar period of centralized bargaining on an all-industry level.

In Britain, on the other hand, employer associations have been regarded largely as "voluntary" associations and, at least in some cases, they have placed a higher priority on taking wages out of competition and mediating disputes with unions than on coordinating resistance to union demands.[13] In the Netherlands, employer associations possess no effective sanctions, and, according to van Voorden, "members who op-

---

12. Bunn (1984). On the other hand, the Labor Court has limited the extent of lockouts by requiring that the numbers of employees locked out in a labor dispute be proportionate to the number of employees whom the union has called out on strike (Gladstone, 1984, p. 41). It should be noted that industrywide bargaining in Germany is often conducted on a regional (and, in some cases, a broad industrial) basis. Employer associations have resorted to lockouts in order to counter the ability of the national unions involved to gain a whipsaw advantage by ordering strikes in key firms and subsectors (for instance, parts suppliers) and using them as pattern setters for the entire jurisdiction. Since lockouts can also be used offensively to drain union strike funds, the rule of proportionality serves to limit the use of the lockout.

13. Armstrong (1984).

pose the policies of their association can easily disregard them."[14] In France and Italy, efforts to establish stable bargaining institutions at the industry level since World War II have been frustrated by political ties of employers and competing unions, by government involvement in wage determination (in Italy), by the power of regional employer associations (in France), and by the absence of effective disciplinary rules in employer associations in both countries.[15]

Strong employers' associations have helped resist nonunion encroachment and the weakening of bargaining institutions. This is evident in the slight growth of unionization in the industrial sectors of Denmark, West Germany, Norway, and Sweden during the first half of the 1980s, despite high unemployment. In France, Italy, the Netherlands, and the United Kingdom densities declined. But not even strong employer associations— and their union counterparts—offer immunity from powerful decentralizing influences. Some of these, especially increased international competition, are of external origin, and, as previously noted, they have contributed to serious structural destabilization in the United States.

Employer associations may also intensify member firms' divergent interests brought on by differences of size, efficiency, profitability, aggressiveness, and so forth. Large firms, especially multinationals, with their greater "ability to pay," more aggressive market strategies, or greater need to motivate, attract, or retain labor in short supply, have often been keener than smaller firms to avoid strikes and worker discontent. Consequently they have been more willing to grant wage increases in excess of those negotiated industrywide. In many instances, such firms remained in their associations and paid wage drift (or premiums above contractual settlement); in a few cases—Volkswagen, most notably— they have bargained independently of the association.

Smaller firms can pay a lower wage while the large firm pays a higher one because the wage negotiated by an association serves only as a minimum. However, this arrangement may threaten to undermine the authority of the association's bargaining partner, the national union, which is motivated to negotiate minimum terms sufficiently high to make drift payments unprofitable. When large firms agree to pay an above-scale increase in independent negotiations, the national union may come under pressure to make up the difference in the next round of bargaining with the association. This leapfrogging process has threatened the survival of

14. Van Voorden (1984, p. 204).
15. Bunel and Saglio (1984); Goetschy and Rojot (1987); Martinelli and Treu (1984); Pellegrini (1987).

some weaker member firms.[16] As a result, there have been instances in Sweden and Germany where national unions successfully struck stray firms to prod them into the fold. In any event, separate bargaining by large firms in Europe for higher wages differs from nonunion encroachments for lower wages in the American manner.

Can an association prevent firms from undercutting negotiated minimum wages or new firms from starting up at wages below the union level? If it is strong enough it can keep the negotiated wage (and hence its differential with a shadow nonunion wage) too low to make it profitable for firms to set up and operate in the industry on a nonunion basis. Otherwise, if its union bargaining partners supported the industrywide bargaining institution, they might be counted on to strike selectively against firms that were no longer parties to the official collective agreement. The credible expectation of such strikes would therefore act as a disincentive to any employer contemplating nonunion operation. This is tantamount to saying that the authority and hence the bargaining power of an employers' association is ultimately a function of union support (the analog to an American employer's recognition of a union and assent to a union shop). But the strike sanction alone cannot constitute a sufficient barrier to nonunion operation.

Associations may also apply economic pressure on nonmembers to force them to join.[17] Such pressure may be exerted by inducing member firms that are suppliers or customers of the outlaw (or even sources of credit) to boycott the firm. This type of sanction is, in effect, an extension of a strong association's power to order lockouts; it involves the association in organizing secondary business boycotts. Where successfully deployed, it can effectively inhibit low-wage operation. (It constitutes impressive evidence of general employer and community acceptance of industrywide bargaining as a wage-determining institution.) Even so, this type of sanction is likely to be more effective in the hands of an association covering a wide, regional and industry jurisdiction (notably Gesamtmetall in Germany) than a narrower one. It may also work better in rounding up the occasional stray than in heading off stampedes.

MANDATED WORKS COUNCIL ELECTIONS. A legal requirement that firms with employees in excess of a stipulated minimum permit the establishment of works councils can also serve as a disincentive to potential nonunion operation. Unlike National Labor Relations Board

16. Flanagan, Soskice, and Ulman (1983, pp. 116, 653).
17. Traxler (1984).

(NLRB) representation elections in the United States, works council elections in European countries are not referenda on whether a works council shall exist; they are solely concerned with determining which candidates shall serve on the council as employee representatives. Usually nonunion candidates may run in works council elections, but they typically receive only a small portion of the vote cast.[18] However, the likelihood of a works council in those countries being dominated by union members has been declining during the past decade, especially in France.

The proportion of votes cast for nonunionists in the German works council elections rose from 17.5 percent in 1975 to 27.5 percent in 1987. However, the blue collar DGB's share of the votes, after declining steeply in the second half of the 1970s, has climbed back to about 65 percent (very close to its 1975 level). In France, the share of votes for nonunion representatives to enterprise committees rose steadily from 14.5 percent in 1976 to 23.5 percent in 1988, while the share of the CGT (the General Confederation of Labor, largely Communist controlled) declined in the same period, from 41.5 percent to 26.7 percent. The share of the CFDT (the French Democratic Federation of Labor), after increasing to 22.8 percent in 1982, fell back to 20.7 percent in 1988. These increases in the nonunion vote may invite comparison with the growing number of union electoral defeats in the NLRB elections in the United States. In Germany, at least, the results are seen as reflecting a rise in the white collar sectors of the work force rather than a decline in the popularity of unionism among blue collar workers; even so, structuralists consider these results as evidence of their position.[19]

How have works councils influenced the stability of union organizations and bargaining institutions? In Europe, collective bargaining with unions has mainly been confined to wages and hours, and it has been conducted by centralized union bodies and employer associations at the industry level or even wider. Unlike their American counterparts, European unions have generally been kept outside the factory gates; such matters as work rules, production standards, technological changes, incentive systems, and employee motivation and training have been outside the purview of collective bargaining.

When codetermination or worker participation arrangements were es-

18. Keller (1991, p. 65); Bridgford (1990, p. 129); and Keller, Jacobi, and Müller-Jentsch (1992, p. 27).
19. Structuralists (such as Troy) maintain that changes in the demographic and occupational sectors of the work force are an important determinant of changes in overall union density.

tablished, management came to share some of its activities with (previously weak) works councils or similar local groups of workers. These groups were prevented from striking (either by law, as in West Germany, or by "peace obligations" in collective agreements with unions), and their relations with management generally remained cooperative rather than adversarial. Moreover, although works councils have always been well stocked with unionists, the interests of both councils and unions— the one centralized and the other local (inside the firm or even the plant)—could differ on specific issues (for instance, the shorter work week versus overtime in Germany) and for political reasons (as in the antipathy of old-style Communist-dominated unions in France and Italy toward decentralized organizational units). Therefore, when intensified international competition and major technological changes obliged management to address problems of rationalization, labor flexibility, and worker involvement in decisionmaking in the interests of greater efficiency, these developments were often interpreted as a shift from union to nonunion domains of activity and from centralized bargaining to decentralized industrial relations.

This has not been the case everywhere. In Sweden and Germany, the national unions, focusing on issues arising from employment problems and technological change, sought to follow the action inside the company without abandoning their negotiations with centralized employer organizations. Sweden's Act on Codetermination at Work, which the unions muscled through parliament in 1976, requires management to consult the unions prior to deciding on major changes (in technology, investment, and so forth) and gives the union the right to veto decisions to subcontract. Despite court enforcement, however, this legislation seems to have had little success in diminishing management's authority in certain areas that have obviously grown in relative importance.[20]

In Germany, the recent shift in emphasis from pay to labor displacement, training, and related issues resulted in management's increased bargaining strength, works councils' heightened importance, and a broadened range of national union activities.[21] Although some of the most prominent union breakthroughs in these areas have been made in single-company agreements, notably between IG Metall and Volkswagen, the industrywide institutions have remained stable. In fact, Streeck and others maintain that the works councils, although autono-

---

20. Brulin and Victorin (1990), Hammarstrom (1987).
21. Müller-Jentsch and others (1990), Fuerstenberg (1987), Rojot (1990).

mous from and sometimes even adversarial toward the national unions and industrywide bargaining, have contributed decisively to the continued stability of these institutions in large-scale industries.[22] The works councilors, themselves strong union supporters, ensure that newly hired employees become union members if they are not already. Although any formal provision for compulsory membership is outlawed, works council members ensure the establishment of "surreptitious union-shop arrangements."[23]

Two distinctive factors make this arrangement possible. First, according to the German Works Constitution Act, works councils are entitled to reject job applicants on certain legal grounds and hence may interview them all. Second is the unitary character of the union movement in Germany—there is no division of union organization along political or confessional lines and, in this respect, no interunion rivalry and little competition for members. This is a strong contrast with the pluralistic unionism of France, Italy, the Netherlands, and Belgium, where works council elections are also mandated. The first three of these countries posted some of the worst organizational showings recorded in table 2-2. It is notable that a mechanism of transforming unions' electoral success on works councils into union shops (as in Germany) is lacking in the first three countries.[24]

STRIKEBREAKING.   Column three of table 2-3 summarizes the most vivid difference between the behavior of U.S. and European employers in the field of industrial relations: the employment of strikebreakers by the former. In the United States, an employer's legal right to hire permanent replacements for workers who exercise their legal right to strike has been established on a qualified basis since the late 1930s.[25] In Europe dismissal of strikers is not legal except in Great Britain. (In most countries, however, dismissal is permitted if strikes violate the peace obligation in the collective agreement.) The prohibition against dismissing strikers constitutes a powerful disincentive to the use of strikebreakers as an alternative to an employer's accepting a shutdown, since employing strikebreakers

22. Streeck (1984).

23. Streeck (1984, p. 32).

24. Nevertheless, even legally mandated union shops have not proved to be a barrier to nonunion entry in the United States.

25. However, workers who strike on economic grounds have the right to reinstatement provided their application is made before permanent replacements have been hired (*NLRB v. Mackay Radio and Telegraph Co.* 304 US333, 1938).

on only a temporary basis can poison management-employee relationships following the cessation of hostilities.

It may be argued that these legal barriers to dismissal are not the foremost reason that European employers refrain from using and hiring strikebreakers. These employers may instead be deterred by the absence of sufficient numbers of willing strikebreakers in the work force or by a taboo against strikebreaking. It is worth noting in this respect that the U.S. employer's longstanding right to hire permanent replacements was not put to use on any significant scale until the 1980s. If an erosion of the inhibition toward strikebreaking occurred in European countries, however, legal constraints would come into force, just as the legal right came into its own in the United States. Nevertheless, even if these laws effectively prevent recourse to strikebreaking on the part of organized employers, they would not necessarily preclude the entry of nonunion enterprises.

EXTENSION OF CONTRACT TERMS.   In all of the EC member countries included in table 2-3 except Great Britain, the terms of collective agreements may be made legally binding on nonsignatory firms—whether by ministerial authority (as in France, Germany, the Netherlands, Belgium, and Austria) or judicial action (as in Italy and Sweden). In Britain, the Central Arbitration Committee had been authorized to extend "recognized terms" or the "general level of pay" to petitioning groups of workers by dint of 1975 legislation, but this authority was revoked in 1980.[26]

Extension of terms appears to be an obvious institutional impediment to the erosion of union membership and bargaining structures for it validates the results of unions' negotiations. If managers of member firms know they will have to pay the minimum contractual wage outside the association, there is little to be gained in breaking away from it. Therefore, this type of legal restraint should deter unionized employers from hiring nonunion workers. It should even induce employers to acquire or retain membership in order to exert some influence over association bargaining objectives and tactics. On the other hand, contract extension also inhibits the extension of union organization, since it offers a free ride to employees in nonunion firms.

In practice, contract extension seems to act as a stabilizing device for well-established bargaining institutions. In Germany and the Nether-

26. Brown (1980).

lands, the applicability of administrative extension has been limited to sectors in which at least a majority of the employees are covered by multiemployer agreements. But it has not served either as a necessary or a sufficient condition of avoiding union membership losses. On the one hand, it has been all but absent in the Scandinavian countries and Belgium where union density has remained high and employer associations are strongly entrenched. On the other hand, despite extensive reliance on contract extension in France and the Netherlands, those countries' unions have undergone organizational decline on par with plummeting U.S. levels.[27]

BARGAINED LEGISLATION. In contrast to the majority coverage set as a precondition in Germany and the Netherlands, contract extension can occur in France "if in a given area for a given branch of activity, either there are no unions able to conclude an agreement, or if although they exist, they are persistently unable to reach one."[28] Yet, while authorized by the ministry of labor, an extension must be preceded by a request either from two unions or one union and an employers' association.

This arrangement is similar to the British system, in which statutory minimum wages have been set in low-wage sectors (retail trades, services, clothing, and agriculture) by the establishment of tripartite wages councils where adequate machinery for effective regulation of remuneration is absent. This system of minimum wage-setting was originally established in 1909 as an exception to the prevailing principles in industrial relations of laissez faire and voluntary association in the hope that the wages councils would evolve into voluntary collective bargaining arrangements. In 1975, the law was changed to increase the councils' authority and also to permit them under certain conditions to drop their public members.[29] In the 1980s, this authority was curtailed, but a proposal to eliminate the councils was shelved.[30]

In France and in Italy as well, where traditions of anarchosyndicalism and communism in the labor movements have for opposite reasons contributed to the fragility of collective bargaining, bargained legislation has become a way of life.[31] In the wake of grassroots unrest in 1968, a series of interindustry agreements was negotiated in France between the central

27. Van Voorden (1984, p. 226), Goetschy and Rojot (1987, p. 153).
28. Despax and Rojot (1987).
29. Starr (1981, p. 19).
30. Brown (1990).
31. Pellegrini (1987, p. 130).

employers' confederation (the CNPF) and the CGT and CFDT, the two largest union confederations. The agreements covered a variety of areas, including aspects of social welfare and unemployment compensation, and were supposed to serve as broad frameworks for detailed negotiations at the industry level. They were more effective, however, as the basis for legislation, although the government's role was to be more than perfunctory.[32] French unions have also been involved in the administration of public policy through representation on the boards of unemployment compensation and social security systems and membership on a variety of councils and commissions. Moreover, unionists are elected to serve on bipartisan labor courts (conseils de prud'hommes).

In Italy, unions have also extensively engaged in bargained legislation in the areas of social security and layoff pay (which is financed by employers, or, in longer-term situations, by the state). The major union confederations have even participated in bargaining over the provisions of a national system of wage indexation (the scala mobile), often at the expense of industrywide bargaining. They are represented in social security agencies and other official bodies and in local commissions for allocating jobs to the unemployed.[33]

UNION PARTICIPATION IN PUBLIC POLICY AND ADMINISTRATION. Participation by unions and employer groups in official policymaking, administration, and judicial institutions is not confined to countries with weak collective bargaining systems, as columns six and eight of table 2-3 might indicate. In Belgium, Austria, the Scandinavian countries, and Germany, both bargaining and welfare institutions have been underwritten to varying degrees by the political power of the union movement.[34] In some instances, on the other hand, the unions' bargaining strength enhanced their ability to influence social welfare policies. This ability was manifest during experiments with incomes policies in the 1970s when central governments and unions exchanged wage restraint in collective bargaining for extended or improved benefits in social welfare programs.[35] In Germany, the central employers' confederation (BDA) endorsed the concept of the social market economy and accepted joint administration of legislated labor and social welfare programs. As Fuerstenberg has observed, "In the course of implementing the different codetermination laws, thousands of new functions and posi-

32. Bunel and Saglio (1984), Goetschy and Rojot (1987).
33. Pellegrini (1987).
34. Blanpain (1974).
35. Bunn (1984).

tions for union officials have been created, thus establishing a network of influence which cannot easily be abandoned."[36]

Bargained legislation and union participation in public administration bear a strong analytic resemblance to contract extension. In both cases, unions have sought to extend their economic grasp beyond the reach of conventional collective bargaining using the instrumentality of the state. In the process of creating a variety of public goods, however, they have stripped away individual incentives to membership. One need not join a union to receive various benefits under social security which might otherwise (as in the United States) be obtainable only under collective bargaining. And if the benefits happen to issue from the participation of a socially responsible union movement in a political exchange for wage restraint, one need not belong to a union to be awarded a pay cut. Nor need an aggrieved employee become a member in order to gain access to a union-supported labor court, which enforces a union-supported law against unjustified dismissal. This is in contrast to American-style grievance procedures under collective bargaining wherein the union "owns" the grievance, and it alone can offer a worker protection denied to non-unionists under laws that permit employers to discharge such workers at will.[37]

FOR MEMBERS ONLY. Two possible remedies for unions afflicted by free riders are compulsory membership (as in the union security clauses found in many collective agreements in the United States and, formerly, Great Britain) and bargaining for members only, whereby unions can privatize some of the benefits they have been instrumental in obtaining (see column seven of table 2-3). For example, in Belgium, where unions are strongly organized and politically powerful, special bonuses for union members have been negotiated as a repayment of dues; they are paid out in a variety of forms (as supplemental unemployment, pension, or other benefits) only to union members in the work force.[38]

The most dramatic restriction of benefits to union members occurs in Sweden and Denmark, where union membership is a condition of eligibility for unemployment benefits. This unusual feature is regarded as a major cause of the high union membership densities in these two countries in comparison to Norway, where the Norwegian Confederation of Trade Unions (LO) is not involved in the system of social insurance and

36. Fuerstenberg (1987, p. 78).
37. In France, where it costs employees nothing to vote in elections for the labor courts, abstentions rose sharply between 1979 and 1987, reaching 54 percent. See Troy (1990).
38. Blanpain (1974).

unemployment compensation. The German labor court system has been said to operate with a bias in favor of membership, since an aggrieved employee is likely to be represented more skillfully and effectively before the court by union counsel than otherwise. But these examples of members-only privileges are exceptions that prove the rule. Thus, according to Goetschy and Rojot, the absence of compulsory membership (closed-shop) and members-only features are important causes of the low degree of organization in France.[39]

Yet these features are largely absent from Germany's robust industrial relations. German unionism's success owes primarily to the scope of union interests and the breadth of union influence, which transcend the limits of collective bargaining.[40] Fuerstenberg attributes German unions' great influence on political and social life and the strong increase in organization in the 1970s to the politicization of younger employees as well as to favorable labor market conditions.[41] While acknowledging the role of the Swedish unemployment insurance system as a union recruiting device, Hammarstrom makes a similar case for Sweden's high membership density: "Perhaps the most important reason is the degree of union influence achieved during the long period of Social Democratic government. The close relationship between the government and the LO has helped the unions to establish themselves as a significant force in this society. Thus, for most Swedes, it is almost automatic to join a union when they enter the labour market."[42]

Labor historians and students of comparative industrial relations have long noted that American unionism is exceptional when viewed in the European context first for its lack of a strong affiliation with parties of the political left and second for its organizational weakness. It is understandable that they find causal relationships, such as the one described by Hammarstrom. Economists see individualistic disincentives to organization in the general availability of benefits issuing from the wider involvement of unions. On that basis, they should expect to find lower degrees of organization in Europe than in the United States, which is, of course, contrary to fact. Other observers, however, stress the importance of group or class identification in making union membership the likely choice for a worker. None of these views can be ruled out before the fact; which one dominates is a function of the relative strength of the individ-

39. Goetschy and Rojot (1987).
40. Fuerstenberg (1987).
41. Fuerstenberg (1987, p. 169).
42. Hammarstrom (1987, p. 192).

ualistic and social incentives at any given moment. But there is reason to doubt the continuing strength of these traditional political sources of social motivation in support of union institutions.

Prospects

While continued European unification will not have proven to be a watershed in the history of European trade unions, it will reinforce prevailing trends toward the Community's economic integration and the attendant reduction of a member state's ability to protect its citizens from competition by producers in other member states. Further, if maintained the recently established regime of nearly fixed exchange rates should sharply reduce national governments' ability to protect output and employment by devaluing their currencies and offsetting idiosyncratic movements of national wage levels.[43] The combined effect of these concurrent developments will be to weaken national unions' ability to influence terms of employment. The state's power to limit nonunion operation within its borders as well as to establish nontariff barriers to imports, to restrict immigration, and to impose wage and price controls has acted as a dike behind which unions have been able to set wages and other terms of employment that are greater than what they would otherwise have been. In this instance state power has reflected the influence of unions and employers as well—with European unions being traditionally more inclined toward politics and governmental regulation than U.S. unionists and European employers somewhat more willing to recognize unions as partners and bargain with them at centralized levels than U.S. employers. The elimination or attenuation of this power could beset European unions with the same dilemma U.S. unions have faced: either to create more highly centralized structures able to cope with unified markets (as U.S. unions were able to do in the nineteenth century and again in the 1930s) or, lacking that capability, to suffer decentralization and organizational loss (as happened to U.S. unions in the 1970s and 1980s under the impact of legal deregulation and intensified international competition).

Apart from valuable research, dissemination of information, and lobbying performed by international trade secretariats, there has been little evidence of tangible progress in the direction of Community-wide unionism. The paucity of examples of unions in different countries following

43. See Eichengreen in this volume.

an agreed-upon strategy of collective bargaining is more easily noted than explained. Usual explanatory factors (differences in language, culture, tradition, and politics) are easy to cite but unsatisfying as explanations. European employers' outright hostility toward negotiating with unions on an international basis differs sharply from their attitude toward collective bargaining in individual countries. This difference in attitude may have had an appreciable adverse effect on European unions' power to cooperate in international collective bargaining. On the other hand it should be noted that, with rare exceptions, European unions have not exerted much effort to promote international bargaining. Perhaps the most important reason for this failure is the tenacity of national union institutions. They have survived the major economic changes of the 1970s and 1980s, sharply higher levels of unemployment, and two other debilitating influences: a tendency toward de facto decentralization of bargaining and a growing disenchantment with unionism and collective bargaining, which have been variously criticized for exacerbating inflation, unemployment, sclerotic inefficiency, and employment insecurity.

Because institutional barriers to nonunion operation present workers with the free rider's disincentive to join unions, they offer unions no protection against worker indifference or disenchantment. Recent declines in European rates of union density, although smaller than those recorded in the United States, may reflect loss of worker support for unions, but it is much too early to be certain.

To the extent that dismantling obstacles to Community-wide trade in 1992 releases previously unexploited comparative advantages, these debilitating influences will be reinforced. Intensified competition in European product markets will lessen union ability to deliver terms of employment that are superior to what market forces would permit in the absence of unions; this will tend to reduce unions' value to their membership and weaken the incentive to join or remain in them. Moreover, with diminished potential for achieving gains on a national scale, industrywide bargaining may be weakened in two ways. National unions will find themselves under greater pressure from workers in more profitable enterprises and from employers in less profitable enterprises to adopt discriminatory bargaining policies (making some multiemployer bargaining in Europe resemble some company-by-company bargaining in the United States). Industrywide mechanisms may also be weakened if wage bargaining, whose payoffs will presumably be lowered by unification, is subordinated to settlement of mainly nonwage issues at the local level through worker participation or codetermination.

Some German national unions claim to have brought codetermination procedures under their control, using them as a complement to rather than a substitute for industrywide bargaining. Elsewhere, however, this local emphasis may lead to either formal or de facto devolution of authority to works councils and other local units. It also may be associated with an accumulation of bargaining power by employers, but it could conceivably invigorate the unions by encouraging cooperative relationships instead of adversarial ones, expanding the scope of union influence within the firm while jointly enhancing job security and cost efficiency.

One can also envisage unions engaging in two functions within an integrated Community that might prompt international organization, although in the political sphere. The first would involve the unions in efforts to protect European labor markets from direct competition by low-wage immigrants from outside the Community, or even from indirect competition from their products. Restricted migration has been a very popular policy in Europe; the fear of massive migration across the EC's eastern and southern borders makes it appealing to the Community as a whole and not simply to unions and their sympathizers.[44] As advocates of restriction, national unions could play a significant role in lobbying the European Parliament and the Council. Forming a Community-wide protectionist lobby may promote international cooperation among labor unions more successfully than the search for common bargaining demands has done so far.

A second political function for union movements—and one they are already fulfilling—is to press the European Commission, the European Parliament, and the member states for the adoption of a Social Charter covering standards of social welfare, health and safety as well as rights of codetermination and union organization. In so doing the unions have encountered opposition from employers and others recruited under the banner of subsidiarity, but they have also met with a sympathetic reception from some employers and others who would not be averse to conveying their neocorporatist heritage to a wider stage. In any event, disparities of legislated labor costs among European countries are, as we have noted, greater than most wage differences; and unionists are more concerned over the prospect of social dumping than they are over wage differentials.

The Social Protocol adopted at the Maastricht summit of December 1991 approaches this controversial area with impressive ambiguity, but it does hold out a prospect that agreements between management and

44. See Hansen in this volume.

labor on such matters as working conditions, information, consultation, codetermination, social security, and even employment conditions of resident third-country nationals might, after approval by the Council of Ministers, become Community (or union) law. This would constitute a Community-wide analog to bargained legislation that would tend to promote and strengthen both labor and management organizations operating at Community-wide levels.

Finally, it must be borne in mind that both union institutions and European Community institutions are the creation of underlying forces that are partially independent of one another. The year 1992 is but a trail marker on a long road from a balkanized Europe to one with an integrated political economy. Trade unions have been organizational chameleons, varying their form and purpose to exploit the opportunities presented by a changing environment. Despite an ideology with strong elements of egalitarian universalism, the ultimate source of trade union organizational strength has been the ability to exclude market competitors. But 1992 may have marked a road to a greatly expanded area within which exclusion of internal competition is impermissible. In the unification process, European unions may nevertheless learn to rely on methods or find objectives enabling them to avoid organizational erosion by competitive forces within the Community.

References

Armstrong, E. G. A. 1984. "Employers Associations in Great Britain." In John P. Windmuller and Alan Gladstone, eds., *Employers Associations and Industrial Relations*. Oxford: Clarendon Press.

Blanpain, Richard, ed. 1987. *International Encyclopedia for Labour Law and Industrial Relations*. Netherlands: Kluwer Law and Taxation.

———. 1974. "Belgium." In *Collective Bargaining in Industrialized Market Economies*. Geneva: International Labour Office.

Bohning, W. R. 1987. "The Protection of Migrant Workers and International Standards." In *International Labour Migration in the Philippines and South East Asia*. Berlin: German Foundation for International Development.

Bridgford, Jeff. 1990. "French Trade Unions: Crisis in the 1980's." *Industrial Relations Journal* 21 (Summer): 126–35.

Brown, William, and Sushil Wadwhani. 1990. "The Economic Effects of Industrial Relations Legislation since 1979." *National Institute Economic Review*, no. 131 (February):57–70.

Brulin, G., and A. Victorin. 1990. "Experts' Report on Sweden." In *Labour Market Flexibility and Work Organization*. Paris: OECD.

Bunel, Jean, and Jean Saglio. 1984. "Employers Associations in France." In John P. Windmuller and Alan Gladstone, eds., *Employers Associations and Industrial Relations: A Comparative Study*. Oxford: Clarendon Press.

Bunn, Ronald F. 1984. "Employers Associations in the Federal Republic of Germany." In John P. Windmuller and Alan Gladstone, eds., *Employers Associations and Industrial Relations: A Comparative Study*. Oxford: Clarendon Press.

Commons, J. R., and Associates. 1936. *History of Labour in the United States*, vol. 2, chap. 3. Macmillan.

Despax, M., and J. Rojot. 1987. In Roger Blanpain, ed., *International Encyclopedia for Labour Law and Industrial Relations*, vol. 4. Netherlands: Kluwer Law and Taxation.

Flanagan, Robert, David Soskice, and Lloyd Ulman. 1983. *Unionism, Economic Stabilization, and Incomes Policies: European Experience*. Brookings.

Freeman, Richard. 1988. "Contraction and Expansion: The Divergence of Private and Public Sector Unionism in the United States." *Journal of Economic Perspectives* 2 (Spring):63–88.

Fuerstenberg, Friedrich. 1987. "Industrial Relations in the Federal Republic of Germany." In Greg Bamber and Russell D. Lansbury, eds., *International and Comparative Industrial Relations*. London: Allen and Unwin.

Gladstone, A. 1984. "Employers' Associations in Comparative Perspective: Functions and Activities." In J. P. Windmuller and A. Gladstone,

Employers' Associations and Industrial Relations: A Comparative Study. Clarendon Press.

Goetschy, Janine, and Jacques Rojot. 1987. "French Industrial Relations." In Greg Bamber and Russell D. Lansbury, eds., *International and Comparative Industrial Relations.* London: Allen and Unwin.

Greenberg, D. H. 1966. "The Structure of Collective Bargaining and Some of Its Determinants." Paper prepared for the Nineteenth Annual Industrial Relations Research Association Proceedings.

Hammarstrom, Olle. 1987. "Swedish Industrial Relations." In Greg Bamber and Russell D. Lansbury, eds., *International and Comparative Industrial Relations.* London: Allen and Unwin.

Hendricks, Wallace, and Lawrence M. Kahn. 1982. "The Determinants of Bargaining Structure in U.S. Manufacturing Industries." *Industrial and Labor Relations Review* 35 (January):181–95.

ILO. 1984. *The Trade Union Situation in Norway.* Geneva: International Labour Office.

Keller, Berndt. 1991. *Einfohrung in die Arbeitspolitik. Arbeitsbeziehungen und Arbeitsmarkt in sozialwissenschaftligher Perspektive.* Munchen-Wien: R. Oldenbourgh.

Keller, Berndt, O. Jacobi, and W. Müller-Jentsch. 1992. "Germany: Codetermining the Future?" In A. Ferner and R. Hyman, eds., *Industrial Relations in the E.C.* London: Blackwell.

Marshall, A. 1927. *Principles of Economics,* 8th ed. London: Macmillan.

Martinelli, A., and T. Treu. 1984. "Employers Associations in Italy." In John P. Windmuller and Alan Gladstone, eds., *Employers Associations and Industrial Relations.* Oxford: Clarendon Press.

Mishel, L. 1986. "The Structural Determinants of Union Bargaining Power." *Industrial and Labor Relations Review* 40 (October): 90–104.

Müller-Jentsch, W., W. Rehermann, and H. Sperling. 1990. "Experts' Report on Germany." In *Labour Market Flexibility and Work Organization.* Paris: OECD.

Neven, Damien J. 1990. "EEC Integration towards 1992: Some Distributional Aspects." *Economic Policy* 10 (April):13–62.

Pellegrini, Claudio. 1987. "Italian Industrial Relations." In Greg Bamber and Russell D. Lansbury, eds., *International and Comparative Industrial Relations.* London: Allen and Unwin.

Rojot, Jacques. 1990. "Synthesis Report." In *Labour Market Flexibility and Work Organization.* Paris: OECD.

Slichter, Sumner H. 1941. *Union Policies and Industrial Management.* Brookings.

Starr, G. 1981. *Minimum Wage Fixing.* Geneva: International Labour Office.

Streeck, Wolfgang. 1984. *Industrial Relations in West Germany: A Case Study of the Car Industry.* London: Heinemann.

Troy, Leo. 1990. "Is the U.S. Unique in the Decline of Private Sector Unionism?" *Journal of Labor Research* 11 (Spring): 111–43.

Van Voorden, William. 1984. "Employers' Associations in the Netherlands." In John P. Windmuller and Alan Gladstone, eds., *Employers Associations and Industrial Relations.* Oxford: Clarendon Press.

Visser, Jelle. 1991. "Trends in Trade Union Membership." *OECD Employment Outlook.* July.

CHAPTER THREE

Prospects for Worker Participation in Management in the Single Market

Lowell Turner

Europe an economic integration's takeoff since the mid-1980s is among the more unexpected and dramatic stories on the world stage in a period in which surprises have abounded. Driven by their own fears of perceived stagnation, "Eurosclerosis," policymakers at national and European levels coalesced around a single European market project which promised to transform the EC's supposedly tired old welfare states into a juggernaut of economic dynamism.

As many have pointed out, business and government have led this project; it is essentially a market deregulatory project into which labor, with little choice or initial participation, was pulled along.[1] The project moves forward at a time of union decline and weakness in most EC countries; and it is precisely in opposition to many labor-supported market regulations that major business actors can agree. As labor has attempted to get back into the rapidly developing European game, a defense of social standards and protections at the European level and within the member states has become a critical union strategy and a major battleground on which employer and worker interests meet.

This paper examines the development of and debates over the so-called social dimension of the single market project, with particular reference to the issues of employee information, consultation, and participation rights. The Social Charter, issued by the European Commission and agreed to in

This paper has benefited substantially from the detailed comments and suggestions of George Strauss, who provided the inspiration for this study. Michael Belzer, Oliver Clarke, Owen Darbishire, Michael Reich, Jacques Rojot, Nick Salvatore, David Soskice, Robert Stern, Wolfgang Streeck, Lloyd Ulman, Harold Wilensky, and John Windmuller also gave careful readings to an earlier draft and provided useful comments and criticisms.
    1. Sandholtz and Zysman (1989); Mosley (1990); Streeck (1991).

December 1989 by eleven of the twelve member states of the Council of Ministers, lists the expansion of such rights as one of its planks. In principle, therefore, most employers, governments, and unions are in agreement; the problem comes in implementation and regulation.

Unions by and large favor expanded legal rights to worker participation in management (WPM), both at European and national levels; this sort of WPM is referred to as *negotiated*.[2] Employers, on the other hand, favor voluntary arrangements that often turn out in practice to be *employer led*. The distinction between negotiated and employer-led WPM is at the heart of the European debate on this issue, a debate that shows every sign of evoking a protracted process of negotiation and political mobilization involving unions, employers, national governments, and the European Commission, Parliament, and Council.[3]

This is a high-stakes issue: for unions attempting to remain major actors in the rapidly changing new Europe; for employers seeking new input and productivity from employees as well as managerial freedom and control; for proponents of new post-Fordist production models that include employee involvement and closer labor-management cooperation; for social democratic advocates of expanded industrial democracy; for national governments balancing conflicting claims of domestic interest groups; for the European Commission and Parliament, each seeking to give substance to a popular social dimension in the unleashed European market integration project. And not only is WPM a critical issue in its own right: the European debates surrounding WPM also serve as a lens shedding light on the broader prospects for social policy in a single European market—the social Europe debate.

While WPM is indeed spreading in Europe as one aspect of market-driven production reorganization, the employer-led variety has largely accounted for this expansion. At the European level, the union-social democratic campaign for negotiated WPM (which has gained in intensity since 1988 but which actually dates to the early 1970s) has met so far with little success.

The reasons for this lie in politics and institutional configurations.

2. For shorthand purposes, the abbreviation WPM is used, as in Strauss (1982).
3. The Council of Ministers, composed of ministers from the twelve member states, is the EC's decisionmaking body. The Commission is the administrative body; it proposes legislation for discussion in Parliament and decision by the Council. The European Parliament, with proportionally represented elected delegates from every member state, is primarily a discussion forum, with little formal power other than certain veto rights.

Employer-led WPM is the default outcome and is often initiated in order to forestall negotiated WPM.[4] Negotiated WPM requires specialized institutions (especially works councils) and unions that are strong and cohesive enough to use these institutions effectively. In those nations where both of these requirements are met, negotiated WPM exists and arguably has grown in importance in the past decade. This is true especially of Germany but also of the Netherlands, Denmark, Belgium, and countries outside the EC such as Sweden. Where one or both of these requirements are lacking, negotiated WPM has made less headway. At the European level, unions have lacked the strength and cohesion to play a leading role in institution building; the necessary institutions for negotiated WPM are absent as well. Employers and their political allies have had sufficient strength within the single market effort to prevent adoption of regulations and creation of institutions that are not to their liking. Therefore, amid the current dynamics of European integration, the political and institutional requirements for expanding negotiated WPM have been missing.

Strauss has identified four principal kinds of WPM: direct (quality circles, teamwork, semiautonomous work groups); profit-sharing; works councils; and company board membership.[5] Broadly speaking, the first two are identified with employer-led WPM initiatives while the latter two are negotiated, including active union participation in the establishment of such forums. The lines have blurred in recent years: while most unions continue to prefer wage increases to profit-sharing, they have in notable cases taken a new interest in direct participation by groups of workers (e.g., the promotion of group work[6]). Employers, for their part, have accepted works councils and employee board membership where these are mandated by law, by central bargaining agreement, or both but have continued to oppose them elsewhere (in particular EC countries and at the European level). Renewed employer interest in direct participation and profit-sharing is driven by changing market circumstances; and these employer-led forms of WPM appear to be spreading in Europe as in

4. Some theorists of worker participation, especially those who fall into the conflict- or opposition-oriented camp, make a distinction between pseudoparticipation (employer-led, in which management defines the issues to be considered) and more substantive participation (negotiated). For a brief, useful discussion of this and other perspectives on participation, see Stern (1988, pp. 397–98).

5. Strauss (1991).

6. Turner (1991, pp. 111–17).

the United States. Nevertheless, the European debate concerns negotiated WPM.[7]

The contemporary expansion of WPM and the surrounding debates are not driven primarily by Europe 1992 processes but by the same forces pushing European governments toward greater integration. These forces include intensified world market competition, the rise of Japanese production models (which include integrated enterprise unions), the rapid spread of microelectronic technologies, and managerial imperatives to reorganize production and work.

Employers have discovered in many cases that reorganization is more effective and that productivity and flexibility can be increased if employees are consulted in advance and on a regular basis. Japanese production models that include some direct WPM in the office and on the shop floor are particularly instructive. Many unions have discovered that in these reorganization processes, union influence is best preserved where some form of negotiated WPM obtains.[8] Both sides have felt pressure within their ranks arising from new demands for participation and voice, especially from younger workers and white collar, technical, and professional employees (whose numbers are growing). Therefore, both employers and unions in most EC countries are promoting various, and often quite different, forms of WPM. In this context, the drive toward European economic integration has served both to accelerate the urgency of these projects and provide a new battleground at the European level where the different concepts contend.

Thus, WPM is spreading but in quite different ways. The specific shape and direction of change or expansion varies considerably from country to country, depending on existing national institutions and the political capacities of employers, unions, and governments. Although WPM has yet to spread widely at the European level (in multinational works councils, board participation, information committees, or bar-

7. Despite their importance profit-sharing or direct employee participation will only be considered in passing. Various forms of direct participation, especially quality circles and teamwork, are gaining in importance in Europe as managers seek to respond to new Japanese competitive challenges by adopting elements of Japanese production practice.

As for the two levels of negotiated WPM, works councils are clearly the more important forum, while EC proposals concerning works councils have provoked the most heated debate. We thus focus on works councils as the critical aspect of negotiated WPM, with a secondary look at company board participation. For a discussion of the problems and usual atrophy of employer-organized direct participation, see Strauss (1991). For an argument that worker directors have little effect on company board operations, see Batstone and Davies (1976) and Stern (1988, pp. 404–5).

8. Turner (1991).

gaining), numerous plans have been proposed—both for individual firms and for multinationals in general. There is currently a major EC-financed effort to establish cross-national information committees at large European firms (see below). But the long-term success of such Europe-wide initiatives will depend to a large extent on WPM developments within the member states as well as on the balance of forces and the outcomes of political debate at the European level.

Left to their own devices, employers would be content to pursue their own WPM initiatives with little help from the EC or the unions. Unions are the major promoters of expanded, negotiated WPM. This is true because intensified international competition has placed national, regional, and firm-level collective bargaining under stress. As employers have moved to reorganize work, negotiations have tended to shift to lower levels, leading to widespread decentralization of bargaining.[9] WPM is a way for unions to maintain their influence under these new circumstances. And at the same time as increasing international competition has put cross-national bargaining on the agenda for unions, new requirements for WPM at the European level (for firms doing business in more than one EC state) afford a possible means for unions to gain a toehold in multinational bargaining.

Germany now has the largest economy in the EC; German employers, unions, and the federal government all make their voices heard in European circles. Moreover, in Germany unions have stayed strong, so that the expansion of WPM, rooted in national legislation, has been negotiated and in some cases even union led (primarily through works councils at the firm and plant levels). In most of the other eleven member states, by contrast, unions have declined over the past decade both in membership density and in influence; and in several of these countries, WPM has neither statutory backing nor the backing of a central national agreement. The expansion of WPM in most of these countries, therefore, has been largely employer led. On balance then, in spite of the fact that Germany has both the dominant economy and most entrenched WPM arrangements, the spread of WPM throughout the EC as a whole has been largely voluntary and along employer models. This is true so far also at the European level, where employers have insisted on guidelines rather than binding legislation in the areas of information, consultation, and participation for employees.

This is the crux of the current debate over the social dimension within

9. Locke (1990).

the Council of Ministers, the Commission, and Parliament. Unions and their political allies want binding measures to "reregulate" the European single market so as to afford the basic social protections currently embodied in national legislation. Employers and their political allies support statements of principle (such as the Social Charter) to guide voluntary implementation of social advances such as WPM at the level of the individual firm.[10]

European-level developments thus reflect national developments and diversity. German unions, following the model that has served the expansion of their own influence so well, are the main proponents of expanded participation rights for workers and unions.[11] They are currently preoccupied with unification, however. Union weakness in other member states combined with overall employer strength in what has so far been a business-oriented single market project has prevented adoption of binding measures for WPM at the European level. It has also ensured that the spread of participation is for the most part voluntary and employer led.

The following sections examine the history of the European debate on negotiated WPM, the recent union-led campaign and current stalemate, the first European-level works councils, and the existing national bases for negotiated WPM. The evidence shows the continued importance of this issue. It points to a substantial amount of national-level WPM in several member states (especially Germany) within an overall pattern of wide cross-national diversity; the great difficulty of building institutions in Europe today, especially those addressing the expansion of employee and union rights; and continued employer dominance within the single European market project.

WPM and the European Community: The History of the Debate

Unions and their social democratic or socialist allies were early postwar supporters of the European Economic Community, hoping to build union influence and social protections through new Europe-wide insti-

10. See, for example, Rhodes (1991) on the broad European struggle between neoliberals and neocorporatists, labor market deregulation and reregulation, competitive flexibility and constructive flexibility.

11. And comparative research supports the notion that participation works best when backed up by legislation. See IDE (1981).

tutions. However, the Treaty of Rome, signed in 1957 mainly by conservative governments of the initial six member states, adopted a minimalist position on social policy.[12]

By the 1970s, however, the European Commission had begun advocating a more interventionist position on social issues. This view gained in influence as the Social Democratic party (SPD) came to power in West Germany, the Labour party took over in Britain (following Britain's entry into the EEC in 1973), and waves of strikes in various countries beginning in 1968 heralded a resurgence in class conflict in western Europe.[13] A new period of European-level social activism began around 1974. The current debates over the social dimension, including those surrounding WPM, have their roots in this period. Thus Mosley identifies three periods for European social policy: 1958–73, the period of benign neglect; 1974–85, the period of social activism; and 1987 to the present, the social dimension period, sparked by the new single market project.[14]

Social Activism: 1974–85

In the mid- to late 1970s, the Council of Ministers approved directives to expand worker rights in health and safety, plant closings and mass dismissals, firm bankruptcies and changes of ownership, and equal opportunity. After 1979, however, further initiatives were frustrated by the rise of conservative governments, conservative economic policy, and most dramatically by Prime Minister Thatcher's "Mrs. No" perspective.[15] Compared to the aspirations of Europeanist social activists, achievements of this period were modest. In particular, several initiatives to expand WPM rights for employees were unsuccessful.

The European Commission made three proposals relating to WPM during this period. First was the Fifth Directive on Company Law, proposed in 1972, aimed at ensuring employee participation on the boards of public companies (that is, most large European firms). The draft directive recognized the need for flexibility in implementation according to divergent existing national arrangements; but the intent was to regularize Community-wide WPM at the top levels of management.[16]

12. Teague and Grahl (1989, p. 170).
13. Crouch and Pizzorno (1978).
14. Mosley (1990, pp. 149–57).
15. Teague and Grahl (1989, p. 170); Dworkin and Lee (1990, pp. 8ff).
16. Pipkorn (1984, pp. 60–66); Northrup and others (1988, p. 529); Teague (1989a, pp. 313–14).

Second was the European Company Statute, proposed in 1975, which offered firms the option of incorporating as European firms for cross-national investment and trade purposes. The proposed statute included provisions to ensure WPM in the new European firms, including a Community-wide works council for each such firm, supervisory board participation for employee representatives, and the possibility of Community-wide collective bargaining.[17]

Third was the Vredeling directive (named after then EEC Social Affairs Commissioner Henk Vredeling, a Dutch socialist), proposed in 1980. It was aimed at expanding and harmonizing employee information and consultation rights in "complex organizations" (again, most large European concerns) throughout the EEC.[18] The Vredeling directive turned out to be the most controversial of all three proposals, giving rise to intense controversy at the European level—in the Council, Commission, Parliament, and other forums.

All three measures were discussed and debated at length at the European level and within the member states. All three were revised and rewritten, shunted back and forth among numerous committees, the Commission and the Council; all the while they were debated, at times quite fiercely, in the European Parliament. The proposals were justified on the basis of articles of the original EEC treaty, such as Article 100, calling for harmonization of economic activities and approximation of laws in the member nations.[19] At various times, the discussion focused on one or the other of these measures. By the early 1980s the debate had become intense and around 1983–84, it came to focus on the Vredeling directive (which is still today referred to as the notorious Vredeling proposal in employer-oriented publications).

The most active supporters of these measures were trade union organizations such as the European Trade Union Confederation (ETUC) and the European Metalworkers Federation (EMF). Employers, organized at the European level through the Union of Industrial and Employers' Confederations of Europe (UNICE), most actively opposed inclusion of mandatory WPM within the two directives and the European Company Statute. Although both the ETUC and UNICE, as well as other organizations

---

17. Pipkorn (1984, pp. 66–68).

18. Pipkorn (1984, pp. 56–60); Northrup and others (1988, pp. 528–29); Dworkin and Lee (1990, p. 11).

19. Pipkorn (1984, pp. 49–54). Eurojargon is an unfortunate affliction with which all students of contemporary European integration must contend. Harmonization and approximation are terms that refer to the necessity for EC member states to bring their diverse economic policies and laws into line with one another—falling short, however, of identity. See, for example, Kolvenbach (1990).

representing cross-national worker and employer interests (for instance, at the sectoral level) were only loosely organized, they provided important forums and lobbying vehicles for their various constituent interests, especially in the debates over WPM.

National unions were far from unanimous on these issues. French unions, for example, were much less enthusiastic about any kind of co-determination than were their German counterparts. But within international forums such as the ETUC, German union support, backed by the Belgians, Dutch, and Danes, was more than enough to overcome indifference (or even occasional hostility) from the French unions and others. Thus the ETUC could for the most part speak with one voice in support of the three measures.[20] Employers, on the other hand, viewed such legislation as an infringement on their authority especially in countries where such arrangements were not entrenched. An oversimplified way to view the debate that nonetheless captures the essence of the political conflict is to see German unions as the primary advocates opposed by French, Italian, and British employers.

By the early 1980s, however, when these debates came to a head, the timing of events worked against labor. Under the leadership of Reagan and Thatcher, conservative economic policy prevailed (by 1983 even in socialist France). Thatcher and the Tories came to power in Britain in 1979; the historic compromise including the Communist party fell apart in Italy in the same year; Kohl and his coalition led by the Christian Democratic Union (CDU) replaced the SPD in West Germany in 1982; and in socialist France unions remained fragmented and weak. Under the impact of a deep recession in 1980–82, combined with employer and government challenges, unions declined in influence almost everywhere in the EEC except West Germany. Unions and social democrats promoted the Vredeling directive vigorously, in part to reclaim at the European level some of the influence they were losing at home. But employer opposition was adamant and powerful. The social dialogue of the previous years bogged down, and no new European social policy was enacted after 1980.[21] Ruling out any vestige of hope of a reemergence, Prime Minister Thatcher perfected the art of casting vetoes on the lawmaking Council.[22]

20. The communist CGT, the French union federation most hostile to participation concepts, remained one of the few European union federations outside the ETUC.

21. Venturini (1989, p. 21); Dworkin and Lee (1990, pp. 8–11).

22. There was an additional factor contributing to the Vredeling directive's defeat in the early 1980s: the expensive campaign waged in Brussels and among the member states by lobbyists for American-based firms. As the *Economist* put it, "Europe's unions are no

Achievements of this period were disappointing compared to the aspirations of the Europeanist social activists. All three WPM initiatives were unsuccessful. The Vredeling proposal was shelved in 1986, precisely the year in which the Single European Act launched the drive toward the 1992 single market.

The Social Dimension: 1987 to the Present

Observers have argued that world economic problems since the mid-1970s, and specifically the intractable economic difficulties faced by western European societies, are related to new challenges faced by the dominant Fordist production system.[23] As the Japanese reinvented production, modifying traditional concepts to produce high-quality goods at low cost and enhancing their capacity to change product offerings quickly, European firms were forced to begin their own processes of reorganization in order to remain competitive. By the early 1980s, these processes included rapid technological change, challenges to union influence and established shop floor bases (contributing to union decline), expanded employer-led WPM (to motivate workers and elicit work force contributions to productivity growth), and widespread decentralization of industrial relations. However, in the eyes of many European business leaders (especially the Roundtable of European Industrialists) and government policymakers, the pace of change was too slow. European firms were falling behind, unable to keep up with Japanese growth rates, productivity increases, investment levels, or market shares. It was also clear that the United States was unable to provide either the leadership or resources to guide Europe out of its economic doldrums. In the face of these new problems, European business and government leaders, organized by Jacques Delors of the European Commission, launched the single market project to spur the needed levels of investment and processes of reorganization.[24]

Thus the same world market forces and political responses were driving union decline, production reorganization, decentralization of industrial relations, expanded employer-led WPM, and Europe 1992. The single market project was initiated, as a product of political negotiation,

---

match for America's multinationals" (October 16, 1982, p. 77). See also a follow-up article in the *Economist*, June 25, 1983, p. 54.

23. See Piore and Sabel (1984); Boyer (1988); Teague and Grahl (1990, pp. 170–72).
24. Sandholtz and Zysman (1989).

by an alliance between large businesses, governments, and European elites based on business and government deregulation goals of the 1980s. Labor was in effect excluded from the project in its takeoff period when unions (and the Left generally) were in decline in much of the Community. At the same time, labor's opposition to deregulation was neutralized by traditional unions' and social democrats' support for European integration.[25]

As events unfolded, the severe threat this deregulatory project posed for established national bases of union influence became clear. Therefore, beginning around 1988, national unions organized at the European level through the ETUC seriously began to take up the banner of the social dimension. Labor would agree to and support open markets in return for upward harmonization of social standards and protections at the European level. But labor was not the only proponent. Several EC governments and even business in some quarters (notably Germany) expressed interest in a social dimension—to prevent social unrest, perhaps, but more importantly to head off capital flight from northern Europe to southern Europe. There were thus two main sources of interest in the new social dimension. Unions saw it as a means to protect and improve worker standards and to maintain or rebuild union influence at national and European levels. Second, certain governments and employers supported it to prevent social dumping, which could choke the high productivity growth anticipated in the single market vision.

Much of the social dimension is in fact noncontroversial, at least for all EC countries except Britain. There is broad agreement on such issues as the free mobility of workers, structural funds (to transfer money from wealthier to poorer countries for training and employment projects, infrastructure, and so on), and the convergence of national labor market policy in such areas as social security, worker training and job creation.[26] But for such issues as the length of the work week, regulation of part-time and temporary work, and employee information, consultation, and participation rights, controversy has been intense. Employers and their political allies continue to resist any binding measures in these areas with the same intensity they demonstrated in earlier battles against the Vredeling proposal and the inclusion of mandatory WPM in the draft Fifth Directive and the European Company Statute.[27]

Jacques Delors, backed by French President Mitterrand, has played an

---

25. Streeck (1991).
26. Teague and Grahl (1989, p. 55).
27. See Teague and Grahl (1989, pp. 55–58).

important role in the social dimension debate. Some observers contend that the turn toward conservative economic policy by these French socialists made the Europe 1992 project possible.[28] But along with his promotion of the single market, Delors called early on for the inclusion of social protections. First, he initiated the so-called Val Duchesse dialogue between representatives of business and labor and charged the Economic and Social Committee of the European Commission (including both employer and union representatives) with developing social proposals. But progress was slow as employers sought mutual understandings rather than binding measures, especially in such areas as labor relations and WPM. The ETUC complained that labor remained excluded in any substantive way from the 1992 project. Delors then chose the ETUC conference in Stockholm in 1988 to launch the campaign for a social charter. Fundamental to this vision of a social Europe were expanded information, consultation, and participation rights for employees, a position that Delors articulated forcefully.[29]

In spite of national differences—German and Dutch unions, for example, strongly favored WPM; others were less enthusiastic—the ETUC passed a strongly worded resolution in favor of a social charter that included significant WPM provisions. In December of the same year, the ETUC officially adopted its own Community Charter on Social Rights, endorsed by all thirty-six member union confederations. The charter included a call for WPM rights for all employees in the European Community, and demanded that the entire charter be legally binding.[30]

The social Europe battle had begun, with WPM as a major focus of the debate. When a social charter proposed by the Commission was adopted in somewhat watered-down form in December 1989 by eleven of the twelve member states, debate merely shifted to the implementation process—the action program and related measures. Proponents of the charter and action program included the ETUC, the European Commission, and the European Parliament. German unionists continued to play a leading role within the ETUC. On the participation issue, they were now backed not only by the Danes, Belgians, and Dutch, but increasingly by the British, Italians, and Spaniards who claimed to have learned from

28. Sandholtz and Zysman (1989).
29. See, for example, the reporting of this event in *Industrial Relations Europe*, vol. 16, (June 1988), p. 1. See also Silvia (1991, pp. 633–34). And Delors kept to this position: in 1990, he continued to place information, consultation, and participation rights among "the most urgent aspects of the Commission's Action Program," Lodge (1990, p. 147).
30. Silvia (1991, pp. 633–34).

their reverses of the 1980s and now saw the value of statutory WPM. Within and beyond the Social Charter, the ETUC promoted information and consultation rights (in works councils or consultation committees), worker directors on company boards, and cross-national Community-wide bargaining for firms with branches in more than one member country. The ETUC supported a new version of the European Company Statute and envisioned revised versions of the Fifth Directive and the Vredeling proposal as aspects of implementing the Social Charter.

Commission officials (including Delors) argued that WPM offered protection against the spread of social dumping, which could wreck the single market project; that WPM made for better management, of which German economic success was strong evidence; and that it was impossible to offer firms an option such as European incorporation unless some form of negotiated WPM was included, since several member states had this already.[31]

The European Parliament also emerged as a strong supporter of the Social Charter and its WPM measures. Many of its members had run on platforms espousing a social dimension (including WPM) in the 1989 elections. The Left (broadly defined) claimed 261 seats to 242 for the Right; and among the delegates of the Right were many Christian democratic supporters of a strong social dimension.[32] Although still mainly a debating forum, the Parliament began to use the popular social dimension to increase its own voice, putting pressure on Delors and the Commission to propose strong measures.[33] In the summer of 1990, the European Parliament, backed by a large majority, called for extensive and binding WPM, declaring that it expected directives to this end from the Commission as part of the action program as well as new legislation to establish a framework for cross-national collective bargaining.[34]

The employers' confederation, UNICE, agreed for the most part with the idea of the charter as a statement of principle, as long as implementation was to occur by means of "subsidiarity" (that is, decisionmaking

---

31. It should be noted that these are three quite different arguments, likely to be supported by quite different interests (German employers, for instance, might support the first, government officials and intellectuals the second, and unions the third). The Commission has thus aimed to be all things to all people, which accounts in part for its great difficulty in producing broadly acceptable specific measures on the issue of WPM in Europe.

32. "European Parliament Election Results," *European Industrial Relations Review*, vol. 186 (July 1989), p. 2.

33. Lodge (1990, pp. 147–48).

34. "Parliament Wants EC Labour Court, Bargaining Rules," *Industrial Relations Europe*, vol. 18 (September 1990), p. 2.

and implementation performed at the lowest possible level). In general, employers favored a social dimension in order to improve industrial competitiveness, but not to expand industrial democracy. UNICE took a consistent and active position against any measures that would obligate firms to expand worker participation. As in the earlier battles over the Vredeling proposal, European employers were reinforced in this position by vigorous and well-financed lobbying by the U.S. Chamber of Commerce delegation in Brussels.

The most vociferous opponent of the Social Charter and any proposed expansion of WPM rights remained the British government. Although the Commission diluted the provisions of the charter to gain British support, the Thatcher government in the end refused to vote for it. Any hint of WPM rights elicited the British government's veto threat in the Council. As Thatcher put it: "I say to people on the Continent: 'Stop talking about worker participation in business management. You are back in the Marxist era!'"[35] Two poles of opinion could, therefore, be defined: a maximalist position on the social dimension supported by the unions, Parliament, and the Commission; and a minimalist position supported by employers and Britain.[36]

In December 1990, as part of the Social Charter's action program, the Commission issued a new draft directive calling for the establishment of European works councils at large firms (those with more than 1,000 employees total and with at least one hundred employees doing business in two or more EC countries).[37] This appeared to be a more flexible version of the defeated Vredeling directive—so flexible in fact that it was sharply criticized by IG Metall President Franz Steinkühler.[38] Criticism of this new European works council legislation escalated in early 1991: while labor found it "too timid and limited," UNICE attacked it as harmful to business, management authority, and free bargaining.[39]

Meanwhile, the Fifth Directive found new life as part of the social dimension; although the possible forms of representation became increasingly flexible as the debate proceeded, employers continued to op-

35. Interview with the editors of *Readers' Digest*, published first in a newspaper advertisement, *International Herald Tribune*, April 19, 1989, p. 13.

36. Teague (1989a, p. 326).

37. "Draft Directive on European Works Councils," *European Industrial Relations Review*, vol. 204, (January 1991), p. 2.

38. Steinkühler criticized it for applying only to very large firms and for allowing firms to withhold extensive information on the grounds of business secrecy.

39. "Euro-Company Statute 'Should Give Workers More Say,'" *Industrial Relations Europe*, vol. 19 (March 1991), p. 1.

pose any attempt to mandate employee participation on company boards. The proposed European Company Statute offered three forms of participation: supervisory board (the German model); works committee (the French model); or any other negotiated version agreed to by both labor and management (the Swedish model).[40]

In the meantime, WPM cropped up in a variety of different forms for specific issues. For health and safety, for example, firm-level joint committees were included in European Commission directives. More controversial, however, were directives concerning the introduction of new technology and the regulation of temporary and part-time work which called for labor-management information sharing and consultation. The WPM issue refused to go away; if anything, the debates showed signs of expanding and intensifying in the early 1990s.

With the opening of eastern Europe in 1989 and the unification of Germany in 1990, European economic (and possibly political) integration took on a new urgency.[41] EC policymakers prepared a second round of integration initiatives, encompassing steps toward monetary and political union. Driven in part by this urgency but also by frustration at the lagging pace of social initiatives, policymakers at the Commission and in the member states began a new effort in late 1990 to expand the concept and practice of qualified majority voting.

A key provision of the Single European Act passed in 1986 was to require qualified majority voting on the Council of Ministers instead of traditional EC unanimity for measures aimed at implementing the single European market. This provision was critical in speeding up the decisionmaking process and making further economic integration possible. But Article 100A of the Single European Act specifically excluded "the rights and interests of employed persons" from majority voting. As a result, social issues such as health and safety were eligible for majority voting; meanwhile others such as WPM, precisely the most controversial issues, required unanimity. And the British government, at least under Thatcher, was outspoken in its intent to use its veto power to block new information, consultation, or participation rights for employees.[42]

40. "Criticism Grows on All Sides over Euro-Council Draft," *Industrial Relations Europe*, vol. 19 (February 1991), p. 1.

41. Story (1990, p. 165).

42. Peter Lange has persuasively argued that Britain's propensity to veto in a voting system requiring unanimity has made possible all kinds of "cheap talk" by the other member governments, who are free to posture to please domestic groups on such issues as the social dimension. In the absence of a British veto threat or given a shift to qualified majority voting, the apparent widespread support for social issues including WPM could become

As the social debate escalated, the demand for majority voting intensified. Already in 1989, the European Parliament had called for broad
majority voting to implement the Social Charter.[43] In August 1990, Italy
proposed that the Council adopt majority voting for labor and social
legislation, to speed up policy-making. At year's end, Belgium submitted
its plan to have qualified majority voting extend to all labor issues. But
the legal and political reality remained unchanged: it required unanimity
on the Council to shift to majority voting.

A breakthrough on the issue of qualified majority voting finally came
in late 1991 in the form of the "midnight surprise" social protocol ap-
pended to the New Treaty on European Union signed at Maastricht.
Eleven countries agreed to shift to qualified majority voting for many
social issues, including information and consultation, but not participation. (Britain again opted out.) In addition, the social partners, UNICE
and the ETUC, were given expanded authority to negotiate broad agreement on issues such as WPM. By mid-1992, however, it was still not clear
whether the Maastricht Treaty would be ratified, nor was it clear
whether the social partners would succeed in negotiating agreement or
whether member governments were prepared to use qualified majority
voting in pursuit of social goals.

So the debate continued. Some were prepared to declare labor's defeat
on the social dimension, at least in the short run.[44] A new strain of Euro-
pessimism took hold, which saw in the 1992 deregulation effort labor's
failure to recreate institutions of regulation at the European level (for
such purposes as collective bargaining and WPM) and the gradual erosion of such bases of union influence at the national level.[45] Outcomes
for all social issues including WPM, however, remained uncertain, subject to political conflict and negotiation.[46] At the very least, the Social
Charter represented a benchmark for those at the national and European
levels seeking to expand social rights in areas such as WPM.[47] But by
1992, although there had been considerable negotiation and debate, no
concrete measures had been adopted by the Council to implement any
controversial aspect of the charter, WPM included. In other words, the

---

much weaker (remarks from a presentation at a Western Societies program seminar, Cornell
University, March 8, 1991).
43. Mosley (1990, p. 157).
44. Silvia (1991).
45. Mosley (1990); Streeck (1991).
46. Teague (1989a); Lodge (1990); Story (1990).
47. Lodge (1990, pp. 140–41).

minimalists have so far won out. This is not surprising given the current balance of political forces, a decade of union decline in most countries, employer leadership in the 1992 project, and the current economic slow-down.

Multinational Works Councils and Community-wide Bargaining

In spite of extensive speculation and discussion as well as occasional advocacy from European unions and the ETUC, there has been virtually no multinational labor-management bargaining in Europe to date.[48] With very few exceptions, unions have yet to produce fully developed proposals for multinational bargaining or to mobilize cross-nationally in support of such a goal. The closest efforts in this direction so far have been a few cases of European-level works councils that have been recognized by management.

In June 1988 the European Metalworkers Federation (EMF) took a position in favor of works councils at the firm level with specified rights to information and consultation for companies with operations in more than one European country. IG Metall President Steinkühler endorsed this concept in a major public campaign including press releases, a conference, and a book on unions and the social dimension.[49] Since then, the European Metalworkers' Federation has worked with numerous cross-national groups of unions seeking to establish such committees or councils, with recent funding support from the European Commission.

Employers, however, have shown great reluctance. The "EMF model" was at first officially recognized only at two French-based multinationals, Bull and Thomson. The latter was the first of its kind, dating from a 1986 agreement between Thomson and the European Metalworkers' Federation.[50] Such agreements, which the federation is working to spread, establish information and consultation committees for union work force representatives from the various countries in which the firm operates. The federation has referred to the Thomson experience as the first European works council.

A similar agreement exists at BSN, a French multinational in the food

---

48. Union initiatives began in the 1970s with the establishment of sectoral International Trade Secretariats, but these were largely ignored by employers.

49. See Steinkühler (1989, pp. 16–19).

50. Northrup and others (1988, pp. 532–33); Baun (1990, pp. 21–22).

business.[51] From a union point of view, the shortcoming in these three experiences is that they have largely proven to be employer led, and the firms concerned are based in a country where unions are weak. Even to the extent that employers are willing to accept such arrangements, they are opposed to allowing them to develop beyond the stage of information committees and into more active WPM. As Northrup, Campbell, and Slowinski put it, "Multinational employers, even those who have participated in such consultative mechanisms, are likely to resist any pressure, whether from union or governmental sources, that would transform consultation into negotiation."[52]

In an effort to provide a more advanced model of European-level WPM, in 1990 the general works council at Volkswagen in Germany initiated the establishment of a European works council composed of representatives from VW and Audi in Germany, VW in Belgium, and SEAT in Spain (owned by VW). VW management was present at the founding meeting and in February 1992 officially recognized the council and its right to meet at company expense, receive information, and discuss issues of strategic importance with management. The VW effort is in part a response to the tedious decisionmaking process at the EC concerning worker rights; and the VW European works council members are explicit in their intent to set an example that will inspire other crossnational union collaborations as well as influence the work of the European Commission.[53] The works council and union at VW have at important junctures in the past served as a model for the German labor movement and for labor-management relations. The extension of this role to the European level is a much more ambitious, complicated, and problematic undertaking.

There is currently an effort under way to establish additional crossnational information committees (now referred to as European works councils, or EWCs) at a number of large European multinational corporations. Organizing meetings are funded by the European Commission at a total amount of 14 million ecus in 1992 and a budgeted 17 million in 1993. Although this may be an important first step, it remains unclear

51. This one also dates from 1986, based on an agreement signed between the company and the International Union of Food and Allied Workers' Unions (IUF) and its European affiliate, the European Committee of Food, Catering and Allied Workers' Unions (ECF), Northrup and others (1988, pp. 535–36).

52. Northrup and others (1988, p. 540).

53. *BR-Kontakt* (newsletter of the VW general works council at Wolfsburg) (June and September, 1990).

both how many of the new committees will walk on their own feet when EC funding expires and to what extent information may expand into consultation and more substantive participation.

To summarize, the evidence presents a consistent picture of an unsuccessful but protracted and continuing union-led campaign for Community-wide WPM rights. Negotiated WPM does exist, however, at the national level, especially in Germany.

WPM at the National Level

Established worker rights will have to be defended in the new Europe from the national level; it is from this basis that cross-national efforts to expand negotiated WPM will be built. The following sections consider negotiated WPM in the member states, with an emphasis on Germany; briefer looks at France, Britain, and Italy; and a glance at the remaining eight countries.

Germany

The German version of WPM, known as codetermination (*Mitbestimmung*), is an integral part of an industrial relations system that has been widely recognized for its success. There are two poles to codetermination: employee participation on company supervisory boards and elected works councils at the plant and firm levels. The rights and obligations of worker representatives and management at both levels are spelled out in detailed national legislation passed in 1951, 1952, 1972, and 1976.[54]

Board representation, although not insignificant, is the least important of the two poles of codetermination. Supervisory boards meet only a few times a year, with day-to-day decisions made by a separate management board, which is, however, elected by the supervisory board. For the worker representatives on these boards (usually works councilors and union representatives), these meetings afford occasions to learn of company financial and strategic planning. The access to information and the ability to speak out at top levels has sometimes served works council and union interests and smoothed labor-management negotiations. Yet except in the iron, steel, and coal industries, which have parity representation on the boards, labor's minority position on supervisory boards has

54. For useful English-language introductions to codetermination in the Federal Republic, see Streeck (1984) and Berghahn and Karsten (1987).

given codetermination at this level a minor role compared to the daily activities of the works councils.[55]

Works councils are legally independent of both union and management, and they are democratically elected by the entire work force, blue and white collar employees. The public sector essentially has the same arrangement in personnel councils. Representatives serve part time at smaller firms, and there is a mix of full- and part-time councilors at larger firms. All works council costs are paid by the firm.

Works councils are empowered by law, precedent, and plant- and firm-level agreements to receive full information and consult with management prior to the implementation of decisions affecting personnel. In specified areas, works councils have veto rights, giving true meaning to the term "codetermination."[56]

How does this works council system work in practice? From a management point of view, there are many actions a firm cannot take without first consulting the works council. In such areas as the introduction of new technology and job design, management is required to inform the works council and listen to comments and suggestions prior to implementation.[57] In these areas, management often ignores the wishes of the works council once the consultation obligation is fulfilled. But in other areas, management must either gain the assent of the works council or, in the event of stalemate, submit the matter to binding arbitration. Under the Works Constitution Act, works councils have codetermination rights in the areas of working hours, piecework rates and bonuses, and performance monitoring (Article 87); working conditions in cases where employers have violated accepted principles of suitable job design (Article 91); hiring, firing, transfers, assignment to pay groupings, or job classifications (Articles 95 and 99); and training and retraining (Article 98).

In spite of West German industry's often cited shop-floor flexibility, given the myriad personnel issues involved, management is not free to reorganize work without extensive discussion with the works council.[58] While decisionmaking may be slowed in this consensus-building process (and the outcome may be altered), once agreement is reached manage-

55. The unions waged a major battle in the 1970s to pass new legislation for parity codetermination on company boards. Although this effort increased the number of worker representatives on the boards of large firms, the goal of parity was not achieved for industries besides coal and steel.
56. Adams and Rummel (1977, pp. 7–8).
57. Works Constitution Act, Article 90.
58. Streeck (1984); Streeck (1987); Thelen (1991).

ment has an important ally in the works council for winning work force acceptance and smoothing implementation.

Germany also has a strong and fairly cohesive labor movement organized into one principal labor federation (the DGB), itself composed of sixteen industrial unions. From 1978 until unification, union membership density of the employed work force in West Germany was stable at around 40 percent.[59] Relations between unions and works councils are typically close: works councils, especially in the larger firms, are usually dominated by union activists who work closely with the local union office.[60]

At the regional level, fairly centralized unions and employer associations conduct nationally coordinated collective bargaining for entire sectors, establishing the framework for wages, working conditions, and hours within which works councils and managers operate. The unions, with substantial resources at the national level, are in a position to offer works councils important advice on strategy, bargaining, key issues, and daily operations. This is especially true of the larger unions such as IG Metall and works councils at the larger firms.

The degrees of influence and independence of works councils within firms differ widely: variations are identifiable by industry, firm size, and plant history. Tensions also exist between works councils and unions. Works councils have been criticized for plant egoism, and there is a considerable literature in Germany on this problem.[61] Nevertheless, observers have maintained that the particular German institutions of WPM have contributed to the stability of union influence in Germany (and even modest expansion in some areas) at a time of general union decline elsewhere.[62] Works councilors' capacity to engage actively in WPM from a perspective independent of management would be much weaker without inclusive unions committed to using the institutions of codetermination strategically. If anything, in the past decade the substance of WPM in Germany has expanded as both unions and employers have focused increasing attention on works councils in an era of industrial restructuring, work reorganization, and decentralized bargaining.

Finally, German codetermination has made a substantial positive con-

---

59. Streeck (1988, p. 20); Niedenhoff (1990, p. 11).

60. In the 1990 nationwide works council elections, 75 percent of elected works councilors were union members, with 92 percent of these coming from unions of the dominant DGB federation (Niedenhoff 1990, pp. 11–12). The DGB share of works council membership has grown steadily since 1978.

61. See, for example, Hohn (1988).

62. See Streeck (1984); Thelen (1991); Turner (1991).

tribution to a level of national economic and industrial success that is unparalleled in Europe. Codetermination has compelled managers to plan carefully, use internal labor markets, train and retrain, and organize personnel effectively. It has pushed management to collect information from and achieve consensus with representatives of its work force, to collect and thoroughly organize information for dissemination to the works council and supervisory board, to rationalize and raise productivity, and to move into more profitable markets in its product strategies.[63] By the same token, codetermination has given works councils and unions (and perhaps workers as well) an enhanced stake in the successful operation of the plant and firm.

As the pace of European economic integration quickens, the minimum requirement for German unions is the defense of codetermination at home.[64] But to the extent that so-called creeping deregulation undermines national institutions, the best defense may be a good offense.[65] German unionists worry that investment will flee to countries where firms are unburdened by codetermination (not to mention high wages) and that European-level decisions will weaken protections at home. (For example, multinationals based in another country might be allowed to produce in Germany using their own weaker versions of WPM.) Unions are concerned that the proposed European Company Statute could displace German national law in areas such as codetermination in the event a merger replaces a domestic employer with a foreign one.[66] Franz Steinkühler, president of IG Metall (the dominant German union), argues that German workers will lose what they have fought for at home if German-style industrial democracy does not spread to Europe as a whole.[67]

These concerns have driven German unions to take leading roles within the ETUC and other European-level groupings such as the European Metalworkers' Federation.[68] They have also driven German unions to seek agreement with their own employers. In 1989, for example, the DGB and the BDA (the German employers association) issued a joint statement calling for general minimum social standards and the alignment of labor law at a high level within the EC.[69] But as one might ex-

63. Streeck (1987).
64. Streeck (1991).
65. Mosley, (1990, p. 163).
66. Mosley, (1990, p. 156).
67. Steinkühler (1988, pp. 7–21). See also "German Involvement 'Must Be EC Model,'" *Industrial Relations Europe*, vol. 16 (August 1988), pp. 1, 8.
68. Streeck 1990, pp. 11–12.
69. "Employers, Unions Unite over EC Labour Reforms," *Industrial Relations Europe*, vol. 17 (August 1989), p. 6.

pect, German employers are of two minds on these issues. While they would love to see other European competitors face the same codetermination constraints they face, they want the opportunity to do business in other countries in a less constrained way and would not protest if the single European market increased their own leverage at home vis à vis their union and works council counterparts. Therefore, as the Social Charter debate escalated, German employers shifted away from their common ground with the unions and arrived at a moderate position supporting concepts such as WPM but opposing their mandatory extension throughout the EC. Chancellor Kohl's attempt in 1989 to bring the two sides together for a common position in the European debate failed.

German unions, however, will continue to lead in efforts to expand European-level WPM. Strategies will vary and evolve. For example, there is only qualified support for Community WPM directives among the ranks of German union leaders, a reflection of their concern that such measures could undermine Germany's own stronger requirements. The DGB favors minimum standards for information and consultation to build up national WPM in the member states and perhaps lay the groundwork for future, more substantial and successful European-level measures.

France

Although less developed and more limited, WPM is nonetheless widespread in France. At plant and firm levels, workers are represented through staff delegations (*délégations du personnel*), trade union sections (*sections syndicaux*), and works committees (*comités d'entreprise*).[70] The staff delegations monitor company rules and present grievances, but they have no bargaining power. The union representatives can engage in collective bargaining and represent worker interests in other ways. They also put up slates of candidates for election to the works committee, itself designated to play a limited role in WPM. Established by law in 1946, works committees are elected bodies at firms with 50 or more employees, with rights to information and consultation. Through the works committees, workers and unionists receive advance informa-

---

70. For brief descriptions of the three basic mechanisms of representation, see IDE (1981, pp. 189–91); and European Trade Union Institute (1990b, pp. 43–47). There is only limited supervisory board participation for worker representatives in France. Two works committee members may attend supervisory or management board meetings in an advisory capacity without voting rights. At state-owned firms and at certain limited liability companies, a small number of worker representatives may sit on the board with voting rights, European Trade Union Institute (1990b, p. 47).

tion regarding company plans, giving them the opportunity to mobilize if necessary. But the committees themselves are chaired by the plant manager and have no formal joint decisionmaking rights except in managing recreational facilities and activities. In most cases this latter area is the major preoccupation of the works committees; on the average they derive two-thirds of their budgets from revenues generated in the recreational programs, with the remaining third provided by the company.[71]

At some large firms such as EDF (the national electric company), the works committees are powerful bodies. Their activities often overlap with union representatives' work. Most of the elected committee members are unionists; at large firms they are often freed from normal work duties by virtue of their positions on the committees. Yet even in these cases, works committees generally have not advanced beyond information rights into more extensive WPM for a number of reasons: employers are opposed; French unions have rejected in principle participation in management decisionmaking although one of the principal labor federations, the CFDT, supports worker decisionmaking or "autogestion"; and plant representation is typically fragmented into several contending union sections who may carry their rivalry into their works committee efforts.[72]

The French labor movement is divided into six principal, often contentious union federations (CGT, CFDT, FO, CFTC, CGC, and FEN). The three largest, the CGT, CFDT, and FO, are all on the left (the CFDT and FO are socialist, but bitter rivals; the CGT is communist and still the largest). Ideological divisions and organizational rivalries among them are intense. Ever since the breakdown of efforts to form a coalition between the socialist and communist parties in 1977, and between the CFDT and CGT in 1980, the French labor movement has been in decline. This has persisted, especially for the CGT, even under socialist governments.[73] France is the only industrial democracy with a lower union membership density (12 percent or less) than the United States. Divided and in decline, the unions have hardly been in a position to promote expanded WPM through the works committees or in other ways, even if they were inclined to go in that direction. In fact, in the 1989 works

71. "Works Councils Cost Firms 'FF1,500 a Head Yearly,'" *Industrial Relations Europe*, vol. 17 (October 1988), p. 4.

72. See Ross (1982, pp. 18–19) concerning the relegation of the works committees to marginal status in the early postwar period after the committees were established by union-backed legislation.

73. Bridgford (1990).

committee elections, nonunion candidates for the first time won the largest number of elected committee positions for France as a whole.[74] The expansion of WPM in France in the past decade has been significantly employer led. Managers have promoted various forms of direct participation, including quality circles and expression groups.[75] Such programs aim at complementing the works committees on the shop floor; they also appear to have had the effect of further undermining the unions.[76]

As for Europe, the socialist party and the government support worker protections embodied in the Social Charter and its action program, including expanded information and consultation rights. But the French perspective, even the socialist and union views, are decidedly different from the German union perspective. As Jansen and Kissler put it: "Radical democratic traditions, overlapping an individualism which has a definite existence in France, give rise to the fact that common interests hardly ever arise in the area of industrial relations. . . . The codetermination model favoured by Germany is rejected virtually universally in France. Political groups and trade unions object that codetermination presumes harmony to exist where, in reality, conflict rules."[77]

United Kingdom

There is little to say about WPM in the United Kingdom, which has no legal provisions for either works councils or committees or worker board participation. Although in the 1970s *The Bullock Report* (issued by a royal committee) recommended participation by employee representatives on the unitary boards of large British firms, this recommendation was never acted upon. Experiments in this direction at British Steel and the Post Office were abandoned when Thatcher took office in 1979.[78]

In the place of formal works councils, employer-initiated or negotiated "joint consultation machinery" has been established at many firms (34 percent of firms surveyed in 1984 in the Workplace Industrial Rela-

---

74. Nationwide works committee elections yielded the following results: nonunion, 26.4 percent; CGT, 25.1 percent; CFDT 21 percent; FO, 11.2 percent; CGC, 5.5 percent; CFTC, 4.6 percent; others, 6.3 percent. "Work Council Elections Blow for Unions," *European Industrial Relations Review*, vol. 200 (September 1990), p. 6.

75. Bridgford (1990, p. 132).

76. Bridgford (1990, pp. 132–33); Delamotte (1988).

77. Jansen and Kissler (1987, p. 392.)

78. European Trade Union Institute (1990b, p. 53).

tions Survey).[79] But according to at least one analysis, these joint consultation bodies are an illusory phenomenon, offering little basis for substantive WPM or its expansion.[80]

As we have seen, the conservative government has been adamantly opposed not only to mandated WPM at home and in Europe, but the entire Social Charter of the EC.[81] The Tories under Thatcher framed the issue as one of employee involvement versus participation. Voluntary employer-led, firm-level involvement is good, they argued; mandated WPM is bad. The former is in keeping with the voluntarist traditions of British industrial relations; as for the latter, however, "formalism and legalism have often been found to be the enemies of effective employee involvement." [82]

There has indeed been an expansion of employee involvement programs at the firm level in Britain in the past decade as employers have responded to market pressures for rationalization and a greater employee contribution to the production process. As in other countries, there have been experiments with shop-floor teams, quality circles, and labor-management cooperation. In many cases, however, these experiments have foundered. The reasons for failure include longstanding adversarial relations, craft demarcations, and the widespread perception that such programs were part of the general offensive by government and employers against union influence.[83] Meanwhile, union membership density in the United Kingdom declined under the Thatcher regime from 54 percent in 1979 to 42 percent in 1987.[84]

In spite of the government's hard line in European circles, 76 percent of British managers surveyed in 1989 expressed a willingness to accept some form of EC legislation on WPM.[85] It is British unions, however, who in important cases have altered their previous views and become supporters of European integration, the Social Charter, and expanded WPM rights. The Trades Union Council (TUC) is explicit in its goal of regaining through alliances and legislation at the European level some of the influence it has lost at home since 1979. Renewed interest in WPM appears to be an important part of this new focus.

79. European Trade Union Institute (1990b, p. 52).
80. MacInnes (1985).
81. Story (1990, pp. 160–13).
82. According to a recent government report on employee involvement cited in *European Industrial Relations Review*, vol. 192 (January 1990), p. 24.
83. See MacInnes (1985); Wood (1988, pp. 231–39).
84. Towers (1989, p. 175).
85. *European Industrial Relations Review*, vol. 192 (January 1990), p. 24.

In 1989, for example, one of the TUC's bargaining checklists cited the proposed European Company Statute "model" for information, consultation, and worker participation on company boards. The TUC encouraged member unions to take up these issues in bargaining, arguing that "the 1992 programme gives unions and management an opportunity to test in practice the claim by many employers that 'voluntary' arrangements are preferable to statutory rights." [86] In 1990, the General, Municipal, and Boilermakers (GMB) union directed its locals to use the Social Charter as a checklist in collective bargaining, a practice that other unions were expected to follow. In its first coup, GMB announced an agreement with Keiper Recaro (a subsidiary of a German firm) that includes, based on the charter, both worker representation on the company board and the establishment of a works council. [87]

The United Kingdom remains, however, one of the least developed EC member states insofar as WPM is concerned. The government under John Major remains the primary opponent in EC government circles of expanded WPM rights, while British employers have banded together with other European employers to oppose mandatory measures.

Italy

Like the British, and unlike the French, Italian unions have become converts to the WPM cause. Also like the British, Italian unions are seeking remedies to reverse a decline that began in 1980, and they are starting from a minimal base regarding rights to information, consultation, and participation.

Italy has no legal provisions for worker participation on company boards. The only major exceptions are agreements signed in the mid-1980s to establish labor-management advisory bodies at the state-owned industrial groups (IRI, ENI, EFIM). Established at the national, regional, sectoral, and firm levels, these bodies receive information and discuss business strategies, organization of work, and industrial relations. [88]

Works councils exist at the plant level, but they have only rudimentary statutory definition aside from their right to exist, provided in the 1970 Workers' Statute. They are essentially union groups, composed primarily of delegates who are members of the three main union confederations

---

86. *European Industrial Relations Review*, vol. 185 (June 1989), p. 25.

87. *Industrial Relations Europe* (June 1990), p. 7; "First Social Charter Agreement," *European Industrial Relations Review*, vol. 198 (July 1990), p. 10.

88. European Trade Union Institute (1990b, p. 71).

(CGIL, CISL, and UIL). The primary function of these groups is to engage management at the local level in collective bargaining. Although national sectoral agreements give them rights to information on investment plans, new technologies, and employment matters, the works councils do not conceive of themselves as instruments for consultation or participation in management decisionmaking.[89]

By most accounts, the works councils have declined considerably in influence from their heyday in the 1970s (the upsurge following the hot autumn of 1969). Part of their problem, and arguably a major cause for union decline in Italy, has been the fragmentation of Italian labor into three rival confederations.[90] Since the breakup of Italian labor's confederation of confederations in 1984, the three groups have often been at odds at national and local levels. Union membership density dropped from 48 percent in 1980 to 40 percent in 1986.[91] The works councils have all too often lacked common strategies both toward management and toward the employees they represent.[92] Meanwhile, as in Britain, managers have pursued new employer-led forms of WPM, such as quality circles, that circumvent the unions and the works councils to involve workers directly.

In an effort to regain influence and to breathe new life into the works councils, Italian unions seek expanded information and consultation rights, from the national and sectoral levels to the plant level. In bargaining with *Confindustria* (the national employers' association) the unions have demanded new consultation rights regarding work reorganization and a reformed works council structure.[93] Among union proposals to reform plant-level representation is one that calls for a dual structure composed of union works committees with exclusive bargaining rights and works councils elected by the entire work force with enhanced participation rights.[94]

Union division and employer opposition remain the major barriers to expanded WPM rights at home, even as Italian unions add their voice to the demand for European-level rights. Italian employers, for their part, ally themselves with the general European employer opposition to mandatory measures, while expanding employer-led involvement programs

---

89. European Trade Union Institute (1990b, pp. 69–70).
90. Pellegrini (1987).
91. Negrelli and Santi (1990, p. 190).
92. Negrelli and Santi (1990).
93. "IR Talks Yield First Fruit," *Industrial Relations Europe*, vol. 17 (June 1989), p. 3.
94. *European Industrial Relations Review*, vol. 202 (November 1990), p. 21.

Table 3-1. *Negotiated WPM in EC Member States, as of 1990*

Country	Works councils	Board membership
Belgium	Yes	No
Denmark	Yes[a]	Yes
France	Yes	No
Germany	Yes[a]	Yes
Great Britain	No	No
Greece	Yes	No
Ireland	No	No
Italy	Yes	No
Luxembourg	Yes[a]	No
Netherlands	Yes[a]	No
Portugal	Yes	No
Spain	Yes	No

Sources: European Trade Union Institute (1990a, various pages); *European Industrial Relations Review; Industrial Relations Europe.*
a. Some codetermination.

at many of their own plants. Meanwhile, the Italian government, like the German government, has taken a middle position but in the runup to Maastricht added its voice to those successfully demanding a shift to qualified majority voting for all social issues, including WPM.

Negotiated WPM in the EC Member States: A Summary

Negotiated WPM is summarized in Table 3-1 for all EC member states. Countries that have only limited works councils or board memberships in certain sectors (such as the public sector) are not counted in this tabulation, which considers broad societywide provisions. Typically, these provisions are mandated by law, although in the Danish case works councils are established by centralized collective bargaining agreement.

In only two of the twelve cases do EC countries have societywide company board representation for employees. In both cases, Denmark and Germany, works councils are generally considered a more significant avenue for WPM than is board representation. Ten of the twelve countries, however, have works councils throughout the economy. In four the councils have some codetermination rights (Denmark, Germany, Luxembourg, and the Netherlands); in the remaining countries the councils have information and consultation rights only, and in Italy they are primarily instruments of collective bargaining rather than WPM. Works councils in Belgium, Denmark, France, Germany, and the Netherlands date to the immediate postwar period or earlier; in Greece, Luxembourg, Portugal, and Spain works councils have been established only since the

1970s. (Greece's are the youngest; its works councils were established by law in 1988.)

A picture of widely contrasting national arrangements for negotiated WPM emerges from the preceding presentation. On the whole, company board participation plays a minor role. Works councils, by contrast, are widespread and appear to be increasing in importance, although they vary substantially among the EC member states in form, influence, and rights. Union members are typically active on the works councils, while the level of union influence on and strategy toward works councils varies widely from country to country. Union interest in negotiated WPM by way of works councils appears widespread.

The evidence shows the importance of the WPM issue. We find substantial national bases for negotiated WPM. This is true especially in Germany, with the strongest economy among the EC members, but it holds in other countries to varying degrees as well. Proponents of WPM, however, can expect to face great difficulties in building new institutions of Community-wide WPM when such broad institutional diversity exists among member states and when negotiated WPM plays only a weak role in many (as in Britain, Ireland, Italy, and France). Contemporary advocates of the expansion of information, consultation, and participation rights—primarily unions and their allies—have a great deal of work to do at *both* national and European levels.

Impacts and Prospects

Because only two of the twelve EC countries have employee representation on company boards, it is difficult to imagine a successful coalition that could institute such a requirement at the European level for European firms. The prospects for European-level works councils seem brighter, however, since all but two of the member states have these in one form or another already. And in both of the exceptions (Britain and Ireland), national union federations have moved away from traditional positions to show new support for negotiated WPM. German unions, with both strong works councils and a strong labor movement (and this is no coincidence), can be expected to continue to lead a pan-European campaign for the expansion of negotiated WPM, primarily in the form of mandated works councils with information and consultation rights (at least) for large firms doing business in the EC.

Industrial relations practices, including mechanisms of participation, are products of national histories. As such, they represent past economic developments and political struggles embodied in present institutions; they tend to be entrenched and quite resistant to change. It is unlikely that current market integration developments will have a radical short-term effect on WPM within the EC. In the longer run, however, the European project may indeed result in or be accompanied by substantial institutional change both within the member states and at the Community level.

New and growing interest in WPM on all sides is rooted most importantly in market-driven pressures that have challenged previously stable patterns of industrial relations.[95] To the extent that WPM is a loose concept and means different things to different people, it sometimes becomes politically possible.[96] Such a dynamic is apparent in the current European case; but the actual shape and content of WPM as it spreads to new areas remain to be determined.

In any case, expanded WPM is on its way in Europe, just as it is in the United States and elsewhere. Managers are inspired by the Japanese example; unionists in many cases by the German example. But the critical question that unions are raising in the current European debate is: will it be employer led or will it be negotiated? Will it depend on employer intention, goodwill, and perhaps enlightenment, or will workers throughout the EC have rights to information, consultation, and participation as they now do in some member states?

A major 1970s research project on industrial democracy in Europe concluded that participation at all levels—shop floor, management, company board—is more effective where backed by legislation.[97] This study also concluded that legislation is more likely to exist where both labor and management have strong central federations. But such institutions do not now exist, and will not come into being in the foreseeable future at the EC level or within several of the member states. Thus, in a single market project that has been significantly business led and deregulatory in intent, employers retain the political advantage and the debate on social issues has reached a stalemate. European-level stalemate leads us to expect the following prospects for WPM: a continuing expansion of employer-led involvement programs on a firm-by-firm basis with no corresponding expansion of workers' and their representatives' formal rights; continued national efforts to expand WPM rights and institutions (as in

---

95. Piore and Sabel (1984); Boyer (1988).
96. Strauss (1982, pp. 182–83).
97. IDE (1981); Strauss (1982, pp. 221–22).

Ireland, Italy, and Britain) driven by unions' growing interest in promoting WPM rights and taking advantage of existing mechanisms, even informal ones; a growing interest among unions in cross-national collaboration; and a continued impasse for efforts to create a European firm and a European industrial relations arena.

On the whole, although WPM has become a major issue and campaign for European unions, so far the outcome has not been favorable to the spread of the formal rights that unions advocate. This lack of success is due to the great diversity of form and substance in WPM among the member states; the difficulty of institution building, especially as concerns new regulation, within the current employer- and government-led European deregulatory project; and unions' relative political weakness. This last aspect is itself a result of great cross-national differences in union structure, influence, and strategy; declining union influence in many member states since 1980; and German unions' preoccupation with German unification since 1990.

One prospect remains, however, that might shift the battle for negotiated WPM in a more favorable direction for its union proponents. Many unionists, disappointed by the European-level deadlock, have shifted their sights toward incremental change. This would include the expansion of WPM rights within the member states as well as the spread of information and consultation procedures initiated at the European level in specific areas such as health and safety.[98] Such incremental change could later provide a stronger institutional basis for more generalized WPM rights in the EC.[99] A shift to qualified majority voting on social issues, now foreseen in the Maastricht Treaty social protocol, would certainly enhance these prospects, as would a possible expansion of the legal powers of the European Parliament.

The long-term outcome of these developments for WPM (as for other social issues) in the EC is contingent on politics and the capacity for institutional transformation within and across the member states. The prospects for unions and negotiated WPM do not at present look promising. But politics is nothing if not uncertain.

98. This perspective counters the commonly accepted notion that European economic integration will devalue national institutions (Streeck 1991). In currently evolving structures, the subsidiarity principle relegates considerable (and in some cases new) implementation and enforcement precisely to national institutions. The EC regulates relations between national governments but does not replace them.

99. See Wallace (1990) on the potentially transformative effects of accumulated incremental change.

References

Adams, Roy J., and C. H. Rummel. 1977. "Workers' Participation in Management in West Germany." *Industrial Relations Journal* 8 (Spring): 4–22.

Batstone, Eric, and Paul Lyndon Davies. 1976. *Industrial Democracy: European Experience*. London: Her Majesty's Stationery Office.

Baun, Michael. 1990. "Europe 1992 and Trade Union Politics: Towards a European Industrial Relations System?" Paper prepared for the Seventh International Conference of Europeanists. Washington.

Berghahn, Volker R., and Detlev Karsten. 1987. *Industrial Relations in West Germany*. Oxford: Berg.

Boyer, Robert, ed. 1988. *The Search for Labour Market Flexibility: The European Economies in Transition*. Oxford: Clarendon Press.

Bridgford, Jeff. 1990. "French Trade Unions: Crisis in the 1980s." *Industrial Relations Journal* 21 (Summer): 126–35.

Crouch, Colin, and Alessandro Pizzorno, eds. 1978. *The Resurgence of Class Conflict in Western Europe since 1968*. 2 vols. Macmillan.

Delamotte, Yves. 1988. "Workers' Participation and Personnel Policies in France." *International Labour Review* 127 (2): 221–41.

Dworkin, James B., and Barbara A. Lee. 1990. "The Implications of Europe 1992 for Labor-Management Relations." Paper prepared for the Bargaining Group Conference, School of Industrial and Labor Relations, Cornell University. May.

European Trade Union Institute. 1990a. "Collective Bargaining in Western Europe in 1989 and Prospects for 1990." Brussels.

————. 1990b. "Workers' Representation and Rights in the Workforce in Western Europe." Brussels.

Hohn, Hans-Willy. 1988. *Von der Einheitsgewerkschaft zum Betriebssyndikalismus: Soziale Schließung im dualen System der Interessenvertretung*. Berlin: Sigma.

Industrial Democracy in Europe (IDE). 1981. *European Industrial Relations*. Oxford: Clarendon Press.

Jansen, Peter, and Leo Kissler. 1987. "Organization of Work by Participation? A French-German Comparison." *Economic and Industrial Democracy* 8: 379–409.

Kolvenbach, Walter. 1990. "EEC Company Law Harmonization and Worker Participation." *University of Pennsylvania Journal of International Business Law* 11 (4): 709–88.

Lange, Peter, George Ross, and Maurizio Vannicelli, eds. 1982. *Unions, Change and Crisis: French and Italian Union Strategy and Political Economy, 1945–1980*. London: Allen and Unwin.

Locke, Richard M. 1990. "The Resurgence of the Local Union: Industrial Restructuring and Industrial Relations in Italy." *Politics and Society* 18 (September): 347–79.

Lodge, Juliet. 1990. "Social Europe." *Journal of European Integration* 13 (Winter-Spring): 135–50.

MacInnes, John. 1985. "Conjuring up Consultation: The Role and Extent of Joint Consultation in the Post-war Private Manufacturing Industry." *British Journal of Industrial Relations* 13 (March): 93–113.

Mosley, Hugh G. 1990. "The Social Dimension of European Integration." *International Labour Review* 129 (2): 147–64.

Negrelli, Serafino, and Ettore Santi. 1990. "Industrial Relations in Italy." In Guido Baglioni and Colin Crouch, eds., *European Industrial Relations: The Challenge of Flexibility*. London: Sage.

Niedenhoff, Horst-Udo. 1990. "Der DGB baute seine Position aus: Die Betriebsratswahl 1990 in den Betrieben der Bundesrepublik Deutschland." *Gewerkschaftsreport* 24 (September): 5–17.

Northrup, Herbert R., Duncan C. Campbell, and Betty J. Slowinski. 1988. "Multinational Union-Management Consultation in Europe: Resurgence in the 1980s?" *International Labour Review* 127 (5): 525–41.

Pellegrini, Claudio. 1987. "Italian Industrial Relations." In Greg J. Bamber and Russell D. Lansbury, eds. *International and Comparative Industrial Relations: A Study of Developed Market Economies*. London: Unwin and Allen.

Piore, Michael J., and Charles F. Sabel. 1984. *The Second Industrial Divide: Possibilities for Prosperity*. Basic Books.

Pipkorn, Jörn. 1984. "Employee Participation in the European Community: Progress and Pitfalls." In Bernhard Wilpert and Arndt Sorge, eds., *International Yearbook of Organizational Democracy*, vol. 2: *International Perspectives on Organizational Democracy*. John Wiley.

Rhodes, Martin. 1991. "The Politics of the Social Dimension: National versus Transnational Regulation in the Single European Market." Paper prepared for the ECSA Biennial Conference, George Mason University.

Ross, George. 1982. "The Perils of Politics: French Unions and the Crisis of the 1970s." In Peter Lange, George Ross, and Maurizio Vannicelli, eds., *Unions, Change, and Crisis*. London: Allen and Unwin.

Sandholtz, Wayne, and John Zysman. 1989. "1992: Recasting the European Bargain." *World Politics* 42 (October): 95–128.

Silvia, Stephen J. 1991. "The Social Charter of the European Community: A Defeat for European Labor." *Industrial and Labor Relations Review* 44 (July): 626–43.

Steinkühler, Franz, ed. 1989. *Europa '92: Industriestandort oder sozialer Lebensraum*. Hamburg: VSA-Verlag.

Stern, Robert N. 1988. "Participation by Representation: Workers on Boards of Directors in the United States and Abroad." *Work and Occupations* 15 (November), 396–422.

Story, Jonathan. 1990. "Social Europe: Ariadne's Thread." *Journal of European Integration* 13 (Winter-Spring): 151–65.

Strauss, George. 1982. "Workers Participation in Management: An International Perspective." *Research in Organizational Behavior* 4: 173–265.

————. Forthcoming. "Workers Participation in Management." In Jean Hartley and Geoffrey Stephenson, eds., *The Psychology of Employment Relations.* Oxford: Basil Blackwell.

Streeck, Wolfgang. 1984. "Co-determination: The Fourth Decade." In Bernhard Wilpert and Arndt Sorge, eds., *International Yearbook of Organizational Democracy*, vol. 2: *International Perspectives on Organizational Democracy.* John Wiley.

————. 1987. "Industrial Relations and Industrial Change: The Restructuring of the World Automobile Industry in the 1970s and 1980s." *Economic and Industrial Democracy* 8: 437–62.

————. 1988. "Industrial Relations in West Germany, 1980–87." *Labour: Review of Labor Economics and Industrial Relations* 2 (Winter): 3–44.

————. 1991. "More Uncertainties: German Unions Facing 1992." *Industrial Relations* 30 (Fall): 317–47.

Teague, Paul. 1989a. "Constitution or Regime? The Social Dimension to the 1992 Project." *British Journal of Industrial Relations* 27 (November): 310–29.

————. 1989b. *The European Community: The Social Dimension. Labour Market Policies for 1992.* London: Kogan Page and the Garfield School of Management.

Teague, Paul, and John Grahl. 1989. "European Community Labour Market Policy: Present Scope and Future Direction." *Journal of European Integration* 13 (1): 55–73.

————. 1990. "1992 and the Emergence of a European Industrial Relations Area." *Journal of European Integration* 13 (Winter-Spring): 167–83.

Thelen, Kathleen. 1991. *Union of Parts: Labor Politics in Postwar Germany.* Cornell University Press.

Towers, Brian. 1989. "Running the Gauntlet: British Trade Unions under Thatcher, 1979–1988." *Industrial and Labor Relations Review* 42 (January): 163–88.

Turner, Lowell. 1991. *Democracy at Work: Changing World Markets and the Future of Labor Unions.* Cornell University Press.

Venturini, Patrick. 1989. "1992: The European Social Dimension." Luxembourg: Office for Official Publications of the European Communities.

Wallace, William. 1990. *The Transformation of Western Europe.* London: Royal Institute of International Affairs.

Wood, Stephen. 1988. "Some Observations on Industrial Relations in the British Car Industry 1985–87." In Ben Dankbaar, Ulrich Jürgens, and Thomas Malsch, eds., *Die Zukunft der Arbeit in der Automobilindustrie.* Berlin: Sigma.

CHAPTER FOUR

The Rise and Decline of Neocorporatism

Wolfgang Streeck

BETWEEN 1979 AND the present, industrial relations as they had been known in Europe since the Second World War changed fundamentally. Ingenious attempts on a broad scale had been made during the previous decade to shore up the industrial relations system of the postwar settlement in the aftermath of the shocks of 1968 and 1973.[1] Ultimately, these attempts failed. Today, an uncertain movement toward a new type of industrial relations is under way; very little is known of it except that it is likely to be very different from its predecessor.

The rough outline of the old regime is familiar. Within it, there were of course variations among countries, and not negligible ones. But even well into the 1970s, it was still possible to believe that within this realm diversity would in the end give way to convergence under the inexorable pressures of technology and economics.[2] According to received wisdom not only did developed industrial societies need autonomous institutions of collective bargaining to mediate between employers and workers, but they also had the capacity to build them and thereby provide orderly governance for the employment relationship. Collective bargaining would transform the disparate social classes into partners, enabling them to settle their differences consensually and avoid a return to the fratricidal conflicts that tore European countries apart in the 1920s and 1930s.

As for labor in particular, under the postwar industrial relations system it was to be represented by strong, independent, broadly based unions or union federations operating primarily at the sectoral or na-

1. Gourevitch (1986).
2. Kerr and others (1960).

tional level where bargaining, basically over wages, was to be conducted. Centralization and inclusiveness were important for several reasons.[3] They permitted unions, imbued with the egalitarian ideal of blue collar working-class culture to control and sometimes reduce wage differentials—between firms, sectors, and regions as well as between occupational and skill groups. As encompassing organizations it was easier for them to bridge the many cleavages among their membership. Where centralized bargaining favored large firms over small ones, it also had the support of the powerful large corporations that were successfully transplanting in Europe the Fordist system of mass production and consumption developed in the United States. Employers also realized that centralized bargaining was less likely than workplace bargaining to interfere with the exercise of managerial prerogative at the point of production—an effect that mainstream union leaders also eschewed, eager as they were to harvest the economic benefits of fast-rising productivity for their members.

Governments, too, supported centralization of both collective bargaining and union organization. Centralization was an indispensable condition of their ability to control the fundamental risk associated with postwar democratic capitalism's commitment to maintain full employment through political means: the risk of inflation caused by ever-higher wage settlements that unions politically protected from the penalty of unemployment might force on employers.[4] National union leaders, with the memory of the Great Depression still fresh, generally recognized the need for such control, and typically their foremost organizational concern became to prevent autonomous wage bargaining at the shop floor or enterprise level, so that national bargains deemed reasonable and moderate could be made to stick. This concern, combined with the unions' acceptance of managerial prerogative and their desire to avoid entangling member loyalties with individual enterprises, translated into an institutional imperative to safeguard the primacy of the "external" over the "internal" union or, even better still, to avoid having local union organizations altogether.[5] When employers felt they needed formal arrangements for consultation with their work forces, unions often tolerated or even supported establishing works councils, all the while clearly indicating that they as unions would have little or nothing to do with them.

3. Visser (1990).
4. Flanagan, Soskice, and Ulman (1983).
5. Visser (1990).

Widespread industrial unrest in 1968–70 laid bare the weaknesses of this construction.[6] Throughout Western Europe, high rates of inflation imported from the international system and the United States in particular, overtaxed governments' and national union leaders' ability to hold wage settlements in line with aggregate productivity increases. Moreover, a decade of relentless technological and organizational rationalization (Taylorism) had given rise to an accumulation of grievances among shop-floor workers, and to concerns for "qualitative" factors or worker interest in exercising a modicum of influence over their immediate work environment. Such interests found no channel of expression in the existing industrial relations system. In addition to this representation gap, there were indications in a number of countries, most prominently in Sweden, that egalitarian wage leveling had finally reached a point at which the losers, or relative losers, felt aggrieved enough to take independent action.[7] Combined with other factors, these conditions compounded into a flammable mixture, ready to explode.[8]

Employers and governments responded very much in the spirit of the postwar settlement. In the immediate aftermath of Europe's various "hot autumns" of the late 1960s, they did their utmost to avoid further confrontation with workers and unions, accepting high wage increases and inflation rates to avoid the political risks of destabilization.[9] Their conciliatory stance lasted into 1973 and 1974, the years of the first oil crisis, as governments continued to assign high priority to full employment, not daring to infringe on unions' rights to free collective bargaining. Instead, governments and employers sought stabilization by giving unions a still greater role in policymaking, increasing rather than curtailing their power and responsibility and helping them strengthen their organizations so that national union leaders could manage shop-floor discontent more effectively. The emerging political configuration later came to be known as "neocorporatism."[10]

Neocorporatism attempted to deal with the economic problems of the 1970s through national-level social contracts among government, employers, and unions. In exchange for cooperating with governments' ef-

6. Crouch and Pizzorno (1978).
7. Among the first to see this coming were Flanagan, Soskice, and Ulman (1983).
8. These factors included generational change, the experience of secure employment throughout two decades of growth and expansion of the welfare state, overlong tenures of conservative parties in a number of European countries, the student protests against the Vietnam War, and others.
9. McCracken and others (1977).
10. Schmitter and Lehmbruch (1979).

forts to restore full employment—keeping wage demands moderate though often entailing losses in real wage levels and distributive position—unions were granted influence over fiscal, monetary, and social policies relating to unemployment insurance, employment protection, early retirement, working hours, pensions, health insurance, housing, taxation, public sector employment, vocational training, regional aid, subsidies to declining industries, and so forth. In addition, governments and employers agreed to a variety of arrangements to help unions reinforce their organizations and, in particular, to strengthen their position at the workplace. Typically this was accomplished through new legislation on industrial democracy or codetermination.

With hindsight, many things explain why the neocorporatist policies of the 1970s eventually proved to be no more than stopgap measures. Even while these policies still functioned reasonably well, various developments began to erode the necessary conditions of stable neocorporatist governance in particular and the postwar industrial relations regime in general. Most prominent among these developments was the transformation in the political capabilities of European nation-states. Budget constraints combined with the fiscal crisis of the welfare state sharply curtailed government's ability to offer unions compensation for restraint in collective bargaining. Similarly, expansionary monetary policies were beset by the new realities of high uncertainty emanating from the post–Bretton Woods international monetary regime as well as an increasingly integrated world capital market enabling investors to divest themselves of and destabilize currencies suspected of inflationary tendencies. Along with the rapidly growing interdependence of national economies, these developments severely limited the ability of national governments, acting individually, to maintain full employment by Keynesian methods and deliver on their part of the neocorporatist social contract.[11] Most importantly perhaps, the Thatcher experience taught governments in all of Europe, contrary to postwar political orthodoxy, that politically guaranteed full employment was no longer indispensable either for social stability or for electoral success and that unions were at a loss to do much about this.

Union weakness reflected ongoing changes in the social structure of European societies and work forces. Informing the old system of industrial-interest representation had been an image of society in which the vast majority of participants in the labor market were male blue collar

11. Van Ginniken (1987).

workers providing for families depending on them as sole breadwinners. While conflicts of interest between different groups of workers certainly existed, as a whole this industrial working class was, at least potentially, homogeneous enough to be represented by inclusive, centralized unions. Moreover, given their relatively clear demarcation from other social groups, industrial workers embodied a reliable electoral base for social democratic and other leftist parties, providing the combination of political and industrial action that typified European industrial relations.

Changing conditions forced contemporary unions and working-class parties to attract and represent a much more diverse constituency of groups and interests: shift of employment to the service sector, the rise of the white collar worker, the transformation of the traditional family structure, the growth of women's participation in the formal economy, increasing ethnic heterogeneity of European work forces, growing individualization of lifestyles and normative orientations, and expanding nontypical part-time and short-term employment. As social cohesion among their clientele eroded, European unions found it difficult to transform special member interests into general demands and policies. The fragmentation of the Swedish model in the 1980s, which more than any other national system had stood for aggregation and centralization of collective bargaining, is indicative of tensions that dogged union leaders throughout Europe.[12]

Finally, the 1970s saw the beginnings of profound changes in the organization of production that were to come into full force in the subsequent decade.[13] Fragmentation of demand in mature markets called into question the economic rationale of large Fordist firms. Market fragmentation was further advanced by greatly intensified international competition both from low-wage countries forcing older industries to seek refuge in streamlining and modernizing, and from Japanese producers capable of an unprecedented rate of product innovation. As a result, the 1980s witnessed a forceful revival of small firms, especially as subcontractors began to account for a rising share of the value-added of quality-competitive products. These small firms were often beyond the reach of unions. The spread of microelectronic information technology reinforced changes in industrial organization. One consequence was the growing heterogeneity of technological and organizational conditions in the workplace, adding to the difficulties unions were experiencing with centralized, uniform regulation of employment standards.

12. Lash (1985).
13. Piore and Sabel (1984).

Fragmentation of demand and flexible technology offered firms and their managements a range of choice unknown in the worlds of Fordism and Taylorism, not least of which was the choice between relatively low-wage, low-price mass production and high-skilled, high-wage, more or less customized, quality production.[14] European unions in the 1980s were unevenly equipped—institutionally, organizationally, and ideologically—to influence such choices, although it was these, rather than distributive bargaining, that increasingly determined their members' income and employment. Moreover, in trying to influence the restructuring process, unions were often dealing with employers who had grown disenchanted with neocorporatist limitations on managerial discretion and had begun to search for ways of recapturing what they saw as "managerial prerogative." At the same time, these developments made shop-floor industrial relations increasingly important, something with which centralized European unions were ill-prepared to cope.

Today, European industrial relations are still adjusting to the new realities of declining state capacities, more complex social structures, and a post-Fordist organization of production. But while these forces were strong enough to bring about the disintegration of the previous system, they seem unable to generate a new model. The result is an unusual and apparently still growing degree of diversity, both within and among national systems.[15]

In the first place, nowhere in Europe has collective bargaining been scrapped. Nor have unions' status and reasons for existence been attacked in any way comparable to, for example, the way they have been in the United States. But the public and semipublic mechanisms that were once used to extend industrial agreements to unorganized sectors have been seriously weakened or even dismantled in some countries, while in others they have remained largely intact. Second, pressures to decentralize bargaining to accommodate more diverse local and workplace conditions have everywhere mounted. In some places, especially in Britain, sectoral- and national-level collective bargaining have been virtually eclipsed by company-level collective bargaining. Elsewhere, however, most notably in Germany, national unions have successfully relied on established institutions of industrial democracy to channel, control and contain decentralization.

Third, union fragmentation, reflecting diverse member interests and visible in conflicts over bargaining objectives, has grown everywhere, but

14. Streeck (1987).
15. Armingeon (1991); Freeman (1988).

to very different degrees. Thus, in Sweden successive breakdowns of national bargaining rounds occurred, whereas in Germany the DGB's unity and predominance remained almost intact at least until unification.

Fourth, workplace cooperation between management and the work force—"worker involvement" as it is called in the United States—is sought by employers even in highly adversarial systems like that in the United Kingdom. But while in some contexts management uses cooperation as a tool to provide a palatable substitute for unions, in others it is embodied in legal rights of worker participation, or it is controlled and regulated by strong national unions. Fifth, tripartism, in its 1970s form of politically bargained incomes policies, has largely disappeared, and governments have ceased to extend to unions additional legal means to reinforce their organizations. However, governments have refrained from attacking the institutional underpinnings of union influence (except in Britain).

Finally, union density has followed different patterns in each country. Swedish and Danish density ratios continued to grow in the 1980s, but Spanish and French unions lost members and now represent only a fraction of workers in the private sector. Where union strength has been sustained, it has been associated with a substantive contribution to economic restructuring toward diversified and high value-added quality production. Certain unions have simultaneously imposed constraints on firms to prevent them from following low-wage strategies to achieve change and have created opportunities for management in search of functional flexibility to gain an edge in quality-competitive production. This seems to have required a combination of strong centralized organizational capacities and a well-institutionalized presence at the workplace, and an ability to coordinate collective action at the two levels, making it possible for unions to intervene from without and within to influence the greatly extended range of firms' strategic choices.

Where unions moved in this direction—as they did to varying degrees in the Scandinavian countries, Italy, and Germany—they may have begun to define a new productivist role for themselves that transcends their traditional, self-imposed focus on the politics of distribution and the political manipulation of aggregate demand. Those European union movements that enjoyed some measure of success during the 1980s seem to have been the ones that found additional functions and power resources for themselves in the organization of production at the level of the individual firm and on the supply side of the economy—providing the economy with the essential institutional underpinnings of advanced, flexible production modes and generating vital factor inputs, broadly speaking, such as social peace, mutual trust, good faith cooperation, and a high skill level.

On the other hand, unions that failed to extend their concerns beyond the traditional domain of distributive bargaining suffered great injury, the prime examples being in France and in part Britain. The same has been true of unions whose main response to industrial change was to demand protection (usually by subsidies) of declining firms and sectors, as in Spain and, interestingly, Austria.[16] Similarly, unions that failed to secure a role for themselves in the organization of work on the shop floor during the neocorporatist bargaining of the 1970s so as not to become entangled in responsibility for economic performance found themselves unable to represent their increasingly heterogeneous membership effectively in ever more diverse workplaces in the 1980s. (In this respect, Britain and France offer a sharp contrast to Sweden, where LO abandoned its longstanding opposition to codetermination at what probably was the latest possible historical moment.) These unions were either pushed aside by a more assertive management that could no longer afford to grant unions control over their labor costs or were cajoled into a kind of cooperation in which the unions were no more than dispensable junior partners (as is apparently the case in some of the Japanese-held companies in the United Kingdom).

Defining a European Industrial Relations System

The rise of interdependence and diversity in European industrial relations in the 1980s coincided with and was closely related to the relaunching of the European Community. From the perspective of national industrial relations systems, such a development appears to carry with it highly contradictory implications. On the one hand, in its more restricted single internal market version, European integration formally ratifies and further increases the interdependence of European political economies, intensifying the pressure of market forces on national regulatory regimes and curtailing control by national institutions. On the other hand, to the extent that the single internal market may have an added social dimension, integration holds out the promise of recapturing political control of the economy through a new system of supranational governance po-

16. Visser (1991).

litically as well as in industrial relations, internalizing the external effects that increasingly preempt the authority of individual national regimes and extricating European industrial relations from the dictates of competition among regimes and market forces.

This second scenario raises the possibility of a genuinely European industrial relations system consisting not of a set of commonalities in otherwise separate national systems but of a unified set of institutions covering the single internal market and the European Community in their entirety. The increased diversity in European industrial relations poses important questions for such a system. On which national systems might a supranational system be modeled? In particular, would it be modeled on the more labor-inclusive national systems? How would it interact with its constituent national systems? Would the economic impact of a system of supranational governance differ from that of a market-driven regime?

Such problems of diversity and interdependence exist not only between European nations but also between Europe and other parts of the developed capitalist world. According to Fordist, Taylorist, and Keynesian premises, the postwar model of industrial relations was intended to apply to all mature industrial societies alike. But much of the pressure affecting contemporary European industrial relations is related to the withdrawal of the Japanese and then in the late 1970s of the Americans from the inclusive adversarialism of the New Deal that the United States instituted and the Western world adopted after 1945.[17]

Today a number of European countries seem to be the last remaining holdouts of what was once a nearly universal industrial order. To many, this position appears highly uncomfortable. By the early 1980s the pluralist labor-inclusiveness of European industrial relations that had been reinforced during the neocorporatist 1970s was widely perceived as a disadvantage in an increasingly competitive world economy in which

17. The Japanese defection dates to the early 1960s, when Japanese employers rediscovered the "three sacred treasures"—lifelong employment, seniority pay, and enterprise unionism—as a means of eliminating adversarialism from Japanese industrial relations while, in a sense, retaining inclusiveness. The United States abandoned the postwar settlement during the 1970s when, in stark contrast to all other major industrialized countries, its rate of unionization in the private sector continued to fall. The defeat of the Labor Law Reform Bill in Congress in 1979, still under a Democratic president, indicated to employers and the Reagan administration that it had become possible to abandon inclusiveness while retaining adversarialism in an effort to restore profitability and stability, if not international competitiveness, through deunionization, expansion of low-wage, unskilled employment, and rapidly increasing income inequality. See Rosenberg (1989).

Europe's two principal rivals had substantially curtailed the role of independent trade unions. Indeed, one of the strongest attractions of the single internal market for European business has been its potential to loosen the purported stranglehold of organized labor over the European economy. Current efforts to add a social dimension to the internal market are best understood as attempts to preserve, if only by default, the historical labor-inclusiveness of European industrial relations against strong economic and political pressures for deregulation by anchoring it in tripartite supranational institutions able to promote a new convergence among national regimes along labor-inclusive lines.

There are many possible lists of concrete institutions that would define a distinctly European, labor-inclusive industrial relations system, distinguishing it from the increasingly nonunion human-resource management model of the United States and Japan's enterprise-based unionism. The debate on the social dimension of the internal market offers a good starting point for an initial inventory of core elements.[18]

—First, in contrast to both the United States and Japan, European industrial relations would provide publicly guaranteed status to strong, independent unions in both the industrial and the political arenas.

—Second, unions and employer associations would be routine participants on the basis of established formal rights in a tripartite policymaking arrangement. Among other things, this would allow for the use of public power to enhance the effectiveness and the reach of private collective bargaining, guarding against erosive competition from a nonunion sector as frequently occurs in the United States.

—Third, compared to the United States and Japan, there would be a relatively high floor of basic social rights for workers, publicly provided and secured, and vested in both an active welfare state and strong collective bargaining.

—Fourth, a European industrial relations system would allow for some degree of coordination of wage settlements at the sectoral level or higher. This would generate smaller wage differentials among regions, industries, and occupations than those resulting from an unfettered labor market such as in the United States or from productivity differentials between firms as in Japan.

—Fifth, at the enterprise level there would have to be some general arrangement for information, consultation, and possibly codetermina-

18. See, for example, the European Trade Union Confederation's 1988 social program, *Soziale Gestaltung des europäischen Binnenraums.*

tion involving workers and unions as a matter of right in managerial decisions that affect employment and working life, distinguishing the European firm from both the U.S. nexus of contracts and the Japanese enterprise community.

Whatever the institutional detail, however, any labor-inclusive European industrial relations system will have to respond to the fundamental condition of external interdependence in a global economy to be able to survive fierce competition from systems that lack the basic commitment to a floor of social and industrial citizenship rights for workers and their organizations. In the absence of a global regime removing labor from international competition, any plan for a European social dimension will have to be evaluated not only in terms of its political and normative attractions but also of its contribution to Europe's economic competitiveness.

It is widely agreed that the only way the high-wage economy predicated by the European social dimension can successfully compete is if it is based on highly skilled, high-quality production. Therefore, the formation of a distinctively European industrial relations system would have to be associated with the convergence of national European economies toward a common pattern of high value-added, quality-competitive production. To the extent that such a production pattern requires specific social relations between capital and labor, a European industrial relations system would have to make a contribution to the institutional infrastructure, understood in the widest sense, on which advanced high-quality production depends and not just to accommodate the struggle for distributional advantage. Whether this is at all possible depends on whether European unionism as a whole will be able to follow the example of the most successful European union movements of the 1970s: that is, shifting strategic attention from the demand to the supply side; developing an effective capacity to intervene in and influence structural change at the microeconomic and macroeconomic level, and to coordinate action at both; and learning to relate member interests to production as well as distribution issues.

Obstacles to Creating a European Industrial Relations System

A labor-inclusive and economically competitive European industrial order could come into being either through convergent development of national industrial relations systems irreversibly joined by the single internal market or through supranational institution building, in particular, the successful creation through supranational politics of a strong social dimension. Either scenario implies a range of formidable limiting conditions. Let us briefly consider five such conditions.

Divergent Industrial Relations Traditions

Industrial relations traditions and institutions differ widely among European countries, and these differences have increased in the 1980s. Divergences include the institutional definition of the employment relationship, the accepted level of wage dispersion and inequality, the status and use of skilled labor, the political status of unions, the role of tripartism, and the existence of formal institutions of industrial democracy. The United Kingdom, in particular, is today closer in its practices to the United States than to Scandinavia or central Europe.[19] Indeed not only do its employers and government but its unions also have ideas very different from those of other EC members about the desirable degree of European industrial relations.[20] Similarly, the rapid deunionization of the French and the Spanish economies does not bode well for union prospects of occupying a pivotal position in a future European political economy. Furthermore, provisions for workplace participation differ widely across Europe, in practice even more than on paper. Disparities in the role unions play in training—a crucial parameter of involvement in the governance of a high-wage and highly skilled economy—are even more pronounced. Although the German pattern of tripartite responsibility for training, organization of work, industrial unionism, and industrial democracy has gained recognition as a plausible model of a labor-inclusive polity remaining economically competitive, its compatibility with long-standing institutions and traditions in other European countries is far from certain.[21] Indeed it appears highly doubtful for the foreseeable fu-

19. In the past these similarities have been hidden under formalistic distinctions between British voluntarism or state abstentionism and American legal interventionism. The Thatcher years showed that there are clear limits to state abstentionism in Britain when it comes to preserving or restoring a free economy. Similarly, the Reagan revolution in the United States demonstrated that legal intervention under the Wagner Act can also be used to subordinate unions to market forces, rather than to help them organize.

20. British union hopes for a transfusion of favorable institutional conditions from the Community to Britain seem limited to certain, very basic legal and political rights that were curtailed by the Thatcher government. They do not seem to extend, for example, to a system of legally based workplace participation, to union involvement in a nonrestrictive universal training regime, or to a union role in incomes policy.

21. Maurice and others (1986).

ture whether supranational European industrial relations institutions will be strong enough to reverse declines in unionism in some countries. Doubtful too will be the institutions' strength to induce unions in other countries to cooperate with industrial restructuring toward quality-competitive production, to support labor-inclusive arrangements for flexibility, or to make employers accept bargaining arrangements imposed from outside individual firms.

Divergent Economic Conditions

Disparate economic conditions among European countries sometimes give rise to conflicting interests in a European industrial relations system and its consequences. Variations in living standards and real wages in northern and southern Europe, for instance between Denmark and Portugal, are far greater than between the richest and poorest states in the United States.[22] Low-wage countries dependent on external investment are likely to be ambivalent toward high common labor standards for western Europe as a whole.[23] They may perceive northern countries' promotions of such standards under the auspices of a social dimension as an attempt to neutralize their main cost advantage over their richer competitors.[24] The same perception would apply to eastern European countries were they to accede to the Community. Moreover, restructuring toward diversified quality production, may not be easily achieved in countries in southern and eastern Europe, given deficiencies in educational, scientific, organizational, and institutional infrastructure. The subsidies that wealthy countries may agree to make available for such infrastructure, even if seemingly considerable, are likely to fall far short of the actual amounts required. The resulting conflicts of interest fundamentally limit the capacity of unions at the European level to press for a Europeanization of industrial relations.[25]

22. In 1991 Greece's per capita income (GDP) was 52.8 percent of the European Community average. Germany's was 112.5 percent. "Annual Economic Report 1990–1991," *European Economy*, no. 46 (December 1990), p. 29.
23. That is, while they may not openly oppose such standards and may even rhetorically demand them, they will not expend much political capital on them and will likely attach low priority to their implementation if they are ever enacted. For a theoretical treatment, see Lange (1992).
24. For further detail, see Streeck and Schmitter (1991).
25. Visser and Ebbinghaus (1991).

U.S. and Japanese Influences

U.S. and Japanese industrial relations practices already exist inside western Europe and are likely to resist Europeanization. Reflecting the globalization of the economy, Japanese firms operate highly successful western European plants, in Britain in particular but elsewhere as well. Their company-centered, privatized industrial relations exercise a powerful influence on the minds of many European employers. Moreover, most U.S. multinationals in Europe oppose any European industrial relations regime that would subject them to the sort of public obligation they have always been able to fend off at home. For instance, the Vredeling directive might have been enacted in its time had it not been for the vigorous opposition of the U.S. Chamber of Commerce in Brussels.[26] In an interdependent world economy, a distinctive economic regime in a given region can be effective only if it manages to extend its authority to centers of economic decisionmaking located outside its territorial jurisdiction. This raises potentially insurmountable legal and political difficulties.[27]

More generally, there are trends toward both U.S. and Japanese practices in European industrial relations that are not confined to those two countries' multinational corporations. The growing heterogeneity of European work forces exerts a powerful tendency to pluralize unions and collective bargaining, just as increased diversity in business strategies, technology use, and work organization invites decentralization of industrial relations.[28] In addition, new forms of management-initiated worker participation at the point of production, such as teamwork and quality circles, may present stiff competition to European-style industrial democracy based on politically endowed rights of industrial citizenship. Although in the United States management typically uses participation to avoid unions, in Japan company unions and management tend to be hard to distinguish; workplace union representatives and first-line supervisors, team leaders, and conveners of quality circles are often the same people. The challenge for European unions in advanced production systems is to combine worker participation in a decentralized, flexible work

26. DeVos (1989).
27. Writing laws for subjects of other sovereign jurisdictions infringes those jurisdictions' sovereignty.
28. This is one important reason why it is unlikely that European business would support centralized, multiemployer collective bargaining at the European level.

organization with independent, authentic unionism, so as to define a role for themselves in which they are neither marginalized nor absorbed by management. Whether the supranational politics of a social dimension could help this role emerge appears doubtful.

The Slow Pace of Institutional Development

The institutional structure of the western European polity will differ greatly from that of a traditional nation-state, and its development is unlikely to follow a federalist path. For a long time to come, Europe as a political entity will consist of separate national regimes competing with each other in an integrated market economy and coexisting with unified supranational institutions layered over them. That layer is likely to be thin, and increases in its depth will be slow. This is so because unlike conventional nation-states, the constitution and the policies of the European Community are determined by intergovernmental bargains struck in the Community's centrifugal core, the Council of Ministers, the European body most keen on preserving whatever sovereignty of national states factually or formally remains. In light of the historical importance of states' capacities to form national industrial relations systems, this leads one to predict that progress toward a social dimension of the European economy will not accelerate beyond its present pace any time soon.

Given the impact of these political realities, it is instructive to note the changes that the notion of subsidiarity portends for a European industrial relations system. Instead of higher levels of social organization providing lower levels with a capacity to govern their affairs autonomously and responsibly, supranational institutions would issue recommendations (most of them nonbinding) to be implemented by nation-states in keeping with their traditional customs. It is difficult to see how progress can be made under such auspices; how significant sectoral collective bargaining could develop at the European level; how a meaningful directive on works councils could become law in the near future; how provisions for codetermination in a European company statute could possibly add to (or create) codetermination rights at the national level; how the present, nonbinding charter of rights for workers could ever become binding, even though its content is strictly limited to the lowest common denominator of national labor law systems; and so forth.[29]

29. Silvia (1991).

In addition, the dynamics of interaction among the different national industrial relations systems in a common market and between the fledgling supranational system and its national subsystems are as yet largely unknown, and they may be rather different from the expectations of optimistic federalists. Regarding the interaction between supranational and national industrial relations in particular, the supranational system need not necessarily develop in the image of the stronger national systems, and structural properties of the strong need not trickle down into weaker systems.[30] In contrast to this federalist scenario, minimalist supranational institutions combined with horizontal competition among national regimes may more plausibly undermine or preempt more developed national systems—for instance, by offering large employers opportunities to switch to more lenient supranational (or national) regimes of codetermination or participation. Fears of erosion of rights brought about by weak supranational institutions are most pronounced in Germany and, in the context of its impending membership application, Sweden—that is, the two countries whose national systems come closest to offering models for a labor-inclusive European system of industrial relations.[31]

Interdependence and Institutional Deadlock

European industrial relations are changing in the midst of converging circumstances that are on the whole unfavorable to union inclusion. Some of the trends that have undermined the postwar industrial relations system, such as the individualization of interests in a more heterogeneous social and economic structure, are also shaping the transition to a new one. In the political sphere, socialist parties throughout Europe are in ideological and strategic disarray and can no longer be counted upon as natural union allies. Moreover, the disappearance of communism has removed an external and internal threat that at two previous historical junctures, after World War I and World War II, made western European economic and political elites offer wide-ranging concessions to moderate labor leaders. Furthermore, competition with the United States and especially Japan tends to rally more support for employer objectives rather than union objectives.

Most important, however, are fundamental changes in the role of the

30. Strangely enough this scenario has seemed to enjoy its highest popularity among British trade unionists.
31. Streeck (1991).

nation-state as manager of the capitalist economy. In part, these changes are another facet of economic internationalization and are themselves reflected in the renewed impetus toward European integration. Public ownership is declining in all countries; deregulation and the restoration of market forces continue to exercise a powerful hold on policy; and as the French experience of the early 1980s demonstrated, a national government's capacity to implement an expansionary Keynesian economic policy has withered in the face of a globalized capital market. As national borders have lost their significance either in practice or, as in the single internal market, by force of law, nation-states have come to resemble regional states—their sovereignty and ability to impose binding obligations on their subjects severely constrained. The decline of socialism and social democracy, dependent as they were on an active, effective, interventionist state, belongs in this context.

Here, as well, belongs the constitutional bargain that underlies the relaunching of European integration in the mid-1980s, concluded essentially among national political elites and large European companies, with organized labor excluded. At its core it involved business support for a collective effort by west European nation-states to recover some measure of external sovereignty in a turbulent, deinstitutionalized world economy by pooling their individual sovereignties.[32] In exchange, business received a commitment of the emerging European polity to a largely deregulated political economy ("a single market without a single state"), for instance, via the founding principle of mutual recognition.[33] The social dimension of the internal market was added later, and largely remains limited to what is necessary to make the market politically and technically possible. Written into the Community's institutional fabric as it is, the basic disengagement of politics and the economy underlying the internal market project will be difficult for labor to reverse in the future, even under the most favorable circumstances.

The chances of a European industrial relations system being institutionally constructed, as it were, from a European political center are small. Institutional intervention is constrained by diversity among existing national systems, economic differences, conflicts of interest among the national actors most predisposed to favor supranational institution building, and a fundamental weakness of politics itself—both of national politics in relation to an internationalizing economy and of supra-

32. Keohane and Hoffmann (1989).
33. For many others see Hoffmann (1989).

national politics in relation to the surviving nation-states. The present situation is best described as institutional deadlock. Because of it, the development of European industrial relations in the coming decade is likely to be driven by global market pressures, local political and institutional circumstances, highly idiosyncratic strategic choices of firms, competition between national regimes in a unified market, and unanticipated consequences of dispersed and fragmented collective action and interest articulation.

Summary and Conclusion

With hindsight, the neocorporatist experiments of the 1970s can be seen as attempts to preserve the labor-inclusiveness of the postwar European political economy under increasingly adverse domestic and international conditions. Because of rapid changes in social structures, growing economic interdependence and the attendant loss of national power, and finally the competitive withdrawal of both Japan and the United States from the worldwide postwar regime of labor-inclusive adversarialism, neocorporatism faltered in the early 1980s.

Today's postcorporatist industrial relations in western Europe are characterized by great divergence among national systems combined with rising interdependence among national economies, creating a growing potential for interregime competition within Europe. The relaunched European integration process to the extent that it aims to complete the single internal market, further adds to such interdependence. At the same time, endeavors to endow the internal market with a social dimension aim to internalize the externalities of national industrial relations systems and make them governable in a comprehensive, supranational industrial order.

The politics of the social dimension is best described as a struggle over whether to leave the formation of a new European industrial relations system to spontaneous convergence among national systems. The alternative is to construct a European industrial relations regime by political means. In fact, to the extent that the postwar European tradition of labor-inclusive industrial relations is not automatically reproduced by market forces, its preservation today would appear to depend on European integration proceeding through political channels.

The development of a unified European industrial relations system is related in complex ways to the present structural transformations of the

European economy. Comparative analysis of national industrial relations in the 1980s indicates that the countries where unions remained comparatively well established were those in which they helped guide economic change toward high value-added production for quality-competitive markets. This raises the question of whether and under what conditions national experiences of this kind can be replicated at the supranational level. It also suggests the possibility that the development of internationally competitive, high value-added production may require the support of, and perhaps even pressure from, independent unions and cooperative industrial relations. If this should be the case, the effective deregulation of the European economy by interregime competition or the failure of a supranational regime may in fact have counterproductive consequences for structural economic change.

Just as there is a social dimension to the internal market, so there is an economic dimension to the social dimension. Any European industrial relations system will have to allow the economy it governs to be globally competitive. Finding a European formula for labor-inclusive economic competitiveness appears to be of particular urgency given that Europe's main competitors, the United States and Japan, have both embarked on paths of deunionization or elimination of union independence.

Although a European response to diversity and interdependence appears indispensable for the preservation of labor inclusiveness and of great consequence for the quality-competitive restructuring of the European economy, the odds against European-level political reconstruction of industrial relations appear overwhelming. Given the endemic weakness of European-wide institutions, the market itself will play a leading role in shaping industrial relations in the future internal market, with the governance of the employment relationship increasingly relinquished to the interplay of disaggregated local economic and institutional conditions and ever-more integrated global firms and market forces.

This is not to say that cooperation between labor and management in Europe will necessarily be abolished by aggressive employers after the completion of the internal market. Neoliberal antiunionism is not the only alternative to neocorporatism. At present, it is as unlikely to dominate European industrial relations as is a supranational reconstruction of national models of labor inclusion. To this extent, optimism concerning the survival of unionism in large parts of Europe appears justified. Still, the future of European industrial relations will be a far cry from its neocorporatist past. While some form of cooperation may continue, because of institutional weakness it will increasingly be based on voluntary profit-driven economic interests rather than the political status of unions and public mandates to employers. Its main site will shift from the level of national politics to the level of the individual, often multinational firm.

Such voluntaristic cooperation will have distinct economic consequences. Where cooperation continues, not only will it be fragmented and dissociated from wider loyalties and solidarities but, in the absence of institutional reassurances, it will also be less reliable and predictable. As a result, cooperation will be less frequent than it would be if generating and maintaining trust were not left primarily to the market.

Reliance on voluntarism as the principal basis of cooperative labor relations could thus effect an ultimately self-reinforcing shift in the path of economic development—making cost-competitive, low-skill and low-wage production not only more possible and attractive, but also more imperative for major segments of the internal market's economy. If society and politics fail to provide firms with the institutions necessary for high performance in quality markets, the firms will seek out product markets in which they can perform well without such institutions— especially if, all else being equal, producing for such markets would have been their first choice to begin with, given their much less demanding politics. If the social dimension project is defeated, neovoluntarism may indeed be the most likely future for European industrial relations. But there are good reasons to be less than euphoric about this outcome— certainly regarding its social and political impacts—but in light of its economic consequences as well.

References

Armingeon, Klaus. 1991. "Towards a European System of Labor Relations?" University of Mannheim, Germany.

Crouch, Colin, and Alessandro Pizzorno, eds. 1978. *The Resurgence of Class Conflict in Western Europe since 1968*, 2 vols. London: Macmillan.

DeVos, Ton. 1989. *Multinational Corporations in Democratic Host Countries: U.S. Multinationals and the Vredeling Proposal*. Brookfield, Vt.: Gower.

Flanagan, Robert J., David W. Soskice, and Lloyd Ulman. 1983. *Unionism, Economic Stabilization, and Incomes Policies: European Experience*. Brookings.

Freeman, Richard. 1988. "On the Divergence of Unionism among Developed Countries," working paper 2817. Cambridge, Mass.: National Bureau of Economic Research.

Van Ginniken, Wouter. 1987. "Wage Policies in Industrialised Market Economies from 1971 to 1986." *International Labor Review* 126 (July-August): 379–404.

Gourevitch, Peter A. 1986. *Politics in Hard Times: Comparative Responses to International Economic Crises*. Cornell University Press.

Hoffmann, Stanley. 1989. "The European Community and 1992." *Foreign Affairs* 68 (Fall): 27–47.

Keohane, Robert O., and Stanley Hoffmann. 1991. "Institutional Change in Europe in the 1980s." In Robert O. Keohane and Stanley Hoffmann, eds., *The New European Community: Decisionmaking and Institutional Change*. Boulder, Colo.: Westview Press.

Kerr, Clark, and others. 1960. *Industrialism and Industrial Man: The Problems of Labor and Management in Economic Growth*. Harvard University Press.

Lange, Peter. 1990. "The Politics of the Social Dimension." In Alberta M. Sbragia, ed., *Euro-Politics: Institutions and Policymaking in the "New" European Community*. Brookings.

Lash, S. 1985. "The End of Neo-Corporatism? The Breakdown of Centralised Bargaining in Sweden." *British Journal of Industrial Relations* 23: 215–39.

Maurice, Marc, Francois Sellier, and Jean-Jacques Silvestre. 1986. *The Social Foundations of Industrial Power: A Comparison of France and Germany*. MIT Press.

McCracken, Paul, and others. 1977. *Towards Full Employment and Price Stability: A Report to the OECD by a Group of Independent Experts*. Paris: Organisation for Economic Co-operation and Development.

Piore, Michael J., and Charles F. Sabel. 1984. *The Second Industrial Divide: Possibilities for Prosperity*. Basic Books.

Rosenberg, Samuel. 1989. "The Restructuring of the Labor Market, the Labor Force, and the Nature of Employment Relations in the United

States in the 1980s." In Samuel Rosenberg, ed., *The State and the Labor Market*. Plenum Press.

Silvia, Stephen J. 1991. "The Social Charter of the European Community: A Defeat for European Labor." *Industrial and Labor Relations Review* 44 (July): 626–43.

Schmitter, Phillipe C., and Gerhard Lehmbruch, eds. 1979. *Trends Towards Corporatist Intermediation*. Beverly Hills: Sage.

Streeck, Wolfgang. 1987. "The Uncertainties of Management in the Management of Uncertainty." *International Journal of Political Economy* 17 (3): 57–87.

————. 1991. "More Uncertainties: West German Unions Facing 1992." *Industrial Relations* 30 (Fall): 317–49.

Streeck, Wolfgang, and Phillipe C. Schmitter. 1991. "From National Corporatism to Transnational Pluralism: Organized Interests in the Single European Market." *Politics and Society* 19 (June): 133–64.

Visser, Jelle. 1990. *In Search of Inclusive Unionism*. Bulletin of Comparative Labor Relations 18. Denver and Boston: Kluwer.

————. 1991. "Trends in Trade Union Membership." *OECD Employment Outlook* (July): 97–134.

Visser, Jelle, and Bernhard Ebbinghaus. 1991. "Making the Most of Diversity? European Integration and Transnational Organisation of Labor." University of Amsterdam, Department of Sociology.

CHAPTER FIVE

West German Labor Market Institutions and East German Transformation

David Soskice and Ronald Schettkat

W HAT PATTERN OF labor market institutions will be conducive to low unemployment in an enlarged and probably more unified Europe in the next decade? Can relevant lessons be learned from the experience of German institutions, both in the former West Germany and now also in the former German Democratic Republic? There is a continuing debate over German institutions and their effectiveness in producing low unemployment and high employment in an open economy subject to external shocks. Certain economists see German institutions as victims of Eurosclerosis and argue that deregulation should govern the development of the institutional landscape in east Germany. The other side of the debate is less cogent, with particular institutions (such as vocational training) singled out for praise but with limited understanding of how the system as a whole works and how it relates to employment and unemployment performance.

This paper aims to articulate this latter side of the debate. First we describe how German labor institutions act to create incentive structures for agents, then we explain a strategy for transplanting west German institutions to east Germany. The macroeconomic consequences of this for both parts of the Federal Republic are considered. We argue that the German institutions of codetermination, coordinated wage setting, and vocational training and education allow flexible adjustment, particularly in conjunction with German companies' and financial institutions' methods of operation. This is conducive to good macroeconomic performance, and unemployment in east Germany should be seen as a necessary transition to the west German pattern.

The first part of this chapter examines west German institutions and describes how they operate to allow efficient labor market adjustment with low inflation and unemployment. The second part attempts to explain economic developments in east Germany and their consequences for west Germany, not as the result of mistaken policies of German unions and employers but as part of a (somewhat) coherent strategy of building the eastern states of Germany into an approximate version of their western counterparts. The strategy that has brought the west German economy close to the maximum level of sustainable activity, together with the development of the exchange rate mechanism (ERM), is seen as changing the relationship between the unions, Bundesbank, and government.

West German Labor Market Institutions

This section examines four main labor market institutions: unions and employer organizations, codetermination, the relationship between the financial system and companies, and the vocational training system. It then shows the principal ways in which these institutions help provide nonprice competitiveness, price competitiveness, and labor market restructuring.

Unions and Employer Organizations

German unions are organized along industrial lines. With few exceptions, workers in the same industry will be organized in the same union. Of the sixteen industry unions, by far the largest and most important is the engineering union, IG Metall. The overall rate of unionization of the employed population, around 40 percent, is not high; but unionization is very high in most large- and medium-sized plants in industry. All the main unions belong to a confederation, the DGB, which performs important functions but does not dominate its members. In particular, in collective bargaining IG Metall plays the leading role.

Unions enjoy many legal privileges. They have a monopoly role in collective bargaining outside the company and in calling strikes; and they play a major part in running the labor courts and in setting policy for the vocational training system. In addition they have considerable quasi-legal authority: they are consulted by federal and regional governments when policy questions of concern to them arise; they have a close working relationship with the Federal Labor Administration; and they work in collaboration with employer organizations and with many large companies. None of this implies, however, that unions identify with the goals of employers. The bitter and hard-fought strikes that occur every so often are a reminder that sharp differences in certain goals exist. Nevertheless, unions are aware of the value to their members of long-term cooperation with business and the benefits their expertise can bring.

Business organizations are also powerful bodies—more so in the 1980s than the unions. There are three types of organizations: industry employer organizations, business associations dealing with nonemployment issues (research and development, export marketing, and so forth), and geographically based chambers of industry and commerce. Membership in the local chamber is required by law, and most companies are also members of industry employer organizations and business associations. Just as the unions run the collective bargaining system from the workers' side, the industry employer organizations have, in effect, run it from the employers' side (with power over lockouts). They also play corresponding roles in the labor courts, the vocational training system, and in business-government relations. The vocational training system is administered by the chambers.

Because governments tend to operate through one or another of these organizations in dealing with private industry, and because they usually enjoy close relations with each other, in principle, the business organizations have considerable power over individual firms. This does not adequately describe their relations with companies, however, since it is not the bureaucrats in the employer organizations who shape their policies so much as do the leading business people in the industry or area in question. What is clear in any case is that business organizations are necessary for coordinating the behavior of businesses, and this role has seldom been contested.

Company Decisionmaking and Participation: The Codetermination System

There are two levels of codetermination in German companies.[1] The first is the works council. In every company with more than six employees, the employees have a right to elect a works council; every employee, whether a union member or not, is entitled to vote and stand for election. In multiplant companies there is in addition a central works council. The second level of codetermination is the supervisory board.

1. For further detail, see Streeck (1984).

Every corporation has two boards: the management board, composed of professional managers and responsible for the day-to-day operation of the company, and the supervisory board, whose major tasks are appointments to and dismissals from the management board, general supervision of the company, and agreement on important decisions. In corporations with between 500 and 2,000 employees, worker representatives constitute one-third of the board. In companies with 2,000 workers or more, shareholder representatives outnumber worker representatives in case of conflict by only one vote.[2] Worker representatives on supervisory boards do not all need to be employees of the company. Those who are not are usually full-time union officials. In practice, employees identify the works council and worker board representatives (nearly all of whom are works councilors or union officials) with the union, especially in larger companies.

Works councils have considerable powers. Among other matters, their agreement is required on any hiring, grading, regrading, or transfers. They must approve plans for compensation and retraining in the event of layoffs. They must also agree to any changes in overtime or working hours and to matters affecting the work environment, including the use of technological devices potentially able to monitor worker behavior. If agreement cannot be reached, the matter goes to arbitration, but this is costly and time-consuming for an employer, especially if the works council is backed by the union. The works council must also be consulted on the employer's work strength planning policies and can demand that vacancies be advertised internally before they are advertised outside. A number of councilors are allowed to work full time on council business, and the employer is required to furnish financial resources for secretaries, an office, and outside expertise. In addition, employee representatives on the supervisory board are allowed access to any company information they wish, under conditions of confidentiality.

What does this mean in practice? First, in larger companies the conjoint representation at works council and supervisory board is reinforcing; the works council chair generally plays a major role in company decisionmaking on employment planning, typically working closely with the personnel director. The power and resources of the works council are further reinforced by external union expertise.

Second, the relation between works council leaders and external

---

2. In the steel and coal industries the arrangement is somewhat more favorable to the unions.

unions is close, but their interests are different. Works council leaders represent the typical established worker in industry—a male, skilled manual worker—and in consequence are concerned for his employment security and real wage growth. The external union is concerned with the whole work force in the industry. Thus it attaches importance to employing apprentices and to semiskilled workers as well. But the external union in most industries has increasingly become the domain of male, skilled workers on account of membership composition and the important role the leaders of the larger works councils play in union decision-making.[3]

Both union and works council support a strategy of continuously retraining and upgrading their skilled manual work force. The union departs from the works council's point of view to an extent in favoring increased numbers of apprentices and a gradual increase in the skilled labor proportion in the company. The works council wants to improve the position of existing skilled workers.

Third, in larger companies in which management cannot pursue individualized strategies toward the work force, the works council has considerable power over the average worker because its leadership's role in planning personnel policy allows it in practice, though not expressly in law, to impose sanctions against individual workers.

Finally, in companies without work force representation on the supervisory board and in most small companies, works councils are not in a strong position despite their formal powers. They have only limited access to important information and weak links to unions and union expertise, and they have to contend with more individualized connections between management and workers.

Banks and the System of Corporate Control

In comparison with the United States and the United Kingdom, there is a close relationship between banks and the business sector. This relationship has been studied at length in the older political economy literature and more recently in the economics press. However, some misconceptions exist about how the relationship works, in part because it has changed over time. Nearly all German banks are now universal banks, acting both for individuals and as investment bankers. For some time, their main preoccupations have been with developing effective "high

3. This trend is not approved of by some union leaders.

street" banking systems and, secondly, with building overseas subsidiaries. Thus it is no longer true that banks' relationship with companies and their role in company strategy are their central concerns. Thus Shonfield writing in the 1960s, and Hilferding at the turn of the century, could describe the role of three banks (Deutscher, Dresdner, and Commerz) as stage-managing industrial planning and exerting extensive control over the largest companies, based on the banks' de facto control over access to finance.[4] These three banks, all private, are still the largest and most important, but their role, control, and sources of power have greatly changed.

In relation to large companies, their role is one of providing a long-term financial perspective, while at the same time ensuring that companies do not behave inefficiently behind the protection of a long-term shelter. They do not directly provide long-term financing, or they only do so to a limited degree. There is no great difference between the sources of finance of large German companies and those in the United Kingdom. Instead, German banks provide the long-term perspective by being able to block hostile takeover attempts. There has been only one hostile takeover in Germany since 1980.[5]

The ability to block takeovers stems from the requirement that a takeover have the approval of 75 percent of shareholdings. In most major companies, large banks are significant shareholders in their own right. More important, they control large proxy shareholdings. In practice, one of the three large banks either controls 25 percent of the voting shares or can assemble an alliance with the other two banks or the biggest insurance companies to control a decisive share.

In exchange for this protection, one of the key members of the supervisory board (often the chair) will be a representative of the bank with the closest ties to the company. That representative plays a major part in the company's main strategic decisions, observes top management closely, figures importantly in their appointment and reappointment, and receives a clear view of company operations. To help evaluate the company, the bank has a research department that studies information on comparative performance of other companies. If the bank believes performance is inadequate, it is in a position to say so and to require change. Thus, roughly speaking, ultimate control of top managers in Germany is held by well-informed banks within a context that permits long-term

4. Shonfield (1965); Hilferding (1981).
5. Franks and Mayer (1990).

decisionmaking. By contrast, in the United Kingdom investors are not so well informed about a company's long-term potential. Companies are careful not to reveal too much to potentially opportunistic investors, and investors are skeptical of company optimism about long-term prospects, suspecting them of behaving opportunistically. As a result, share prices tend to reflect current profitability, and short-term cost reductions to improve current profits can dominate decisionmaking when the hostile takeover looms as the ultimate sanction.

The Vocational Training System

The majority of German young people go through a highly structured apprenticeship, usually lasting three years, begun between the ages of sixteen and eighteen. About 60 percent of German youth are apprenticed, 30 percent go on to higher education (with some doing both), and 10 percent leave school at age sixteen and receive no further education or training. Apprenticeships are offered by companies in all fields of economic activity. Apprentices spend three or four days a week at the company and one or two days at a public vocational training school where they receive more theoretical education. Regulations govern what apprentices learn within the company and to some extent how their time is spent. At the end of the three years the apprentice has to pass both written and practical exams conducted by the relevant chamber in order to become a certified skilled worker. Companies are free to train apprentices to meet higher standards than are required for certification, and in practice larger companies have training programs to match their more sophisticated requirements. With one important exception, companies tend to keep their apprentices after they have qualified and provide a career path for them.

What happens if not enough apprenticeships are available, or if the demand in an occupation does not match the supply? Apprentice wages, although varying among occupations, seem not to vary in response to excess supply or demand. These wages are set by collective bargaining. Apprenticeships are allocated by a selective process whereby the young people most attractive to companies on the basis of their school records get the most desirable apprenticeships, and so on down. If there are serious shortages, pressures may be exerted on companies in two directions. For instance, in the early 1980s, deflation made companies want to reduce their work forces. At the same time there was a demographic increase in the number of young people of apprenticeship age. Employer organizations put pressure on some companies not to reduce the number of apprenticeships and to lay off older workers. Such an institutional arrangement is a potentially critical mechanism in labor market restructuring.

Companies pay for training. It is reasonable to ask why they are willing to do so, since much of the benefit goes to the workers. They may sometimes respond to pressure in taking apprentices. The apprentice's wage is normally about a third of the skilled worker's, and it is probably less than the value of the apprentice's contribution to production. Moreover, the company can train the apprentice in company-specific skills. By offering career conditions in practice that are better than a worker can get by changing companies, there is a reasonable guarantee that the trained apprentice will stay with the company.

Unions, works councils, employer organizations, and chambers are all significant participants in the vocational training system. Unions and employer organizations spend considerable resources on research in vocational training and are involved with the federal and regional governments in developing policies, including new regulations. Works councils monitor how effectively training is being carried out within the company. Chambers of commerce and industry administer the system at the local level.

According to some critics, the length of time required for regulations to be altered makes the apprenticeship system slow to respond to changing needs. Others have suggested that such a bureaucratic system is inherently unresponsive to market forces. These criticisms are misplaced on three counts. First, the system is in practice a differentiated one. Large companies carry apprenticeship training beyond the minimum requirements, to whatever level they believe appropriate given their likelihood of employing the apprentice for a long time. Second, apprenticeship training is only the first (albeit most intensive) training experience for many workers. Companies develop the skills of their work force to meet the companies' needs. Third, the regulations covering many occupations underwent major changes in the 1980s, and the process of change appears to be accelerating.

Nonprice Competitiveness

Unions, works councils, employer organizations, and chambers all help promote certain conditions for nonprice competitiveness. The first set of conditions relates to the skills and organization of the work force.

The technological revolution brought about by the development of the microprocessor has enabled companies of all sizes and in most industries to engage in diversified-quality production, in customization and modification of products and services, and in some cases product innovation. This is possible in part because the microprocessor gives an appropriately skilled and cooperative work force the ability to operate in semi-autonomous teams and to work with equipment workers can program themselves, facilitating rapid changes in production organization.

But the precondition of a highly skilled and cooperative work force may be difficult to satisfy. First, there is the standard public goods problem—workers are trained in marketable skills; they may leave and take their training with them to the benefit of a new employer.

A less visible, but equally important problem is ensuring that the work force behaves in a cooperative way. The nature of teamwork and semi-autonomous responsibility precludes detailed monitoring of individual effort and output. Moreover, long tenures are important for workers to acquire the company-specific skills needed. These skills are also marketable, placing these workers in a strong negotiating position. The implicit bargain between company and works council serves to resolve this situation. According to its terms, workers behave cooperatively and in exchange receive employment security, growing real wages, and participation by the works council in decisions concerning them individually. The works council mediates as follows. On the one hand, it guarantees effective worker behavior because councilors can informally monitor and sanction workers. On the other hand, since it has access to company decisionmaking and information, the works council can ensure that the company is keeping its side of the bargain.

The second condition for nonprice competitiveness relates to companies' ability to make decisions and develop relations within a long-term context. The decisions to invest in training and product development are cases in point. In both, the cost of the investment is incurred before the return is realized—often long before. In principle those who lend money to the company or who own the company (where ownership and management are divorced) bear the risk that the return will not be realized. Clearly this does not matter where the investment is itself marketable. The problem arises when the owners or financiers of the company have to rely on its managers for information on these returns. Under some circumstances, managers build up a reputation of truthfulness, but this is not always possible. Truthfulness about what might happen is not easily verifiable ex post. The German system circumvents this problem through close long-term relations between companies and banks, with the banks possessing considerable knowledge of the companies. By contrast there are few such relationships in the British or U.S. financial systems, and owners (or lending banks) are happier to use a clear criterion, in particular current profits, about which there can be little disagreement. This encourages a style of management wary of long-term investments.

Recent research on innovation and customization of products suggests the importance of long-term relations among producer and customer companies and subcontractors, with development being a joint process. These relationships are difficult to put in legal contractual form because of the multitude of future contingencies. But they involve investments specific to the relationship on all sides. In some contingencies these are likely to put one side or the other at risk. A high degree of trust is therefore needed that one partner or the other will not terminate the agreement. This requires companies to make credible commitments to maintain these implicit contracts over the long term. Two elements of the German system help make this possible. First is the long-term framework provided by the financial system; second is the general environment of close relations between companies and well-organized business associations, which would make life difficult for companies that did not behave responsibly.

Finally, it is important for companies to make a credible commitment to reasonable employment security for their employees. If companies were frequently taken over or likely to make major cost reductions to maintain profitability, such a commitment would be difficult to sustain. Employees might themselves approach employment within the company from a shorter-term perspective and be inclined to extract immediate concessions from management. Thus the underpinnings of the works council's implicit bargain would be removed.

Wage and Price Competitiveness

There are many misunderstandings about the German system of wage determination.[6] In particular, it should be emphasized that there is no formal system of joint discussions at the national level among the social partners, nor between them and the government or the Bundesbank. Such a system existed between 1967 and 1977, with formal concerted

6. This section is partly based on Soskice (1990).

action meetings among unions, management, the government, and the Bundesbank. That system collapsed for reasons unconnected with wage determination. Unions withdrew from the system as a symbolic protest of employers' legal challenge to the 1976 legislation extending codetermination. Moreover, most observers considered the system little more than a ritual; unions would have been unlikely to withdraw had it been more important. Despite the lack of a formal mechanism the German system provides a high degree of coordination across the entire economy.

The most important formal locus of wage bargaining in Germany is the industry at the regional level; second is the company or plant level. Wage determination occurs on an annual basis, and settlements tend to take place in the first quarter of the year. The tone of the wage round is usually set by a key leading settlement, often an engineering regional agreement. Before the settlement, a great deal of informal discussion will have taken place among the DGB, the union confederation, the BDA (representing employer organizations), and other industry unions and employer organizations. There are also extensive contacts—particularly on the employers' part—with the government and the Bundesbank. However, discussion primarily takes place within IG Metall, within the engineering employers' organization, and between the two. It may appear, in fact, that coordination takes place within but not between industries. An examination of the decision problem that confronts IG Metall shows why this is not the case.

IG Metall's principal objective is to increase employment in the engineering industries (including autos and steel), or at least to minimize reductions. This reflects its desire to maintain membership. It therefore needs to be sure that monetary wage developments in the engineering sector do not erode the competitiveness of engineering in the world economy. There are three elements involved here given the evolution of world prices and costs: German unit-labor costs in deutsche marks; the deutsche mark cost of nonlabor inputs into engineering; and the nominal effective exchange rate. IG Metall discusses at length with the engineering employers' organization the development of world engineering prices and export prospects as well as prospective productivity increases in engineering in Germany. Assuming the exchange rate remains constant and given the growth of nominal nonlabor unit costs, the permissible growth rate of nominal wages is determined.

The exchange rate cannot be taken as exogenous in these calculations, however, because of the Bundesbank's perceived strategy. Essentially, the social partners expect that increases in the rate of inflation will meet with bank action to produce exchange rate appreciation. Why is this relevant to wage bargaining in engineering? The key settlement sets the broad percentage increase that most sectors of the economy follow within 1 or 2 percentage points. With a fixed exchange rate, price inflation is substantially determined by the nominal increase in engineering wages less economywide productivity growth—or so the social partners see it. To avoid the risk of deteriorations in international competitiveness (brought on by the Bundesbank's tightening monetary policy to quell inflation and bringing about an appreciation) engineering wage settlements have to be in line with existing inflation plus economywide labor productivity growth. This relationship is reinforced by the need to hold down inflation in nonlabor inputs into engineering. This inflation rate will likewise be indirectly determined by the key wage settlements. A rate of nominal wage growth in engineering that is too high will also lead to an increase in nonlabor costs by this process, further eroding competitiveness.

An important element of this leveling process is that settlements in other industries and supplementary settlements in companies stay sufficiently in line with the initial key settlements. Were that not the case—if for instance the effect of even important settlements on the "going rate" of wage increases were individually small as in the United Kingdom—the threat of the Bundesbank's tightening money would not be of as much concern. Why these other settlements usually stay roughly in line is evident from an examination of other regional-industry settlements and company negotiations.

There are temptations for unions at the industry level to settle above the going rate. Settlements later in the wage round have less of an effect on the inflation rate; and settlements in the public sector and the non-trading sectors generally are hardly affected by the Bundesbank action vis à vis the exchange rate; indeed, they gain from it because it raises real wages without affecting their employment position. Such temptations can cause great problems: either the settlement raises the going rate or it puts strains on unions and employer organizations in the next round. Therefore, any sector that attempted to settle at a significantly higher than normal rate would experience considerable pressures from unions and employers at the national level. The ability of the BDA or the DGB to exert pressure is substantial, because many contacts between industry organizations and central or regional government take place through these associations. Moreover industry unions and employer organizations (smaller ones especially) greatly rely on the DGB and the BDA respectively to provide services. Industry organizations are loathe to fall out of favor with them.

There is somewhat more flexibility in bargaining at the company level.

Almost all basic rate agreements are concluded at the regional-industry level.[7] Company agreements are supplemental, arising from negotiations between senior management and the senior members of the company or plant works council.[8] These company agreements are carefully watched by the social partners at regional-industry and local level. Both the industry employer organization and the industry union clearly recognize that a generous settlement in one company can lead to pressures for increases in other companies. They are also aware that companies using high wages as a recruitment strategy can destabilize local labor markets, especially if incentives are put in place for skilled workers to move.

But both the employer organization and the union want to afford some flexibility to the company. Employer organizations believe in giving companies as much freedom as possible, so long as it has no damaging effect on other members. Unions want to help works councils, which in large- and medium-sized companies are generally close to the union. The negotiation by the works council of a supplementary increase strengthens union members' position among employees.

These supplementary agreements are, however, carefully controlled. Both the employer organization and the union have a range of sanctions they can impose on management and works council respectively. In the German system, employer organizations and the business associations to which they are closely related provide a far greater range of services than their counterparts in the United States or the United Kingdom. For instance German employer organizations help in export marketing, research and development, and vocational training. They function as conduits to government at regional and national levels, and amass extensive strike insurance funds. Along with the unions, they provide assessors for the labor courts, which in turn exercise extensive powers over individual and collective dismissals. In an industrial system in which long-term but frequently noncontractual relations exist among companies for product development and other purposes, employer organizations can function as mediators and facilitators. Along with the banks, they embody a collective memory of companies' strong and weak points, including their lapses. Thus employer organizations are in a position to restrain companies if the need arises. In a parallel manner, unions supply a wide range of services to works councils and can restrain them in company-level wage negotiations.

7. Volkswagen is an exception, but its basic rate agreement is very similar to the engineering agreements for auto sectors.
8. In a technical legal sense, works councils are not allowed to negotiate wages, so these agreements are formally unilateral management decisions without legal force.

There are problems with this system. Overall, however, it provides a clear incentive structure. Its reliable functioning depends on three things. First, the union and employer organization involved in the key settlement believe that subsequent regional-industry settlements will more or less follow the initial one, and that company supplementary agreements will not significantly distort this pattern. Given the exchange rate and world price developments, this key settlement has a major impact on the inflation rate. They believe that the Bundesbank has an inflation objective and will tighten monetary policy with a likely exchange rate appreciation if actual inflation exceeds the target. Second, the union involved in the key settlement is employment oriented, so it is concerned to keep as low a real exchange rate as possible.[9] Third, employers are able to coordinate their activities sufficiently to ensure that other sectors and profitable companies are held in line.

The Beveridge Curve

The critique that German institutions are beset by Eurosclerosis focuses on the Beveridge curve, and the effectiveness of restructuring.[10] Some critics may be prepared to accept that German institutions aid wage restraint, even perhaps that they favor high-quality production. The cost, however, is a slow pace of restructuring. Critics claim that this ineffective labor market adjustment is visible in the Beveridge curve's shift out and to the right, evidencing higher levels of both unemployment and vacancies. They give two reasons for this movement: unemployed workers have increased their search activities and companies have become more selective in filling vacancies because of the high cost of firing workers. The evidence cited for the first factor is an increase in the duration of unemployment, attributed to generous unemployment benefits.

9. In any case they must not be concerned with maximizing short-term real wage growth. The incentive structure set up by the Bundesbank would then work in the wrong direction, for it would translate high nominal wage growth into high real wage growth as a result of exchange rate appreciation. This is why it is a problem for the system if public sector unions with high employment security and limited concern for international competitiveness become too important in the wage bargaining process.

10. The Beveridge curve defines the relationship between unemployment and vacancies. During a normal business cycle an economy will move from a state with high levels of economic activity, a low unemployment rate, and a high vacancy rate to one with low economic activity, a high unemployment rate, and a low vacancy rate and then back again. If both the unemployment rate and the vacancy rate go up simultaneously, it is an indication that unemployment is not due to standard business cycle problems but to structural factors such as mismatches between workers and jobs, a higher restructuring intensity, and so forth.

An alternative possibility is that lengthier unemployment has a different effect. As long periods of unemployment reduce their skills, job seekers' attractiveness to employers is reduced. The evidence for the second point is the ostensibly tough procedures businesses have to follow in order to lay off workers. Both problems shift the Beveridge curve out because matching workers and jobs has now become less efficient for the same level of unemployment and vacancies.

There is a mixture of fact and fantasy in these arguments. On the one hand, unemployment duration did lengthen in the 1980s; it is also true that layoff procedures are in principle rigorous in Germany, in effect requiring the consent of the works council. On the other hand, there is little backing from the official figures for the view that the Beveridge curve has shifted to the right to any significant degree. That view is based on adjustments to the figures,[11] which are quite controversial.[12] Moreover Schettkat, using a dynamic analysis of cyclical movements in vacancies and unemployment, makes a strong case that vacancies have fallen with each cycle.[13]

We take a different approach, and ask how institutions prevented the Beveridge curve from shifting out if unemployment duration lengthened and companies faced difficulties in firing employees. There are three parts to the answer. For any given exogenous product market shocks, German companies tend to respond with only slight changes in output because they are usually in higher value-added ends of the market and they attach great importance to maintaining links with customers. Jobs, rather than workers, are more stable in every sector of the German economy compared with the United States.[14] Financial institutions help to make this minimal response possible. This is reinforced by an emphasis on internal company retraining when the skills required by product market developments are not initially available. Behind this behavior lies another implicit bargain between the works council and management: the works council will not impede firings so long as companies are pursuing appropriate product development and internal retraining policies. This ex-

11. Franz (1991).

12. The argument is that reported vacancies have fallen as a proportion of new hires. Therefore, reported vacancies are divided by the ratio of accumulated vacancies to accumulated hirings over the year, on the assumption that true vacancies are measured by hiring activity. But there is no reason why this should be the correct interpretation of the decline in the reported vacancy-to-hiring ratio. Equally plausible, in line with our interpretation, is that the intake of apprentices (who count as hires) has been maintained during the recession while the number of actual vacancies has fallen.

13. Schettkat (1992).

14. Leonard and Schettkat (1991).

plains the apparently paradoxical findings that, on the one hand, German exports respond less than American to real exchange rate shocks,[15] and on the other that the responsiveness of employment to output shocks in Germany is similar to that in the United States with respect to hours worked but not to employment in the short term. In the medium term (after one year) the employment response is similar in the two economies.[16]

Thus the works council does not impede necessary layoffs despite its natural role as the representative voice of those currently employed. What is more surprising in considering worker interests is the form that labor force reductions take. Schettkat argues that when companies reduce their labor force they do not cut back on apprenticeships but on the employment of older workers.[17] These older workers are, in effect, taking early retirement. They have generous severance payments and a relatively high rate of unemployment. They are likely to stay technically unemployed for some period of time before becoming formally retired. This implies that the duration of unemployment will be long.

In Britain, this would pose many problems because long-term unemployment is by no means concentrated among older workers. Where the long-term unemployed attempt to find work, they face a difficult situation. Their skills and their confidence tend to decay, and British employers interpret lengthy unemployment as signaling that job seekers have had difficulty finding work and that they are problem cases. The Beveridge curve shifts right as businesses find it harder to fill vacancies from the pool of unemployed. The German situation is quite different. Companies take on apprentices and train them with an eye to future skill needs, including potential retrainability. A significant part of the mismatch problem is avoided by company training and retraining. In addition, those who are unemployed and not taking early retirement generally have marketable skills and experience. Thus the increase in unemployment duration has not worsened the problem of mismatch.

Transplanting West German Institutions in the East

The optimistic view that the transformation of a planned into a market economy would take place easily has dimmed. According to that view, all that was necessary was for property rights to be established, planning

---

15. Knetter (1989).
16. Sengenberger (1987); Abraham and Houseman (1992).
17. Schettkat (1992).

mechanisms and other restrictive policies abolished, state ownership eliminated, and proper systems of accounting and law set up. Bringing about such conditions, it was assumed, entailed no great hardship. Now, only elemental free marketeers can fail to be struck by the enormous difficulties and pains that attempted transformations have brought in their wake.

The difficulties are of two very different sorts. First, there is a growing realization among Western economists that the freeing of markets has not led to marked improvement in performance in the countries that most strongly embraced them: the United Kingdom and the United States. The capitalist economies that were successful in the 1980s were those such as Japan, Germany, and South Korea—hardly exemplars of the deregulated marketplace. Ironically, the collapse of the communist system, widely accepted as rotten, shielded from public view the manifest failures of Thatcherism.

But not only has Thatcherism failed; so too has the Swedish version of social democracy. How serious the latter failure is, and whether the Swedish system can be repaired rather than totally replaced, is unclear. For those disillusioned by Thatcherism, however, there is no longer a readily available Scandinavian social democratic alternative.

From this perspective, the west German institutional system appears an obvious candidate for a model in the rebuilding of eastern Europe. Moreover, west German institutions have proven their effectiveness at solving some of the problems of modern capitalist economies—in particular creating the conditions for low unemployment.

Before considering the advisability of transplanting west German institutions in the east, the second type of difficulty encountered in the transformation process needs to be broached, namely, the disjunction between political and economic change. In short, the transformation of a political system toward democracy may undermine economic transformation toward a market economy. The transition to the market creates great losses for particular groups. These can form the basis, in a nascent democracy, of political groupings opposed to market progress. Where political groups are already well identified and can reach an understanding with each other during the transition to democracy (and where those represented by the groups accept their leadership) a long-term agreement to proceed toward the market may be possible. But across much of eastern Europe, the embryonic push for democracy has occurred in a context of relatively fluid political groupings. Thus problems perceived as generated by the market may easily lead to populist political movements and a conflict-ridden society.

In this section we examine the strategy for transforming east Germany and the effect this strategy has had so far on the labor markets in both parts of Germany. The process of transforming the former GDR has been carried out almost completely by west German institutions, most notably the federal government, the employer organizations, and the principal unions. This strategy is one of transplanting the west German economic institutional system into east Germany. It has two related goals, corresponding to the two main obstacles to transformation. The first has been to ensure political integration of east Germany into the federal system to avoid the problems of populist political reaction and to guarantee the continued functioning of the federal system. The second has been to bring into being a working economy that is internationally competitive in high value-added goods and services.

The political argument underpinning this strategy is this: the modus operandi of the federal system of government in west Germany emphasizes the consensual resolution of disputes between regions based on a principle of equitable distribution of resources. Moreover the process of making and administering policies stresses the close involvement of interest groups in vocational training, unemployment administration, labor market policy, and social policy. This is reinforced by the common application of legislation for industrial relations and collective bargaining across the former West Germany.

Thus, there were strong political reasons why a strategy of transformation in east Germany should seek to replicate the west German institutional system. An alternative strategy, notably the creation of a low-cost, weakly regulated labor market would have put intolerable stresses on the long-term operation of the federal system. First, two classes of regions, and citizens would have required a principle of decisionmaking different from consensus based on equitable distribution. Second, the role of interest groups would have been quite different in the two parts of Germany, and the carefully constructed common policies in vocational training, employee participation, social policy, and collective bargaining would have had to be reconstructed. So, while an alternative strategy was clearly feasible from an economic point of view, the political reality of the way the west German system worked ruled it out. In any case, the enthusiasm the deregulated model enjoyed in the United Kingdom and the United States through much of the 1980s was not shared in Germany. The German institutional model was seen by and large as economically successful. Thus, if it were possible to transplant it, the performance of the west German economy provided a prima facie case for doing so.

Implementing the transplantation strategy has had major effects on east German wage development and on west German aggregate demand growth. These effects have given rise to sharp criticism by economists who argue that these developments have created massive unemployment in east Germany and sharp inflation in the west. The most common argument claims that German wage and public expenditure policies have been simply mistaken, demonstrating a failure on the part of policymakers and unions to understand elementary economics. This view, however, misconstrues the implementation strategy and the nature of the German institutional economy. These policies are not the reflection of uninformed choice of an inefficient system; they represent a decision to accept a massive medium-term rise in unemployment in east Germany given the promise of eventual political and economic equality. The alternative would have been to pursue a deregulation strategy with low real wages and a smaller rise in unemployment, but with an enduring second-class political and economic status for the East.

Implementing Transplantation

A major element of the transplantation strategy has been to devise an appropriate structure of incentives for businesses moving into east Germany. The primary incentives for companies are the availability of long-term finance and a well-trained and cooperative labor force. There are, however, constraints on employment policy: clear limits on wage and employment flexibility exist. The incentive structure effectively pushes companies to pursue an employment strategy based on the development of skills within internal labor markets.

How was this incentive structure to be reproduced in the east? Wages were the first consideration. Setting the exchange rate between the deutsche mark and the ostmark at one to one as the basis of currency reunification did not in itself set east German wages in terms of the deutsche mark, except in the short term. West German unions and employer associations established collective bargaining resembling west German processes, and agreed to set basic wage rates so that they would rise to west German levels over a period of four years.[18] This agreement relied on the idea that companies should regard skills and labor productivity in east Germany as partially endogenous and partially a function of investments in training and equipment and the introduction of west German managers and patterns of work organization.

18. West German companies, especially medium and large ones, pay wages that are substantially above basic rates, so this does not literally mean wage parity by 1995.

Second, the unions recognized that east German companies were generally greatly overstaffed. The extension to the east of the Federal Republic's codetermination legislation establishing the rights of works councils and so forth put the unions in a strong position to block or at least retard layoffs. Such a power was very tempting for unions, since it would have helped build support and membership in the east. Indeed, if German unions competed along the lines of British unions, they might well have exercized it. Instead, the main unions cooperated at both the company and the societal level, allowing necessary layoffs to take place. The incentive structure for the new owners of east German companies as far as firing was concerned was effectively modified: companies would bring employment to the proper level, then the west German rules would apply.

The third element of the incentive structure was the availability of business infrastructure: long-term credit, the services of business associations, vocational training systems, and so forth. In addition, the government undertook a huge program of rebuilding road, rail, and air transport, and telecommunications, constructing and refurbishing buildings, and setting up a west German administrative system.

East German Macroeconomic Consequences of Transformation

Unification's first effect was a large reduction in east German aggregate demand. This fall took place for four reasons. With the opening of the economy to free trade, east Germany's low level of nonprice competitiveness contributed to a drop in export demand. The preexisting markets in eastern Europe and the Soviet Union declined sharply, further reducing export demand. Labor productivity increased as a result of the widespread layoffs. And government purchases could no longer fully compensate for the lack of aggregate demand as they had in the GDR.

In the absence of German employment institutions, wages might have been expected to fall, since high unemployment and the unions' limited influence should have enabled employers to drive wages down. The basic agreement between unions and employer organizations, however, raised wages above their market level. In the incomes policy literature it is customary to speak of unions "restraining" their bargaining. Here, the employer organizations were restrained. The organizations' ability to impose wage increases on their members stems from collective bargaining legislation that prevents employers from undercutting the agreed industry rates.

However, these same forces that kept wages high in the face of diminished aggregate demand promise to ameliorate inflation should Keynesian policies be pursued at the regional level. Furthermore, because east Germany is only a small part of Germany from an economic standpoint, aggregate demand policies may be pursued without fear of serious consequences for the external balance. Therefore the current levels of government-led investment in the east are likely to lead to an expansion of employment and a fall in unemployment with little rise in inflation or need to revise the deutsche mark's value.

There are, however, two problems with such a simple Keynesian solution. The first is long term and concerns the growth of wealth in the region. The change in wealth is equal to net investment plus accumulation of foreign assets, that is, the current account surplus. Thus from a longer-term perspective, an external deficit represents a cumulative drain on regional wealth. The second problem concerns the implications of financing the demand growth in the region (east Germany) for the rest of the currency area (west Germany). Before examining this, we need to consider the longer-term strategy for the east.

There are three main longer-term institutional pressures. The first concerns the complex of incentive structures operating on companies' product market strategies and associated effects on employee productivity. These incentives, which make it difficult for companies to avoid high real labor costs through a low cost labor strategy, should lead companies to invest in training in order to raise productivity and increase the quality of their goods and services. The higher quality of goods should increase export demand and hence reduce unemployment. Improved labor productivity has two opposite effects on unemployment: it decreases the cost of goods, which can increase real demand, but it also requires less labor to produce the same amount of goods. There is no way to know a priori which effect will dominate.

The second institutional effect is the operation of the wage bargaining system. As the demand increases, the wage bargaining system may be able to prevent pressures for real wage increases even though unemployment is falling. To this effect is added the third factor, that the vocational training system will prevent the Beveridge curve from imposing a major constraint on expansion. This could come about either through increased vacancies creating upward pressure on wages or through the spillover effect into imports as companies fail to satisfy demand because they cannot hire needed labor. Thus the system of wage bargaining and vocational training creates the conditions for a reduction in unemployment with little increase in inflation.

West German Macroeconomic Consequences of Transplantation

The principal economic condition of the transplantation strategy's success has been that a large percentage of the resources required be available from outside eastern Germany. Insofar as these resources physically come from west Germany, this amounts to an increase in exports on a major scale for west Germany. This is true whether these resources take the form of private investment or government expenditure. In the case of private investment, the financial counterparts are claims held by west German companies or individuals on assets in the east; and in the case of government expenditure, these are financial claims on the government in the form of bonds, currency, or increased tax receipts. The direct effect, therefore, on the west German economy is an increase in aggregate demand, mitigated to some extent by increased taxation and higher real interest rates.

The net effect on aggregate demand has been massive. Between the fourth quarter of 1989 and the third quarter of 1991, employment rose by 1.6 million. Some 1.35 million people came from outside the labor force—many from east Germany—rather than from the unemployed. Unemployment fell from 1.99 million to 1.73 million over the period. To give an idea of the magnitude, the increase in employment was close to the total number of those unemployed in 1989. This occurred, moreover, after a marked expansion in 1988. Unemployment fell from 2.24 million in 1988 to 2.04 million on average in 1989, a cumulative decrease in unemployment of 0.5 million and a rise in employment of 2.1 million since 1988 in west Germany.[19]

The west German economy operated with unemployment above its minimum sustainable level during the 1980s. The increases in aggregate demand from the transplantation strategy have brought the west near the limit. To understand the limits of expansion in west Germany, we need to see the effects of the increase in labor supply and the changes implied by unification on the minimum sustainable unemployment rate (in the west). First, an increase in the domestic labor supply with no increase in foreign demand for export goods means an increase in the minimum sustainable unemployment rate.[20] The second effect is that of unification. This implies that the postunification external balance constraint to west German expansion is the current account of the united

19. Deutsches Institut für Wirtschaftsforschung (1991).
20. A complete macroeconomic model that yields this result is described in an earlier version of this paper available from the authors.

Germany. This worsens the west German balance for two reasons. West German net exports to east Germany no longer count as part of the external balance, and the net imports of east Germany (besides those from the former West) now have to be added into the balance. This further increases the minimum sustainable unemployment rate. How much of this effect will be felt in the east and how much in the west is an open question.

Beyond these questions of external balance, the minimum sustainable unemployment rate is also affected by domestic considerations: the role of union strategy in collective bargaining and the behavior of the Beveridge curve. The Beveridge curve for west Germany has shifted slightly to the right between 1983 and 1990.[21] During that seven-year period, the vacancy rate rose only by 0.5 percent.[22] This small increase suggests there is little reason to suppose that the matching institutions—particularly the apprenticeship system—have failed to function normally.

The operation of wage bargaining in west Germany in 1990–91 has, however, been subject to almost as much criticism as it has been in the east. There is reason to believe that the system may change, and that more direct negotiations will take place between unions and the government, or at any rate, that there will be greater union involvement in certain aspects of policymaking. The potential weakness of the system is that the public sector unions have no good reason to restrain their demands. Because it is hard for the government to fire public-sector employees and because the Bundesbank's threats are irrelevant to them, public-sector employees are constrained only by the government's willingness to allow a prolonged public-sector strike. Unless the unions were to insist on increases greater than those received in the rest of the economy, the government would not take the political risk. Thus the compromise is that wage increases in the public sector match those elsewhere in the economy.

In the industrial sector the Bundesbank's threats have generally proved sufficient in the past. But the more firmly embedded the Federal Republic becomes in a fixed exchange rate system, the less credible the threat of the Bundesbank. If an increase in German interest rates leads to an appreciation of the deutsche mark within the exchange rate mechanism (ERM), this certainly hurts German exporting industries. But this outcome is increasingly unlikely as other countries (notably France and

---

21. That is, the trade-off between vacancies and unemployment has worsened slightly.
22. Schettkat (1992, pp. 169–70).

Italy) insist that they will not devalue their currencies against the mark. If others do not devalue, the Bundesbank's interest rate increases must be followed by the other members of the ERM. This would result in massive international political protest against enforced deflation in other ERM member countries by the Bundesbank and an appreciation of all ERM currencies against the dollar and the yen, making for a much weaker threat. Thus the unions are in the process of calling the Bundesbank's bluff.

What is IG Metall's agenda? The union is certainly not concerned about gaining major increases in nominal wages. The mark is not going to be devalued, and wage increases elsewhere in the economy would follow IG Metall's lead, so there would be only minimal increases in real earnings and an appreciation of the real exchange rate. What the union seems to want is greater respect from the government and participation in certain major decisions. In particular, IG Metall considers unacceptable the government's offer to pay for much of the transfer of resources to the eastern states through increased personal taxation, an offer made without consulting the unions. IG Metall is in effect presenting the following ultimatum to the government. Although it does not want to have to risk an appreciation of the real exchange rate if it can be avoided, the union feels compelled to compensate its members for tax increases imposed on them without consultation. At this stage, the risk of a real appreciation of any size is limited by the Bundesbank's increased inability to mount a credible threat of nominal appreciation.

It is, of course, possible that this challenge may lead to a period of disequilibrium in wage bargaining: that the government may continue to impose tax increases without consultation and the union may continue to bargain for high nominal wage increases, with each side stubbornly believing the other will capitulate. So long as this pattern continues, price competitiveness will be reduced and the minimum sustainable unemployment rate increased. This may require further deflationary measures and limit the transfers to east Germany.

In the longer term, however, an equilibrium solution appears more likely. The advantages are not wholly on the union's side, and three outcomes are possible. The one most favorable to the unions is that they be included in consultation and policymaking in matters of importance to them. In exchange they would allow the government to raise taxes. Alternatively, the government might decide to limit its reliance on increased taxation. Finally, the government might continue to finance transfers to the east through personal taxation and risk ignoring the unions.

Any outcome is possible, but there is some reason for attaching importance to the first. East Germany's problems will not disappear and will continue to demand huge resource transfers. The ability to supply these without taxation—and wage restraint—is restricted, since the limits to expansion of aggregate demand have already been reached. Moreover, the cost of increased union involvement may not be excessive, given the generally difficult state of economic management. As a net effect, internal considerations should not increase the minimum sustainable level of unemployment, except perhaps in the short term. However the institutional mechanism behind unemployment may alter significantly.

References

Abraham, Katherine G., and Susan N. Houseman. 1993. *Job Security in America: Lessons from Germany*. Brookings.

Deutsches Institut für Wirtschaftsforschung. 1991. *Wochenbericht* 46 (November 14).

Franks, Julian, and Colin Mayer. 1990. "Takeovers: Capital Markets and Corporate Control: A Study of France, Germany and the UK." *Economic Policy* 10 (April): 189–231.

Franz, Wolfgang. 1991. "Match and Mismatch in the German Labor Market." In Fiorella Padoa-Schioppa, ed., *Mismatch and Labour Mobility*. New York: Cambridge University Press.

Hilferding, Rudolph. 1981. *Finance Capital: A Study of the Latest Phase of Capitalist Development*. London: Routledge and Keagan Paul.

Knetter, Michael M. 1989. "Price Discrimination by U.S. and German Exporters." *American Economic Review* 79 (March): 198–210.

Leonard, Jonathan, and Ronald Schettkat. 1991. "A Comparison of Job Stability in Germany and the U.S." *Labour* 5 (Autumn): 143–57.

Schettkat, Ronald. 1992. *The Labor Market Dynamics of Economic Restructuring. The United States and Germany in Transition*. Praeger.

Sengenberger, Werner. 1987. *Struktur und Funktionsweise von Arbeitsmärkten: Die Bundesrepublik Deutschland im internationalen Vergleich*. Frankfurt and New York: Campus.

Shonfield, Andrew. 1965. *Modern Capitalism: The Changing Balance of Public and Private Power*. Harper.

Soskice, David. 1990. "Wage Determination: The Changing Role of Institutions in Advanced Industrialized Countries." *Oxford Review of Economic Policy* 6 (November).

Streeck, Wolfgang. 1984. "Co-determination: The Fourth Decade." In Bernhard Wilpert and Arndt Sorge, eds., *International Yearbook of Organizational Democracy*, vol. 2: *International Perspectives on Organizational Democracy*. John Wiley.

CHAPTER SIX

Employee Benefits in the Single Market

Daniel J. B. Mitchell and Jacques Rojot

EMPLOYEES IN MANY countries depend on their work affiliation for various types of benefits, including pensions and health insurance.[1] Their ability to change jobs may be impeded if these benefits are attached to a particular employer—as in the United States—rather than simply to being employed. Thus, an exogenous shock pushing an economy toward greater mobility affects countries differently. Countries with portable benefits will have an easier adjustment than those with benefits that act as barriers to mobility. The changes associated with the single market project represent such a shock for the European Community nations. They may well experience the kinds of pressures that have already weakened the relationship of employee and employer in the United States. However, largely for reasons of historical accident, some EC countries have benefit programs that are portable. Such countries are in a better position than the United States to cope with future pressures arising from mobility.

Special thanks are due to the following individuals: Jacques Amzallag, Claude Baudot, Gunter Becher, John Blackwell, Keith Bradley, Phil Calderbank, J. Chaperon, R. Oliver Clarke, Jan Degadt, Betty Duskin, François Eyraud, David Foden, Alan Gladstone, Rolf Jacob, Peter Jacques, John A. Jolliffe, B. Keller, David Metcalf, Peter Scherer, Winfried Schmähl, Werner Sengenberger, Zafar Shaheed, Alistair Steven, Helen Sudell, Michéle Tourne, Francine Van den Bulcke, Michel Voirin, Manfred Weiss, Harold L. Wilensky, A. D. Wilkie.
1. An extensive bibliography on European benefits, social insurance, and related matters is contained in Mitchell and Rojot (1991).

Benefits and Social Europe

As a general rule, EC countries are more likely than the United States to have public policies mandating benefits of all types. But pensions attract special interest because of the impending retirement of the baby boom generation in the next century. And containing health care costs is a problem for all nations. Thus, a focus on these two types of benefits allows common concerns of the European Community and the United States to be explored.

Table 6-1 provides a profile of benefits in France, Germany, and Britain, the three EC countries on which this chapter focuses. France has diverted the largest proportion of pay into social benefits and workplace supplements. Britain has diverted the smallest proportion and would closely resemble the United States, were it not for its national health care system. Germany appears in an intermediate position.

The countries vary in the degrees of employer discretion in choosing benefit plans. French wages have a large component officially designated by the EC statistical authorities as legally required. Yet much of what the EC calls a customary expenditure for France in fact represents payments to quasi-official funds. These funds are private in form, although they resemble social security in other countries. Of the three European states, Britain gives employers the greatest freedom in setting the mix of direct pay and benefits. Differences in employer discretion arise from variations in the corporatist traditions of the three states. Where there has been a tradition of government involvement in economic affairs and government consultation with the social partners, employer discretion may be limited. Some of this tradition is reflected in the growing EC machinery of governance, so that national policy may be increasingly influenced by EC social policy. That policy, in turn, is articulated by EC Directorate General Five, Employment, Social Affairs, and Education. Some corporate managers and the considerable financial services industry also consider benefit issues from the vantage point of Directorate General Fifteen, Financial Institutions, Company Law, and Taxation.

As part of the movement toward a single European market, there has been considerable discussion of a Social Europe. There is concern that competition within the EC from low-wage areas would lead to social dumping, a reduction in labor standards. In response, a Social Charter and action program were produced and adopted by eleven of the twelve EC heads of state (Britain dissenting). The charter touches on various aspects of remuneration that could eventually affect benefit arrange-

Table 6-1. Social Insurance and Benefits in Three Countries

Item	France	Germany	United Kingdom
Percent of indirect pay in manufacturing			
1975	25.7	19.4	11.5
1989	31.4	21.9	15.1
Percent of labor cost in industrial sector, 1984[a]			
Legally required	19.4	16.4	7.6
Customary expenditures			
Insurance	0.2	0.1	n.a.
Retirement	4.7	4.4	n.a.
Other	3.8	0.1	n.a.
Total	8.7	4.6	7.0
Kind of pension system	Social security plus quasi-official defined-benefit programs external to the employer. Portable for employees. Pay-as-you-go funding.	Social security plus employer-provided defined-benefit plans. Significant barriers to portability. Funding often by company book reserves rather than separate prefunded trust.	Two-tier social security plan: basic flat-rate plan plus earnings-related second tier. Employers can opt out of second tier and set up prefunded private pensions. Employees can opt out of both and set up personal pensions. Recent reforms increase portability.
Kind of health insurance system	Basic medical plan provided through social security. Employers may provide supplementary plans. Because of basic plan, portability has not been an issue.	Basic medical plan through social security. Employer-provided plans are rare due to comprehensive nature of basic plan.	National Health Service supplies basic plan. Employer plans for private care are growing but only cover a small portion of work force. Portability is not an issue under basic plan.

Sources: Bureau of Labor Statistics (1990b, tables 10–13); European Communities (1986, pp. 184–85, 316–17, 354–55, 356–57).
n.a. Not available.
a. "Industrial" refers to manufacturing, mining, construction, and utilities establishments with ten or more employees. Similar results were reported for other sectors but are not reported here.

ments. A country's social obligations before the Community are subject to judicial review by the Court of Justice. Court decisions can in some cases override national legislation, as happened in a 1990 case overturning disparate retirement ages for men and women under a British pension plan.[2]

Economic and Political Implications for the Labor Market

Undoubtedly, most public policy toward the labor market in EC countries will remain at the national level. Any attempt to move, for instance, to a uniform social security system across EC countries would run afoul of national traditions and the problem of making a transition in twelve national systems with millions of people already covered under existing arrangements. Even the vaguer notion of a harmonization of social security systems through general EC guidelines is a concept confined solely to internal discussions within the EC bureaucracy. In any case, the major impact of the single internal market is the increased uncertainty in national product markets it will create.

INCREASED COMPETITION. Movement toward a more competitive product market is also bound to bring a more competitive labor market. Directives and programs in the spirit of Social Europe may cushion some of this impact, but cannot prevent it. Even apart from Europe 1992 competitive adjustments, there are other changes in labor markets that are difficult to reconcile with traditional views of how the employer-employee or the employer-union relationship should be conducted. Along with other aspects of economic life, the labor market is becoming "disorganized" in the EC and elsewhere. Heightened product market competition will restrict employer's ability to pay or make it less certain that their ability to pay will continue. Member countries will be less capable of protecting favored employers. Moves toward deregulation intensify this problem, as does the easing of policy toward corporate takeovers and restructuring.

INTERNAL LABOR MOBILITY. Data on comparative national mobility rates are limited. Table 6-2, which compares French, German, and British data on job tenure with comparable figures from the United States, confirms the impression that labor is less mobile in the European countries. European unemployment also seems characterized by long-term idleness in contrast to the United States.

2. *Barber* v. *Guardian Royal Exchange Assurance plc* (1990).

Table 6-2. Employee Mobility Measurements, Selected Years, 1978–84[a]

Measurement	France	Germany	United Kingdom	United States
Percent of workers with tenure of:				
less than two years	17.8	18.6	27.5	38.5
twenty or more years	13.2	15.1	10.0	10.0
Mean tenure (years)	9.5	10.0	8.5	7.8
Percent of job losers and leavers searching for six or more months	65.2	59.1	68.1	19.1
Structural adjustment index[b]				
1967–77	8.5[c]	7.2[c]	7.5[c]	6.8[d]
1977–87	9.7[c]	6.9[c]	10.0[c]	5.8,[d] 5.0[c]

Sources: OECD (1986, table 2-1); EC (1989, table 69); International Labour Office, *Yearbook of Labour Statistics*, various issues; Bureau of Labor Statistics (1988, table B-11); *Employment and Earnings*, various issues.

a. Data on France and Germany are for 1978; data on the United Kingdom are for 1984; data on the United States are for 1983. European data are for individuals aged 14 and older; U.S. data are for those aged 16 and older.

b. Calculated using the eight industrial classifications appearing in the *Yearbook of Labour Statistics:* agriculture, mining, manufacturing, utilities, construction, commerce, transportation, finance, and services. Employment not classified by sector was excluded. Index is equal to one-half the sum of the absolute changes in the percentages of employment in each sector.

c. International Labour Office (ILO) data.

d. U.S. data approximating ILO industrial classifications.

But pressures for increased EC mobility have grown. Table 6-2 provides an index of structural pressures experienced in France, Germany, the United Kingdom, and the United States from 1967 to 1987. The index is equal to one half the sum of the absolute changes in the percentage of each country's employment in each of the nine one-digit sectors used by the International Labour Office (ILO) in its industrial classification system.[3] The index can vary between 0 (no change) and 100 (maximum change in employment patterns).

From 1967 to 1977 the three European countries showed levels of structural pressure roughly the same as or somewhat higher than U.S. levels. But during 1977–87, France and the United Kingdom showed higher levels of structural adjustment than the United States. Notably, they showed the most marked departure from U.S. levels in their unemployment rates. By contrast, Germany, which made a lesser adjustment, experienced unemployment in the U.S. range. With pressure for increased mobility already evident in EC states, it is logical to consider social insurance and benefit structures and their possible role in facilitating or obstructing job mobility.

INTERNATIONAL MOBILITY VIS-À-VIS THE EC. It may seem surprising to relate the mobility implications of the single European market largely to mobility within the member states. In principle, incompatible

3. The sectors are agriculture, mining, manufacturing, utilities, construction, trade, transportation, finance, and community services.

benefit arrangements could interfere with cross-border movement. But language and culture have been the chief limiting influences to international mobility. The proportion of EC nationals working in EC countries other than their own amounts to only 1 percent of the total EC labor force. In fact, more than half of the foreign workers employed in EC countries are from outside the EC.

Intra-Community migrants come mainly from areas with low wages or high unemployment. They are unlikely to be constrained by incompatibilities between domestic company-level benefit arrangements in their native countries and their countries of employment. Most are unlikely to have been part of such benefit arrangements in their native countries. Only one out of ten intra-Community migrants are estimated to have any significant vested pension rights in their home countries.[4] For those few who have worked under pension schemes in their home countries, private pension vesting rules pose no more of a barrier to international mobility than they do to domestic mobility. Vesting rules vary widely across EC countries but are not based on the national destination of a worker who changes jobs.

The problem is more serious with regard to the value of the vested benefits. Some EC countries have mechanisms for transferring pension value entitlements from one scheme to another so that a worker does not lose pension value by changing jobs. However, the formulas under which such interplan transfer payments are calculated vary from country to country. Absent the creation of Community-wide rules for such factors in the calculation of actuarial tables, cross-border fund transfers would be difficult.

With regard to public social security arrangements, the least pressing mobility problems for intra-Community migrants arise with current benefits such as health care. For example, anyone employed in Germany or France and any resident of Britain is covered by the national health benefit program. Other current benefits, such as family allowances, are also available to migrants. Various totalization agreements coordinate national social security systems for migrants including those from countries outside the EC. It is unlikely that greater harmonization would have much effect on intra-Community mobility.

There is a small population of European executives who are transferred across national boundaries by multinational enterprises. Because social security accounts for a relatively small percentage of executives' pay and private executive benefit plans can be extensive, there are special

---

4. A total of 256,000 EC migrants fall into this category. See Jolliffe (1990, p. 5).

mobility issues for this group. A 1990 survey of European, U.S., and Japanese multinationals revealed a general expectation that the completion of the single market would mean more intra-European executive mobility. For short-term transfers, most companies expected to keep their executives under the home country's private pension and social security arrangements. For longer-term transfers (and for medical coverage), there was a somewhat greater propensity to use the plans of the receiving country.[5]

Employee Benefits as Employer Costs

European employers, like employers everywhere, think about benefits in different terms than economists do. Employers view benefits as additions to labor cost. The possibility that benefits influence the mix of labor costs, rather than their level, is usually not considered. Seen as added costs, benefit increases threaten enterprise competitiveness. From the added cost perspective, countries that have high ratios of benefits to wages will be uncompetitive; those that cut benefits will be more competitive and will expand employment.

Unfortunately, the tendency to view benefits as added costs rather than as a way of dividing total compensation distorts public policy. It is true that if a given firm could reduce its benefit costs relative to others in the labor market, it would obtain a competitive advantage. However, a tax or premium for benefits across the board does not change the relative competitive position of firms within the labor market. And as far as costs relative to other countries' labor markets are concerned, the possibility that labor absorbs the cost of benefits—except in the very short run—must be considered.[6] The fact that there is no free lunch does not imply that the benefits are not entirely paid for through lost labor-cost competitiveness.

Employee Benefits, Growth, and Productivity

The matter of savings and growth arises principally with regard to pensions. Pensions can be funded in advance, representing a potential

5. Hewitt Associates (1990a, pp. 21, 35, 36, 38).
6. Zoeteweij (1986, p. 63). Generally, labor compensation can be expected to be correlated with productivity. It will be found that GNP per employee (national output per worker) is a better determinant of total compensation than just wage compensation across countries. This finding, in turn, suggests that benefits affect the compensation mix rather than the level.

form of saving. If a national pension system is based on pay-as-you-go financing (as in France), covered individuals may save less than otherwise. But the effect of pay-as-you-go systems on saving behavior is uncertain. For instance, if retirement would otherwise be financed through private intergenerational transfers (the elderly cared for by their children), creation of an alternative system need not have any effect on saving.

At this point, therefore, a modest, pragmatic assessment is best; it is unclear that public retirement programs substitute for private saving. However, increased saving in public or quasi-public systems (moving from pay-as-you-go to prefunded retirement) will probably increase national saving and is certainly unlikely to reduce it. Substituting private enterprise-level or individual-level savings schemes for public pay-as-you-go programs will also probably increase total saving, if the private schemes are prefunded. However, the transfer between savings and investment is not one-to-one, and the connection among investment, growth, and productivity is also loose.[7]

Related to the proposition that privatized pension arrangements will stimulate investment is the idea that private schemes will invest in financial instruments different from those that public schemes invest in. Private schemes might be more likely to hold private securities than government bonds. For instance, in the mid-1980s, more than one-third of U.S. private pension assets were held in stocks, as were two thirds of the assets of British plans.[8] In the case of many German pensions, the assets are effectively invested in the employer itself.[9] Thus, some argue that private arrangements make more funds available for private investment.

There are problems with this approach. Financial markets are fluid. If public pension schemes tend to hold public debt in their portfolios, fewer such instruments remain in the capital market to be absorbed by private investors, hence more private funds are available for private investment. The preference for the kind of asset is not critical. At most, the asset propensities of public funds may have an impact on risk premiums.

Clearly, public pension schemes can be used to favor public borrowers artificially. But a similar problem also occurs under private savings schemes. For instance, investing pension funds in the firm itself can create a hidden subsidy to the employer providing the pension. German em-

7. For further discussion see Mitchell and Rojot (1991).
8. Turner and Beller (1989, p. 334).
9. Noninsured German pension plans that were not directly invested in the employer held more than 40 percent of their assets in stocks. Turner and Beller (1989, p. 334).

Table 6-3. *Public Social Insurance Provisions, 1989*

Country	Date of first law	Pension[a]	Medical insurance for active employees[b]	Financing[c]
Belgium	1924	E	X	ER, G
Denmark	1892	F, E	X	ER, P
France[d]	1910	E	X	ER, EE, G
Germany	1883	E		ER, EE, G
Greece	1914	E	X	ER, EE, G
Ireland	1908	F	X	ER, EE, G
Italy	1919	E	X	ER, EE, G
Luxembourg	1911	E	X	ER, EE, G
Netherlands	1913	F	X	ER, EE, G
Portugal	1935	E	X	ER, EE, G
Spain	1919	E	X	ER, EE, G
United Kingdom	1908	F, E	X	ER, EE, G
United States	1935	E	Y	ER, EE, SG

Source: Department of Health and Human Services (1988).
a. E = earnings-related pension; F = flat-rate pension.
b. X = publicly provided medical coverage; Y = public coverage for employees and retirees aged 65 and older.
c. ER = employer tax; G = government subsidy; P = personal tax; EE = employee tax; SG = government subsidy to specialized programs.
d. Excludes national ARRCO (Association of Complementary Retirement Systems) and AGIRC (General Association of Cadre Retirement Institutions).

ployers' tenacious defense of the book reserve system of pension finance raises suspicions that such private subsidies in fact occur.

Benefits and the Employment Relationship

National benefit systems can have public and private components; the mix varies substantially across countries. The modern state-run social insurance pension is usually attributed to Bismarck's Germany, whence it spread to other European countries and eventually to the United States. National medical insurance is provided in all EC countries, but in the United States it applies only to retirees and employees age 65 and older. State subsidies to social insurance funds are common in the EC, along with payroll tax financing. In most cases, retirement benefits are related to earnings, although some minimum benefit amounts may apply. Two countries, Denmark and Britain, have explicit flat-rate and earnings-related pension programs. (See table 6-3.)

Private pension and insurance arrangements existed on a limited scale before World War II in both Europe and the United States. In Europe, these became known as occupational plans. In the postwar period, some countries followed policies that encouraged the expansion of such schemes through tax incentives. Enterprise-based pensions currently ex-

Table 6-4. *Tax Status of Employer Contributions to Private Pensions and Health Insurance, 1988*

Country	Pensions[a]	Health insurance	Country	Pensions	Health insurance
Belgium	T[b]	T	Luxembourg	T	T
Denmark	0	T	Netherlands	0	T
France	T[c]	T[c]	Portugal	0	T
Germany	0[d]	0[d]	Spain	T	T
Greece	0	0	United Kingdom	0	T
Ireland	0	T[e]	United States	0	0
Italy	0	0			

Source: OECD (1988, table A).
a. T = taxable; 0 = not taxable.
b. Contribution is part of taxable income but employee receives a tax deduction for the same amount.
c. Although listed as taxable, there is some ambiguity in French law, and tax avoidance is possible for benefits provided by collective agreement.
d. Tax-free up to specified limit.
e. Contribution is part of taxable income, but employee receives tax relief on payment.

ist on a significant scale (in Germany, Britain, and the United States for instance) and are typically related to earnings. Under the French system, national funds have supplanted enterprise-based pensions for most workers.

Widespread national health insurance arrangements have drastically limited the scope of enterprise-based medical insurance in Europe. In the United States, however, most full-time workers at medium to large firms are covered by employer-based health insurance. And about two-thirds of all U.S. wage earners and salaried workers had employment-related health insurance in the mid-1980s.[10]

There are bound to be substitution effects between public social insurance and private employee benefits. Once a substantial private benefit system exists, it is unlikely to be supplanted by a public system. Sometimes public policy may build on existing private arrangements. Examples include the state earnings-related pension scheme in Britain, which applied in cases where private firms did not already provide pensions, and recent U.S. proposals to require private health insurance from employers not providing it.

Employers' willingness to provide significant pensions or health insurance to employees depends partly on the tax treatment afforded enterprise-based benefits. Most countries allow deductions from corporate income taxes for benefit expenditures. The crucial tax variable is whether

10. Bureau of Labor Statistics (1990a, p. 4); Bureau of the Census (1987, table 17); Bureau of Labor Statistics (1988, p. 185).

employees are subject to tax on the value of the benefit contribution. As table 6-4 indicates, most EC countries allow the employer's pension contribution to escape immediate taxation. But most EC countries tax private health plans, discouraging such programs.

Various motives may account for the degrees to which countries encourage private employer-provided benefit arrangements. Countries may encourage such benefits because they want to promote social harmony by putting employees in a position to be grateful to employers for benefits received. If it is national policy to help employers to be perceived as beneficent, then company-by-company programs of social insurance are a logical tool. A second motivation for encouraging a link between social insurance and employment is to provide an incentive to participate in the work force. Fulfilling this motive does not require insurance to be provided at the firm level, however. It could be offered through a national social security system in which eligibility for benefits was tied to work experience. A third motivation is ideological. If the alternative is viewed as state-run social insurance and if there is an aversion to individual dependence on government, employer-operated plans may be preferred. Of course, the middle ground of quasi-private national funds remains available.

All of these motivations seem to have played a part in the formulation of the systems of countries that make heavy use of company-based benefits. The difficulty with this approach is that its implementation ties employees to particular firms. Of course, the mobility issue did not arise in previous eras when lifetime careers with an employer were assumed to be the norm.

Pension Issues

Government-run social security schemes (often operating on a pay-as-you-go basis) require significant tax increases as the elderly population increases relative to the active work force. Consequently, private pensions and private individual savings programs are turned to as a solution to the future problem of supporting retirees.

The attractions of this solution are partly illusory. Private savings and pensions involve anticipatory funding for retirement. Shifting from pay-as-you-go funding to prefunding will be equally painful whether done by converting public systems to prefunding or substituting prefunded private arrangements for pay-as-you-go public systems. In either case, current workers make a double contribution to support existing retirees and to prefund their own retirements. Moreover, private pensions and officially encouraged individual savings plans (called personal pensions in Europe) often entail considerable government involvement through tax incentives and regulations. The plans themselves may not be recorded in the government budget, but their tax consequences are reflected there. Thus, the degree to which they are strictly the result of free-market incentives is open to question.

THE IMPORTANCE OF PRIVATE PENSIONS. Data on the proportion of pension income reported by retirees for their households at the beginning of the 1980s are available for the United States, the United Kingdom, and Germany. For those aged 65 to 74, the proportions of pension income in total income were 20 percent, 22 percent, and 14 percent in the respective countries. The proportions provided by social security were 50 percent, 61 percent, and 82 percent, with the balance of income supplied by investment and property income, work, means-tested benefits, and other sources.[11] In short, in the early 1980s, German pensions were less significant as a source of retirement income (and social security was more significant) than in the United States or the United Kingdom. Although data for France are not available, the relative absence of company-based pensions in that country would have revealed much greater reliance on public and national funds than in the other three countries.

Data on retirement incomes for more recent periods are available from private sources. The data in table 6-5 assume a career worker in a firm with a private pension plan; the proportion of income coming from the pension will thus be higher than an average for all retirees. Many retirees will not have had the service with a single firm assumed in table 6-5. Once again, even among those German workers best situated to receive significant private pension income, the amounts from that source are substantially less than can be expected in the United States or the United Kingdom (and German social security benefits are proportionately larger). The typical career French worker does not have a company-level pension at all. In all four countries, public plans benefit lower-paid workers the most. Private pensions partially offset this effect.

MOBILITY ASPECTS. Enterprise-level pensions are of two basic designs: defined contribution and defined benefit. In the former, money is put aside for workers based on a formula. The worker has a tax-favored savings plan through the employer that earns interest and is available

11. Turner and Beller (1989, p. 328).

Table 6-5. *Typical Retirement Incomes as Share of Final Earnings,*
1989[a]

Percent

Worker	Private company pension	Social security and national funds	Other	Total retirement income as percent of final earnings
Factory worker				
France	...	70	2	72
Germany	15	50	...	65
United Kingdom	39	40	...	79
United States	42	40	...	82
White collar worker				
France	...	70	2	72
Germany	15	45	...	60
United Kingdom	50	35	...	85
United States	53	25	...	78
Middle manager				
France	...	58	2	60
Germany	25	30	...	55
United Kingdom	50	25	...	75
United States	63	12	...	75

Source: Towers Perrin (1990).
[a]Figures are for men retiring in 1989 after a full career at a medium-sized industrial firm. Lump-sum and savings plan distributions are converted into equivalent annual income. Figures are based on estimates from graphic presentations.

upon retirement as a lump sum or annuity. The value of that account and the monthly pension it will buy at retirement are not specified in advance. These amounts depend on returns to assets while the worker is employed and interest rates and actuarial considerations at the time of retirement. Thus, the risk of providing an adequate pension is borne by the employee not the employer. A defined-benefit plan specifies a retirement benefit the amount of which is fixed independently of the return on assets, interest rates, and actuarial factors. Typically, a formula based on past earnings, age, and service determines the monthly pension. The employer bears the risk entailed in coming up with the resources needed to fund the promised pension.

A major advantage of defined-contribution plans is that they can easily be made portable. The employee can be allowed to "roll over" the amount in his or her account into another plan upon changing jobs. If the contribution is not portable, that is if it remains in the old plan with the former employer, the employee can still retain full rights to the account. Thus, it is not a barrier to mobility.

In practice defined-benefit plans do not shift all risk to the employer.

Absent a government guarantee, an inadequately funded plan may be unable to pay all of its promised benefits. And, unless the plan is indexed, retirees may face an inflation risk due to the specification of benefits in nominal terms. Still, the precise cost of the promised benefit cannot be known in advance, and inadvertent inadequate funding can create unforeseen pension costs in the future for which the employer may be liable.

The uncertainty surrounding eventual liability creates a portability problem for enterprise-level defined-benefit pensions. Under a defined-benefit portable pension system, if an employee moves from one plan to another, the receiving plan accepts the uncertain liability incurred by the sending plan. A financial transfer between the plans must be made to offset the liability. But in a decentralized pension system the prefunding assumptions may differ among plans. In order to have financial transfers common assumptions must be imposed, in effect converting the plans into a de facto national system. The problem is compounded if the sending and receiving plans do not have identical benefit formulas.

Small homogeneous countries (such as the Netherlands) with relatively few players to coordinate are better able to develop acceptable common transfer assumptions than large diverse countries. Indeed, the Netherlands has made significant steps in harmonizing its enterprise-level pensions to allow transfers. The Dutch were aided in this effort by the existence of industrywide pension schemes that already permitted mobility among member firms.[12] Developing common transfer assumptions within larger countries is more complicated.

Although the imposition of common assumptions raises technical issues, the most important barriers to portable enterprise-level defined-benefit plans are cost and behavior consequences. Defined-benefit plans tend to subsidize the benefits of immobile workers with the contributions made on behalf of mobile workers who eventually lose their benefit entitlements. There are two components of this loss: nonvested service and postvesting upward tilt of pension accrual with service.

Vesting is simply a period of minimum service before a pension entitlement begins. In the United States the typical vesting period is five years. Individuals who quit or are terminated before the vesting period ends have no benefit rights; any contributions made on their behalf can be used to meet other liabilities of the plan. Wage inflation cuts benefit costs because vested benefit entitlements are commonly based on final earnings or earnings history up to the date of departure from the plan. Thus, a

12. P. R. de Vlam (1990).

Figure 6-1. *Pension Accrual as Share of Final Wage*[a]

Percent

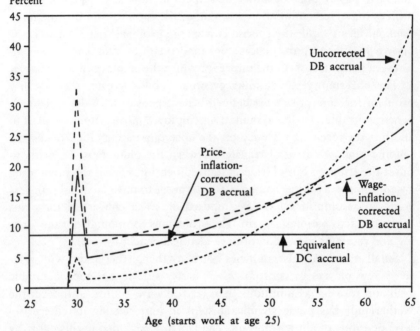

Age (starts work at age 25)

Source: Author's calculations.
[a]DB = defined benefit; DC = defined contribution. Inflation of 4 percent, wage growth of 5.5 percent, and interest of 7 percent are assumed.

worker who departs at age 50 and who would have normal retirement benefits at age 65 loses the wage-inflation effect of 15 years of nominal wage increases between ages 50 and 65. Even at relatively modest rates of wage inflation, a substantial erosion in pension value will occur. The erosion caused by wage inflation can be broken down into two elements. Some of it reflects general price inflation, and some is due to individual real wage growth, which could be positive or negative. Moreover, because of promotions and merit increases, individuals may experience faster rates of real wage advance than is exhibited by the average wage in the firm or economy.

Some options to correct for wage inflation are depicted in figure 6-1. The figure shows the annual accrual for a worker who spends a career from ages 25 to 65 with a single firm. The figure assumes 4 percent price inflation, 5.5 percent nominal wage inflation, 7 percent interest (for discounting), and a 5-year vesting rule. After retiring at age 65, the person is assumed to live for 10 years. The plan formula is assumed to provide

1.5 percent of final earnings (defined as an average of the last 3 years of service) for each year of service. Thus, after a 40-year career, the individual would have a pension of 60 percent of final earnings.

Without any correction for wage inflation, pension accrual (the amount of discounted present pension value obtained by staying an additional year) shows a spike at vesting (30 years of age) and a sharp upward acceleration as the worker approaches retirement age. With an adjustment offsetting just the price-inflation effect, the curve shows a bigger spike at vesting but a more gradual upward slope. (Such a correction makes up for the loss of purchasing power resulting from early departure but not for the loss of the effects of real wage growth.) A correction for all erosion (the price and real wage effects combined) increases the vesting spike, but further flattens the curve.

As the curve is flattened, the antimobility effect is reduced at higher age brackets. But the sharp increase of the vesting spike reduces mobility incentives in prevesting years. Moreover, the curve cannot be completely flattened because of the impact of discounting on the present value of the pension. Even a pension entirely corrected for price and wage effects will still be worth more in later years when the worker is close to receiving it than it is in earlier years. To remove the antimobility effect entirely, it is necessary to have immediate vesting and to give the employee an entitlement to an equivalent of a defined contribution that would produce the same 60 percent pension after 40 years of service. Such a completely flattened equivalent is also shown in figure 6-1.

Governments in some countries have pressed employers to reduce the mobility barriers of defined-benefit pensions by requiring early vesting, transferability between plans, or both (table 6-6). Mobility barriers can also be overcome through laws against the adverse preretirement inflation effect that affects those who depart before retirement age. Governments may impose such mandates for several reasons.

First, the worker-retention advantage perceived by the employer at the microeconomic level is less impressive at the macroeconomic level at which governments operate. Every employee who is discouraged from quitting a current job is one more worker who is difficult to recruit by some other employer. What one employer gains, another loses. Second, there is an obvious question of whether the tax subsidies that go into defined-benefit pensions should be channeled into penalizing labor mobility. Employers who want to discourage workers from quitting can do so without a tax subsidy by paying wages that are higher than average. Third, even from the standpoint of the employer, economic circum-

Table 6-6. *Policies Relating to Enterprise-Based Pension Plans, 1991*

Country	Legally mandated vesting	Common vesting period (years)	Transferability rules
Belgium	No	5	Under consideration
Denmark	Yes	5	Yes
Germany	Yes	10	No
Greece	No	10[a]	No
Spain	Immediate	Immediate	Yes
France	. . .	. . .	. . .
Ireland	Yes	5	Yes
Italy	No	. . .	Under consideration
Luxembourg	No	5-10	No
Netherlands	Yes	1	Government encourages
Portugal	No	Unvested	No
United Kingdom	Yes	2	Yes
United States	Yes[b]	5	No

Sources: Steinmeyer (1990); R. Watson and Sons (1990).
a. Only a few multinational firms have plans.
b. Limited alternatives allowed.

stances change. The tight European labor markets of the 1960s gave way to softer markets of the 1970s and 1980s, reducing employers' labor-retention concerns. When layoffs are required, mobility-inhibiting pension plans make dislocations more painful.

PENSIONS AND RETIREMENT. Labor mobility generally concerns movement from job to job, but there can also be pension-related incentives to drop out of the labor force entirely. Incentives in public schemes to encourage later retirement (to minimize the resource drain as the baby boom generation approaches retirement, among other things) could be offset by early retirement incentives in private pensions. Defined-contribution plans and personal pensions have different effects, since they do not have benefit formulas based on age and seniority. If a worker with a defined-contribution plan or a personal pension chooses to delay his or her retirement, the annuity payment at retirement will be enhanced actuarially by an appropriate amount.

PENSION PROTECTION. In a system of enterprise-based defined-benefit pensions, there are two pay-as-you-go options to meet the retirement liability. The firm can simply make a pension promise without putting money aside. Or the firm can set aside a reserve on its books for future liabilities, as is common in Germany. The reserve method produces a more accurate profit calculation than a simple promise, since it recognizes accrued liabilities. And because recorded profits are smaller at the time of liability accrual, income tax payments by the firm will also be lower. But despite the device of a bookkeeping reserve, the plan's assets are effectively invested in the firm. Whether the pension is based on a promise or is carried as a reserve, the plan's eventual ability to meet its obligations depends on the economic fate of the enterprise.

Such risk is substantially lessened if the employer prefunds the pension promise through an independent pension trust, as occurs in the United States and the United Kingdom, or contracts with an insurance company to provide the pensions, as some German firms do. Risk to workers then depends on the eventual return on the pension portfolio and the adequacy of employer funding. Deficiencies in either category could still lead to default on future payment promises.

Pension protection can be provided for any type of plan by external insurance. In some cases, as in the United States and Germany, quasi-official insurance funds are created to back private pension promises and to provide benefits when defaults occur. These systems can create complex moral hazards, since employers may have incentives to default on their obligations and transfer liabilities to the insurance fund. Even with state-backed pension insurance (or with defined-contribution plans and personal pensions), there is a potential inflation risk to retirees if benefits are calculated nominally. Social security plans are typically indexed in Europe as in the United States to consumer prices. Formal indexation of private plans is rare in the United States but more common in Europe. The two French national pension plans are indexed to point values (as opposed to price inflation); these point values reflect forecasts of future revenues and costs of the plans. German pensions can be said to have de facto price indexation of retiree benefits, at least for companies not in financial difficulty. In Britain, legislation passed in 1986 effectively indexes pensions.

THE FINANCIAL SIDE OF PENSIONS. Within the context of the single European market, there is a drive to reduce barriers to cross-border activities of financial services firms. The market for providing pension services in countries such as Great Britain, where enterprise-level pensions are common, becomes attractive for insurance firms in countries such as France, where enterprise pensions are rare. But there is a counterpart to insurance companies' crossing borders to manage other firms' plans. For multinational employers this counterpart is a European pension fund. Essentially, if financial services firms have the freedom to cross borders in a single European market, employers that provide such services for themselves should be given the same freedom. This is the goal of the proposal for European pension funds. Such a fund would draw

Table 6-7. *National Health Expenditures and Health Outcomes,*
1987, 1988

Country	Health expenditures as percent of GDP, 1987	Health expenditures per capita as percent of U.S. spending, 1987[a]	Life expectancy at birth, 1988	Infant mortality rate, 1988[b]
Belgium	7.2	43	75.4	8
Denmark	6.0	39	75.3	7
France	8.6	54	75.7	9
Germany	8.2	53	75.8	8
Greece	5.3	16	77.0	12
Ireland	7.4	27	n.a.	n.a.
Italy	6.9	41	76.7	8
Luxembourg	7.5	51	n.a.	n.a.
Netherlands	8.5	51	77.1	8
Portugal	6.4	19	74.1	16
Spain	6.0	25	77.1	11
United Kingdom	6.1	37	75.1	9
United States	11.2	100	75.3	11

Sources: *Statistical Abstract of the United States, 1989,* pp. 817–18; OECD (1990, p. 10).
n.a. Not available.
a. Converted to U.S. dollars in purchasing-power parity terms.
b. Deaths per 1,000 children aged less than one year.

contributions from all subsidiaries of the firm within the EC that have pension schemes. Each subsidiary would make its own pension promises in accordance with local law. Assets of the European funds could be invested throughout the EC, however.

In short, there is a coincidence of interests between financial services firms seeking wider markets in the EC and multinationals seeking European pension funds. Thus the likelihood that such funds will be created pursuant to policies of the EC's Directorate General Fifteen is substantially greater than the possibility that pension benefits will be harmonized.

Health Insurance Issues

Seen in monetary terms at the national level, the United States outspends its EC counterparts on health care both relative to GDP and in absolute terms per capita (table 6-7). Indeed, in 1987 even the most prosperous of the EC countries spent barely more than half the amount per capita on health care that the United States did. Moreover, the EC countries provide national systems of medical coverage, so that almost all their populations are covered by basic systems. Yet the U.S. ratio of health expenditure to GDP is about 3 percentage points higher than would be expected based on its per capita GDP.[13]

COSTS AND BENEFITS.   There is a tendency in many countries for health care costs to rise relative to GDP. From 1975 to 1987, for example, the ratio of health expenditure to GDP rose in ten of the twelve EC countries (and in the United States).[14] In the United States, the rise seems to have resulted from relative health care service inflation (a price effect) and greater use of those services (a quantity effect). Within the EC, the price effect has been more mixed, and the quantity effect has been the more general cause of the rising ratio. When measured by the most encompassing health index, life expectancy at birth, it is hard to discern any relationship between health spending and this ultimate national outcome.[15]

The U.S. enterprise-based health insurance system has not been especially effective at containing health care costs compared with EC countries' systems. Indeed, there is little reason to suppose that employers— whose main preoccupation is producing the goods and services they sell—should also be adept at controlling health costs. From the perspective of human resource management, the most striking contrast between U.S. and European employers is the lack of involvement of the latter in issues related to health. U.S. employers are overwhelmed with issues of health care cost containment. European employers, on the other hand, would not know an HMO from a PPO; they are largely content to let questions of health care be settled at the national—not the firm—level.

MOBILITY ASPECTS.   Enterprise-based health insurance arrangements raise portability and labor mobility issues similar to those raised by pensions. With European-style national programs, however, individ-

---

13. A simple regression of the health expenditure to GDP ratio (*HGDP*) in 1987 across the twelve EC countries and the United States against (1/1,000 times) per capita GDP in U.S. dollar purchasing-power parity terms (*GCAP*) and a dummy value of 1 for the United States (*DUMUS*) produces the following result:

$$HGDP = 4.97^a + 2.82^a\, DUMUS + .19^b\, GCAP \quad \text{adjusted } R^2 = .61$$

a. Significant at the 5 percent level
b. Significant at the 10 percent level
14. OECD (1990, p. 10).
15. Regressions of life expectancy against either per capita health spending, per capita GDP, or both reveal no significant trends.

uals can change jobs without losing health care coverage. Thus the labor market changes that may accompany the completion of the single European market do not conflict with typical European health programs. In the United States, however, two kinds of portability issues arise. First, the coverage provided by employers may vary considerably in terms of expenses eligible for reimbursement and the extent of reimbursement. Thus even if an employee is accepted by a new employer, he or she may lose elements of coverage. Some U.S. employers, especially small ones, may not provide health insurance. Second, employers and their insurance companies are anxious to hold down costs by screening out bad risks among newly hired persons and their dependents. One method is to exclude coverage for preexisting illnesses.

Variations in plan coverage and the issue of preexisting illnesses are barriers to voluntary labor mobility. Moreover, not all mobility is voluntary. For some employees the loss of health insurance is an additional cost of being laid off.[16] In summary, the labor mobility pressures that can be expected to accompany the internal market integration do not conflict with European health plans. For the United States, in contrast, mobility is an ongoing problem.

Benefit Plans in Three Countries

EC data are available by detailed (mainly two-digit) industry on benefit expenditures in France, Germany, and Great Britain. Table 6-8 illustrates the variables associated with greater pension spending in each of the three countries. Industries were ranked by the percentage of labor costs going to pensions (other than government-run social security), and the mean characteristics of the top half and bottom half of the ranking were computed. Because pension costs were not available for Britain, the ranking and computation was based on so-called customary expenditures as a percentage of labor costs, a category that contains pensions.[17]

Industries that devote more pay to pension spending tend to be those with higher pay, more nonmanual workers, and larger establishments.

16. U.S. law requires employers to offer continued health care coverage to laid-off workers. But the employee must pay for the coverage (and in after-tax income), which can be difficult for someone who has just lost a job.

17. Such expenditures include payments for nonpublic schemes of insurance, retirement, guaranteed remuneration, unemployment payments, family allowances, and other payments. In Britain, pension spending is likely to predominate in this category.

Table 6-8. *Characteristics Associated with Pension and Benefit Spending, 1984*[a]

Item	Germany		France		United Kingdom	
	Bottom 18	Top 18	Bottom 20	Top 19	Bottom 18	Top 18
Pension spending as percent of labor costs	1.6	6.5	3.2	5.8	n.a.	n.a.
Customary expenditures as percent of labor costs	1.6	6.9	6.9	10.0	4.3	11.1
Monthly labor cost (ECUs)	1,610	2,269	1,497	2,203	1,160	1,700
Workers per establishment	54	714	125	530	n.a.	n.a.
Percent female	48.2	25.4	45.7	24.0	n.a.	n.a.
Percent part time	18.0	6.2	5.6	2.1	12.6	8.2
Percent nonmanual[b]	22.3	36.7	28.5	51.3	n.a.	n.a.

Source: EC (1986, various tables).

n.a. Not available.

a. Composition of available industries varies slightly across countries. Data refer to establishments with ten or more workers. "Top" and "bottom" refer to the number of industries listed in the source publication ranked by percentages of total compensation devoted to pensions or, for Britain, customary expenditures. "Top 18" means the top-ranked eighteen industries, for example.

b. Excludes data from banking, trade, and insurance sectors.

They tend to have fewer women and part-time workers. In short, pensions are associated with large size, high pay, white collar jobs, and male, permanent workers. Even in France, where the figures are distorted by the dominance of the quasi-public national pension schemes, these relationships seem to hold. Those few French industries that do have independent, enterprise-based pensions include banks and insurance companies (with large white collar work forces) and utilities (which are male dominated). These industries also tend to be relatively well paid.

All the characteristics associated with increased pension spending suggest low labor turnover. Thus pensions tend to be linked statistically to reduced mobility. The linkage need not be causal; the high overall pay levels associated with higher pension spending would tend to reduce turnover independently of the pension. Nonetheless, the pension-immobility link is a useful one to consider.

Britain

From the standpoint of pensions, Britain resembles the United States more than many other EC countries. It has a substantial sector of employer-provided pensions funded through trust arrangements. Within Great Britain, 47 percent of the employed work force (full and part time) had an occupational pension in 1987. In the private sector, pension cov-

Table 6-9. *Membership in Employer-Provided or Personal Pension Plans in Great Britain, 1987*

Percent of employment

Workers	Membership in employer-provided pension plan			Ever covered by personal pension plan
	All	Public sector	Private sector	
Full-time, men	62	92	51	15
Full-time, women	51	89	32	5
Part-time, men[a]	8	12	7	n.a.
Part-time, women[a]	11	21	6	n.a.

Source: Great Britain, Office of Population Censuses and Surveys (1989, pp. 146–48).
n.a. Not available.
a. Part-time work is defined as thirty hours a week or less.

erage is closely associated with firm size; 78 percent of employees at firms with 1,000 or more employees were covered in 1987 compared with less than one-fourth at firms with fewer than 25 employees.[18] As table 6-9 shows, pension coverage was generally higher among public employees and full-time workers than among private employees and part-time workers. About half the uncovered part-time workers at firms with pension plans indicated that they did not participate because their particular job was not covered.[19]

Mobility issues mainly involve defined-benefit plans, which are predominant in Britain. Nine out of ten workers under pension systems are covered by plans that gear retirement payments to final earnings. Only 6 percent are under defined-contribution plans as their primary pension; these are inherently portable. However, about 11 percent of covered employees make additional voluntary contributions toward their pensions, the funds from which are mainly handled as money-purchase plans.[20] Such funds—similar to U.S. 401k plans—are also portable.

Personal pensions are completely portable, but until recently they have not been major retirement income vehicles for employees. As of 1987, only 11 percent of employees had ever contributed to a personal pension. Higher-paid workers were more likely to be contributors than lower-paid workers. Workers at small firms (where employer-provided pensions are less common) were more likely to contribute than those at large

18. Daykin (1990, p. 26).

19. Great Britain, Office of Population Censuses and Surveys (1989, pp. 145–146). Data cited later in the text can be found on pp. 33–40, 82–83, 149–50.

20. The balance of workers are reported to be under plans using other formulas, presumably flat-rate or lifetime earnings plans. NAPF (1990, pp. 32, 35).

firms. But changes in government regulations are likely to increase the importance of personal pensions.

There is some evidence of a retreat from employer-provided pensions in Britain. For full-time male workers, coverage rates fell from 65 percent in 1985 to 62 percent in 1987; for female workers, from 56 percent to 51 percent. The drop has been concentrated among younger workers. New entrants to the work force seem less likely to be covered by employer-provided pensions, even if they work for employers that have pension programs and even if they hold full-time jobs. This development suggests that more young people and new entrants are taking up contingent jobs.

In the area of health insurance, Britain and the United States differ greatly. For nonelderly individuals, the United States relies on private insurance coverage, in large part through employers. The elderly are generally eligible for medicare through social security, but that scheme is a reimbursement arrangement. In Britain, the entire population is covered by the National Health Service (NHS), which is both insurer and provider.

Because the NHS rations its services, a private sector exists in Britain for patients who wish to avoid queueing. In 1987, about 8 percent of those aged 16 or older held private health insurance policies, up from 5 percent in 1982. Fifty-four percent of individuals with private health care policies obtained their coverage through their employer, although about one-fifth of these paid for the entire cost directly. However, health insurance contributions by employers in Britain do not receive the tax advantages afforded pensions, so the formality of who is said to pay for such insurance is of little consequence.

HISTORICAL BACKGROUND. Nineteenth-century Britain and the United States had much in common regarding the origin of employee benefits. There was concern about supporting persons too old to work. For the majority of the population, income for old age support was largely a matter of savings, family help, and limited poor law relief. Some unions acted as beneficial societies, and a few provided formal pensions. Burial insurance became available from commercial insurance companies.

Certain employers had informal practices of taking care of long-serving employees by providing them with reduced workloads (and pay) in their later years, or—as a last resort—with a pension. A few large firms, especially railroads, evolved formal defined-benefit pension plans, as did the civil service. By the early part of the twentieth century, recognition of the potential impact of inflation helped bring into use pension formulas based on final earnings rather than career earnings. Some defined-contribution plans were also developed. Formal plans covered perhaps 5 percent of the work force in 1900.[21] Trust funds for pensions began to develop around this time and tax concessions were granted.

The development of German social security arrangements in the late nineteenth century stimulated calls for British government programs. Important voices among British employers supported some type of state-run system to head off socialist pressures. A national noncontributory, means-tested pension program was begun in Britain in 1908. In 1925 more generous pensions were provided under a contributory scheme without a means test. U.S. social security with pension entitlements was not established until 1935.

In part, the spread of pensions was a matter of marketing. Private insurance companies, importing U.S. practices, began selling group pension plans through employers. These plans helped meet the needs of employees at smaller firms, which were not easily able to administer their own programs. Eventually British unions began to negotiate pensions with employers as well as with certain multiemployer systems, which permitted pension portability. By the mid-1930s, one in eight British workers was covered by some kind of occupational pension. But by the mid-1950s the proportion had reached one-third. As in the United States by that era, tax law had evolved into an important policy lever influencing the operation and growth of the pension system.

The state social security pension was a flat-rate system, unrelated to earnings, until the late 1950s when various European countries with flat-rate schemes began to create an additional earnings-related tier of social security. The British state scheme was supplemented in 1959 by a limited earnings-related second tier that covered pay above specified levels and permitted employers to contract out.

Benefits under the state earnings-related pension system (SERPS) and the private pension schemes that contracted out of it were substantially increased in the late 1970s by the Labour government. This shift set the stage for the dramatic changes in pension provisions that occurred under the Conservatives in the 1980s. Under the Thatcher government, contracting out was taken to the individual level by permitting workers to set up their own personal pensions in place of SERPS or a substitute employer-run plan.

---

21. Hannah (1986, p. 13). Hannah's book is the source of much of the historical material in this section.

Britain's system of national health insurance followed a different path from its pension arrangements. As in the United States, health insurance evolved initially as a way of covering income loss through disability rather than as a way of paying medical bills per se. Various state schemes, friendly society programs, insurance plans, and employer schemes were created in response to the fear of lost income during periods of ill health, and there was a limited offering of private policies to pay medical bills. However, programs to pay such bills were largely preempted in the late 1940s with the creation of the National Health Service. Only during the Thatcher period did the private sector for medical care and insurance begin to take on nonnegligible proportions.

Although the NHS's position as a provider of health services was in greater conflict with the Thatcher government's political tilt toward privatization than other nationalized industries were, no official proposal to privatize it was ever made. The NHS appears to be the most popular form of British social insurance.[22] Privatization of the system is not an idea that could win broad public support, even though employees of the NHS accounted for about 4 percent of total British employment in the late 1980s.[23] Even attempts to structure the NHS on a more cost-sensitive model are politically difficult for the British government.

BENEFIT PORTABILITY. The existence of the NHS means that even those who elect private health insurance have a backup health plan regardless of job change. Were the private sector to become the major health care provider, the kinds of mobility questions related to health care found in the United States could develop in Britain. Such a development seems unlikely, hence, issues of portable benefits largely concern private pensions.

Important changes in British laws governing pensions were made in the Social Security Act of 1986. There were several reasons for them. The Thatcher government was nervous about the pay-as-you-go funding of the SERPS component of social security and wished to shift more of the burden of the coming baby boom generation's retirement to employers (who prefund) and to personal saving. A shift away from SERPS to prefunded private arrangements could conceivably increase national saving.

In addition to various budgetary and saving concerns, the Thatcher government harbored an ideological attraction for individual responsibility. In this regard, even private pension plans provided by employers

22. Hennessy (1987, pp. 248–60); Crewe (1988, p. 43).
23. Great Britain, Central Statistical Office (1990, pp. 67, 109).

were a reflection of welfare-state policies accumulated over several decades. As noted before, the private pension system has been closely tied to public social security. Therefore, improving occupational pensions would not really wean British society from past collectivism.

Under the 1986 legislation, which took effect in 1988, the individual employee controls his or her participation in all retirement systems except the mandatory flat-rate part of social security.[24] If the individual works for an employer that does not offer coverage under an occupational pension plan, he or she would ordinarily be covered by the SERPS part of social security in which size of the pension depends on earnings. However, the 1986 law allows the individual to contract out of SERPS and maintain a personal pension instead. If the person would ordinarily be covered by an employer-provided plan contracted out of SERPS, he or she in turn can contract out of the employer plan and maintain a personal pension. If the employee elects the personal pension option, the employer's contribution, which would otherwise go to its own occupational plan or to SERPS, goes to the personal pension.[25] Obviously, the decision involves the risks of a defined-contribution plan (which is, however, completely portable) versus the security (but incomplete portability) of a defined-benefit arrangement.

Although the 1986 legislation enabled saving by means of a personal pension, it also attempted to make defined-benefit schemes more portable. Vesting was cut to two years and a price-correction factor was introduced for workers who leave a plan before retirement age. As noted earlier, defined-benefit plans produce seniority-related upward-sloping costs of quitting due to price inflation, real wage growth, and discounting. Price correction tends to flatten the cost-of-quitting curve (figure 6-1) but does not completely even it out.

The British price-correction factor is the increase in the retail price index up to a cap of 5 percent a year.[26] Thus, if inflation runs above 5

24. The description that follows relies heavily on Great Britain, Department of Social Security (1990).

25. Occupational pension plans often go beyond the minimum required for contracting out of SERPS. The employer is not obligated to contribute beyond the minimum to a contracted-out personal pension, however, and many will not do so.

26. This rule also applies to pension plan terminations. As in the United States, there were complaints that overfunded plans were being terminated as part of corporate takeovers or otherwise. Terminations are not forbidden but the price correction of promised benefits increases the liability of the plan and makes it less likely to appear overfunded. Moreover, overfunded plans are required to increase benefits, provide contribution holidays, or issue refunds subject to tax. The objective is to keep overfunding at or below 105 percent.

percent, even the required price correction will not be complete. Nonetheless, the official recognition of the mobility problem in Britain goes far beyond attempts in the United States, which have been limited to cutting normal vesting from ten to five years. Moreover, the cash equivalent of the promised pension can be transferred to another employer's plan (if the plan will accept it), a personal pension, or an annuity. In addition, the new rules allow defined-contribution plans to qualify for contracting out for the first time. Such plans are inherently portable. The rules also encourage voluntary employee contributions to supplemental pensions similar to U.S. 401k plans.

Various subsidies to the private pension system are provided. First, defined-benefit plans are responsible for paying at least a guaranteed minimum pension (GMP). Once the retiree begins to receive the GMP, the private plan is only required to index benefits up to a cap of 3 percent a year. Should inflation exceed 3 percent, the social security system pays the additional amount needed to protect purchasing power. This government guarantee of a pension in real terms provides a stimulus to private pensions.

Second, employers with their own occupational pension plans may deny supplemental payments to employees who contract out of the plans and establish personal pensions. Such policies could in principle discourage this contracting out. However, to promote personal pensions, the 1986 legislation provided for a subsidy of 2 percent of pay beyond the contribution to social security of 5.8 percent that was rebated to personal pensions until April 1993. (The 2 percent subsidy is also available to employers creating new occupational pensions.) An estimated 500,000 employees were expected to open personal pensions in 1986 with an expansion to 1.75 million by April 1990. In fact, by then the number had risen to 4 million. The net cost to SERPS (reduced liabilities minus rebates) has been estimated at £6 billion through April 1993. Part of the eventual cost reflects incentives to contract back into SERPS at later ages; many persons are expected to play the system by contracting for personal pensions and back in to obtain a greater combined pension from the two sources.[27]

OBSERVATIONS ON THE BRITISH EXPERIMENT. The British experiment in creating more labor market flexibility through benefit reform is especially instructive to the United States, where little creative effort in that area has been made. But British policy could in theory have gone

27. Great Britain, National Audit Office (1990).

much farther. It could have terminated defined-benefit pensions and substituted personal pensions and money-purchase plans. But such a change would have been far more radical than was politically possible, given the millions of employees already in defined-benefit programs. Termination of defined-benefit plans would have created complete portability, but it would have exposed the work force to greater pension risk. Thus the 1986 reform was a compromise.

It is ironic, however, that the ideological bias against public social security reduced the role of the SERPS plan, which offered perfect compatibility with an atomistic labor market while ensuring retiree income security. That is, SERPS would be completely portable if no contracting out were permitted; all employers would be covered by the same plan. Shifting from pay-as-you-go funding to prefunding would require an increase in employer contribution rates to SERPS, but these would not necessarily be greater than the increased costs of shifting to personal pensions and other contracted arrangements. In that regard, the French approach to pension provision is instructive.

France

As early as 1793, an official French decree refers to securing the means of survival for citizens unable to work. However, the modern system of French social insurance is largely a creation of the years after World War II, with some absorption of earlier programs.

PENSION PROVISIONS. After World War II, French policy aimed to make the basic pension component of social insurance universal. Thus there exists a government-run (but theoretically private) social security system, supplemented by programs administered by various other quasi-public entities. Over the years, these many "regimes" have been coordinated. As a result, though operating procedures and formulas may be complex, the individual pensioner generally deals with a single administrative institution. In addition, there are a few private pensions.

Although there is some balkanization of the basic system, the outlines are roughly similar for all subcomponents. All components are supported through a combination of compulsory employer and employee, or self-employed, contributions. All are funded on a pay-as-you-go basis (*répartition*). Pension payments from the basic system (which tend to be low) are defined for employees by a formula linking the highest ten years of earnings, labor force experience, and age.

The French approach to social insurance and benefits diverges dramatically from the U.S. approach with respect to complementary systems of retirement income. In the United States, benefits beyond basic social security are left to the discretion of the individual employer, albeit with tax incentives. In France, however, there is a second tier of national arrangements that are compulsory, though not created by statute. These arrangements were established through interindustry collective agreements between employer and union federations.

Creation of the complementary systems had its roots in the ceiling on wage levels on which the basic social security system bases its pension. The first level up to the ceiling is termed the "A-slice" (*tranche*) and is somewhat analogous to the taxable wage base in the U.S. social security system. For higher-paid employees, coverage of successive slices (B, C) became an issue. The issue was especially important to employees classified as *cadres*, a term that roughly corresponds to managerial and professional.

Pressure for retirement income based on higher wage levels prompted the creation of the AGIRC (General Association of Cadre Retirement Institutions) immediately after the war. In later years, AGIRC pensions came to be based on the A-slice of wages as well as higher slices. This program and similar arrangements for noncadres eventually came to be covered by ARRCO (Association of Complementary Retirement Systems) in the early 1960s. Complementary systems are in principle run by the social partners but are tightly regulated by the social security code.

Because there are a variety of retirement schemes, mechanisms for benefit coordination are provided for employees who have established eligibility in more than one system. Financial transfers between the various systems also occur. These transfers sustain plans applying to such industries as railroads, where the ratio of pensioners to active workers is high.

Table 6-5 provides one estimate of expected benefit levels for career employees under the French retirement system. Unfortunately, there appears to be no ongoing data base concerning the system's average results. However, it does appear from other sources that the career outcomes are generally in keeping with the data shown in table 6-5. Generally, the replacement rates of the highest paid workers are less than those of employees earning average or below-average wages.

Within the ARRCO-AGIRC framework, firms have some discretion over the size of the pension their employees receive. Thus, the principle of independent internal corporate policy regarding retirement remains alive in France despite the high degree of intervention. Beyond the vari-

Table 6-10. *Lifetime Number of Enterprises by Which Workers Who Became ARRCO Pensioners Were Employed, France, 1989*

Number of enterprises	Percent of pensioners	Cumulative percent of pensioners
1	6.4	6.4
2	12.0	18.4
3	13.0	31.4
4	12.4	43.8
5	9.6	53.4
6	7.6	61.0
7	6.2	67.2
8	5.2	72.4
9	4.4	76.8
10	3.6	80.4
11	3.0	83.4
12	2.6	86.0
More than 12	14.0	100.0

Source: Unpublished data provided by ARRCO.

ation allowed within the ARRCO-AGIRC framework there are instances of supplementary enterprise-based retirement programs.

MEDICAL INSURANCE. Employees who work a certain number of hours a year, along with pensioners, the unemployed, and dependents of persons in these groups, are covered by medical insurance through the social security system. The system is based on reimbursement with co-payments. Doctors' associations and other health providers enter into agreements with the authorities regarding costs. Some providers who are outside the system charge more than the agreed costs; patients who use such providers are reimbursed at a lower rate and must pay the difference. The system is supported by a combination of employer and employee taxes.

The system does not reimburse all medical expenses. Thus supplementary health insurance provided by private carriers or beneficial institutions is often available through larger employers. Policies for cadres and noncadres appear to be the norm in larger firms.[28] Unlike the U.S. practice, employers do not exclude new hires from coverage on the grounds of preexisting illness, probably because so much of the risk is borne by social security. Hence, the mobility issue this creates in the United States is not significant in France.

LABOR MOBILITY. Although table 6-2 indicates that French workers tend to be less mobile than their U.S. or British counterparts, in ab-

28. Hewitt Associates (1990b).

Table 6-11. *Job Changes in France, 1975–88*[a]

Percent of work force

Worker date of birth	Job changes			
	Never	One	Two	Three or more
1925	44.1	29.5	12.1	14.3
1930	32.7	30.6	16.0	20.6
1935	26.9	27.5	17.6	28.0
1940	23.9	27.2	18.2	30.7
1945	22.6	24.2	19.2	34.0
1950	19.8	24.4	18.0	37.8
1955	13.7	18.7	17.2	50.4

Source: Unpublished data provided by the French social security system (CNAVTS).
a. Active workers under basic social security.

solute terms there is considerable mobility. (French workers who change jobs are less likely than workers in other countries to experience benefit losses because of national social insurance arrangements.) An indication of the extent of employee mobility is given in tables 6-10 and 6-11.

Table 6-10 is based on the reconstructed lifetime work histories of workers who retired under ARRCO in 1989. The median reported number of employers these retirees had over their careers is between four and five. About one-fifth of the retirees reported having had ten or more employers. Since employment that took place during these retirees' youth may not be fully recalled, figures shown in table 6-10 are certain to be underestimated.

A different measure of mobility is given in table 6-11. These data consist of the number of job changes active workers made during the fourteen-year period 1975–88, organized by age cohort. Within the youngest cohort—those born in 1955 and who were just entering the labor market in 1975—about half are recorded as having made three or more job changes during the period. Among the oldest group (those born in 1925) a majority report at least one job change. Thus, even among age groups that are the least mobile, job changes are very possible, and the fact that the changes will not entail benefit losses is an advantage.

The French system of national and nearly comprehensive health insurance relegates private enterprises in retirement and health care to a small role. Certainly, there are problems with the system. The pay-as-you-go aspect of retirement income financing may become troublesome as the baby boom generation retires. And although health care spending is well below U.S. levels, French health expenditures as a percent of GDP (table 6-7) are high by European standards. However, if the single European market creates added pressures for job mobility, the French approach to social insurance and benefits will not be an obstacle to needed structural shifts in employment.

Germany

The unification of East and West Germany has distracted German policymakers from other social issues. Nonetheless, more conventional issues remain.[29] The single market poses potential problems for the German benefits system, especially pension provision. Germany is the largest economy within the EC, and its markets will certainly feel the impact of the competitive forces unleashed by the 1992 reforms. These pressures can already be seen in legislation in the 1980s designed to regularize the use of temporary workers in Germany. The use of part-time workers and changes in work hours (initiated by employers) have begun to be negotiated in collective agreements.

BASIC SOCIAL SECURITY. With respect to state-run social insurance, Germany has long been regarded as the pioneer of the nineteenth century. To fend off a socialist threat, the early German social insurance system provided for pensions as well as accident and sickness insurance. However, as in most industrialized countries, the modern system of German private benefit provision is largely a post–World War II creation.

German social security covers almost all workers other than civil servants, who have their own program. Administration of the system is shared by federal and state authorities, although social security policy is a federal responsibility. As in France, the system operates on a pay-as-you-go basis. Thus, concern about the cost of the baby boomers' retirement has been reflected in recent system changes. For example, early retirement options are scheduled to become less generous, and increased employer and employee contributions are being phased in.

MEDICAL INSURANCE. German social security includes medical insurance for all employees earning less than a specified maximum. The insurance is administered by more than 1,100 decentralized funds con-

29. In principle, German laws concerning employee benefits cover east Germany. The social security systems of East and West Germany were broadly similar with the exception of unemployment insurance (which did not exist in the east on the grounds that full employment was guaranteed). (U.S. Department of Health and Human Services, 1988, pp. 92–95). A complicating factor was the role official unions in East Germany played in administering the system.

trolled by boards representing employers and the insured. About 90 percent of the population is covered by the program as a whole.[30] Medical insurance is intertwined with a program of paid sick leave under which employers must pay 100 percent of earnings for an initial specified period during medical leaves; thereafter, statutory sickness funds pay 80 percent of earnings for an additional period. Medical care is provided by doctors, hospitals, and pharmacists under contract with the funds.

Persons earning more than the specified maximum can participate in the social security medical system or obtain private insurance. In either case the employer must make a designated contribution. The private health insurance market mainly covers higher-paid individuals who decide not to belong to the social security plan.

The medical insurance system is generous; most health expenses are covered in full or with only a small deductible. Because the system remains so comprehensive, even large firms are unlikely to provide supplemental medical programs.[31] Thus, issues of employee mobility based on health insurance are absent from the German system.

RETIREMENT BENEFITS. Retirement benefits in Germany come from two primary sources: social security and enterprise-administered pension programs. In that respect, Germany resembles Great Britain and the United States more than France, although its basic social security arrangements are more generous. Contributions to social security are divided between employee and employer, as in the United States, although employees with very low incomes are exempt from contributing. Social security retirement benefits are based on work force experience and on earnings (up to a cap). They are indexed to the average pay of active workers.

As in other countries, some large firms in Germany had pension plans by the late nineteenth century. But the modern (West) German pension system developed after World War II in part because of a perception that pensions could be used as a source of enterprise finance, and hence, a tool to stimulate growth. Despite the widespread belief that pensions are important to the economy, data on the operation of German pensions are remarkably sparse.

There is no mandate requiring German firms to provide pensions. Roughly two-thirds of German employees, however, are reported to be

30. Goebel (1989, p. 462).
31. Of the twelve firms Hewitt Associates used to illustrate sample German employee benefits, only one had a supplemental medical program. (Hewitt Associates, 1990c).

covered by some form of pension arrangement. But not all will necessarily qualify for pensions as a result. A long vesting period of ten years' service is the legal maximum. Nine out of ten plans are of the defined-benefit type.[32] However, defined-contribution plans are experiencing increased popularity.

Four types of funding mechanisms for pensions are found in Germany: book reserves (70 percent of total reserves in 1989), solidarity funds (10 percent), direct insurance (5 percent), and pension trusts (15 percent).[33] Pension trusts are similar to the U.S. model; monies are invested in an independent trust to provide for future liabilities. Direct insurance refers to a contract between the employer and an insurance carrier whereby the latter undertakes to meet future pension commitments and charges the employer sufficiently to pay for it. In effect, the insurance carrier acts as a pension trust. Solidarity funds are multi-employer pensions; a central trust receives payments from various employers in an industry and pays benefits to retirees. Finally, the book reserve system, which is by far the most important funding mechanism, involves carrying a "reserve" on the books of the employer against pension liabilities.

With the exception of direct insurance plans, all pension arrangements are required to be (partially) insured with the Pension Security Fund (PSV), a specialized insurance company created by employers and private insurance carriers. Contributions are based on the experience of the fund. Major corporate bankruptcies, such as AEG Telefunken's in 1982, can deplete the fund's reserves and call forth increased contributions from active employers.[34]

German pension liabilities are not fixed in nominal terms, as is the U.S. norm. By law, retirement benefits must be reviewed every three years, taking into account price inflation, pay increases of active workers, and the firm's economic state. Except in periods of financial stringency, this means that pensions are increased by the lesser of the first two factors.

32. Turner and Beller (1989, p. 338). However, there is provision for salary reduction plans similar to U.S. 401k plans which resemble defined-contribution programs.

33. Data from Maillard (1990, pp. 145–47).

34. During the period 1975–89, the PSV made pension payments to about 140,000 retirees as the result of 3,800 bankruptcies (Swiss Life, 1990, p. 170). Contribution rates have varied substantially as the result of PSV experience. Rates have been as high as 0.69 percent of payroll in 1982 and as low as 0.06 percent in 1989 (Foster, 1990, p. 212).

THE BOOK RESERVE SYSTEM. The book reserve system of pension finance is in fact varied. In its simplest version, book reserves are difficult to differentiate from unfunded pension liabilities. The firm creates a "reserve" equal to its accrued liabilities. This accounting transaction reduces recorded profits (and taxes) but no asset other than the commitment of the firm stands behind the liability. Workers have their pensions invested in their employer. Without the backup PSV scheme, an employer's bankruptcy would threaten receipt of pensions. Even with the PSV, bankruptcy still puts some pension risk on retirees because its coverage is partial.

Book reserves have been seen by German employers and policymakers as giving a national advantage in providing for corporate finance. Yet it is not obvious at the national level that efficiency is encouraged if firms can borrow more cheaply from their workers than from the outside market. Having a source of funds available without external scrutiny creates a classic principal-agent problem. And there is a potential for inefficient allocation of resources.

Without full backup insurance, investing employee pensions in a single employer puts workers at special risk in the event of bankruptcy. Some economists might describe such an arrangement as an ersatz profit-sharing plan designed to achieve group incentives. However, German employers can institute more typical profit-sharing if they wish; there is no evidence that pensions were developed in place of profit-sharing. Although the PSV does act as a partial guarantee of pension promises, this system simply transfers the problem of having a risky claim on a single employer to another institution. And workers still bear some risk because the insurance is incomplete. As U.S. experience with compulsory pension insurance indicates, ethical hazards can arise from such arrangements, threatening the solvency of the backup plan.

GERMAN PENSIONS AND THE SINGLE EUROPEAN MARKET. Compared with French and British arrangements, German pensions seem most in need of scrutiny in light of the single European market. Their book reserve funding is predicated on continued corporate stability, a questionable assumption. Their lengthy vesting period assumes long-term worker attachments and an absence of involuntary separations, again questionable assumptions. Unlike some other EC countries, Germany has not been developing policies aimed at providing transferability of pension rights across pension systems. Finally, the assumption that book reserves stimulate economic growth (relative to other forms of financing) is at best an unexamined assertion.

Conclusions

European countries have almost uniformly tended toward public provision with respect to health insurance. That tendency has left less room for an employer role in health care than is typical in the United States. As regards pensions, although Europeans have tended to develop a larger public presence than is found in the United States, there is wide variation in the employer role vis-à-vis retirement. In seeking to harmonize policies in various economic spheres, EC countries are being forced to make comparative assessments. The impact of cross-border mobility is in fact not great. But growing awareness of differences in approach to benefits among countries could have important long-term effects on benefits and social insurance within Europe. The existence of alternative routes to retirement income and health care is becoming evident.

Internal labor mobility pressures may also have important long-term effects. The single European market is likely to require significant structural change; greater labor mobility, both voluntary and involuntary, can be expected. Countries with benefit structures external to the firm have one less barrier to labor mobility about which to worry. Thus, French workers can change jobs without jeopardizing pension rights. British workers can obtain new employment without losing health coverage due to preexisting illnesses.

European benefit and social insurance arrangements are better adapted to changing labor markets than are corresponding U.S. arrangements. This feature is mainly a historical accident rather than the result of either prescient planning or economic forces; in the past, there have been higher rates of labor mobility in the United States than in Europe. Nonetheless, some European countries—notably Britain—whose pension systems might pose mobility barriers are experimenting with reforms. That is more than can be said about the United States, where reform has meant little more than unproductive tinkering with the tax code and hand wringing about health care cost containment.

References

Bureau of the Census. 1987. *Receipt of Selected Noncash Benefits: 1985.* Washington.
Bureau of Labor Statistics. 1988. *Labor Force Statistics Derived from the Current Population Survey, 1948–87.* Washington.
———. 1990. *Employee Benefits in Medium and Large Firms, 1989.* Washington.
———. 1990. *Supplementary Tables for BLS Report 794.* October.
Crewe, Ivor. 1988. "Has the Electorate Become Thatcherite?" In Robert Skidelsky, ed., *Thatcherism.* Cambridge, Mass.: Basil Blackwell.
Daykin, Christopher D. 1990. "United Kingdom Pension Statistics." Paper prepared for U.S. Department of Labor international conference, "Private Pension Policy and Statistical Policy." February 21–23.
Department of Health and Human Services. 1988. *Social Security Programs throughout the World—1977.* Washington.
———. 1988. *Social Security Programs throughout the World—1989.* Washington.
De Vlam, P. R. 1990. "Transfer within a Country, with Express Reference to the Netherlands." Working paper for Directorate-General of the European Communities. September.
European Communities. 1986. *Labour Costs 1984.* Luxembourg: Office for Publications of the European Communities.
———. 1989. *Labour Force Survey—Results 1987.* Luxembourg: Office for Publications of the European Communities.
Foster, Howard, ed. 1990. *Employee Benefits in Europe and U.S.A.* London: Longman.
Goebel, Willi. 1989. "Reform of Health Service in the Federal Republic of Germany." *International Social Security Review* 42 (4).
Great Britain, Central Statistical Office. 1990. *Annual Abstract of Statistics, 1990 Edition.* London: HMSO.
Great Britain, Department of Social Security. 1990. "Occupational and Personal Pension Provision in the United Kingdom." Paper prepared for U.S. Department of Labor international conference, "Private Pension Policy and Statistical Policy." February 21–23.
Great Britain, National Audit Office. 1990. *The Elderly: Information Requirements for Supporting the Elderly and Implications of Personal Pensions for the National Insurance Fund.* London: HMSO.
Great Britain, Office of Population Censuses and Surveys. 1989. *General Household Survey, 1987.* London: HMSO.
Hannah, Leslie. 1986. *Inventing Retirement: The Development of Occupational Pensions in Britain.* Cambridge University Press.
Hennessy, Patrick. 1987. "Public Opinion about the Social Security System in the United Kingdom: Continuity and Change 1961–83." *International Social Security Review* 40 (March).
Hewitt Associates. 1990a. "Europe 1992: Business Outlook and Human Resource Planning in Multinational Companies." Lincolnshire, Ill.

————. 1990b. "Sample Employee Benefit Specifications, France, August 1990." Lincolnshire, Ill.

————. 1990c. "Sample Employee Benefit Specifications, West Germany, August 1990." Lincolnshire, Ill.

Jolliffe, J. A. 1990. "The Portability of Occupational Pensions within Europe," discussion paper. Surrey, England: Watsons Europe. January.

Maillard, Paul. 1990. *Votre Retraite? Regimes de Base: Epargne Salariale: Regimes Complemaintaire en France et dans 9 Pays Etranger.* Paris: Castellange Diffusion.

Mitchell, Daniel J. B., and Jacques Rojot. 1991. "Employee Benefits in the Context of Europe 1992," working paper 191. UCLA Institute of Industrial Relations.

National Association of Pension Funds (NAPF). 1990. *Annual Survey of Occupational Pension Schemes, 1989.* London.

OECD. 1986. *Flexibility in the Labour Market: The Current Debate.* Paris.

————. 1988. *The Taxation of Fringe Benefits.* Paris.

————. 1990. *Health Care Systems in Transition: The Search for Efficiency.* Paris.

R. Watson and Sons. 1990. "A Paper for Directorate-General V of the Commission of the European Communities." R. Watson and Sons for EC Directorate General Five.

Steinmeyer, Heinz-Dietrich. 1990 "Expert Group on Supplementary Pension Schemes Report on Vesting." EC Directorate General Five.

Swiss Life. 1990. *Employee Benefit Reference Manual, 1990.* Zurich.

Towers Perrin. 1990. *Retirement Income throughout the World.* New York.

Turner, John A., and Daniel J. Beller, eds. 1989. *Trends in Pensions.* U.S. Department of Labor, Pension and Welfare Benefit Administration.

Zoeteweij, J. 1986. *Indirect Remuneration: An International Overview.* Geneva: International Labour Office.

CHAPTER SEVEN

European Wage Equalization since the Treaty of Rome

Robert J. Flanagan

THE 1957 TREATY of Rome establishing the European Community sought to raise living standards and to promote improved conditions of employment in Europe "so as to lead to the equalization of such conditions in an upward direction" (Article 1). One mechanism through which such equalization could occur is the labor market, and the treaty sought to reduce barriers to the movement of workers among the six member countries, Belgium, France, West Germany, Italy, Luxembourg, and the Netherlands. By broadening the scope of the effective labor market, the benefits of high wages in one country could in principle spread to countries with low wages through the forces of labor market competition. Indeed, the Treaty of Rome was notable for its emphasis on competitive mechanisms rather than regulatory approaches (such as the implementation of labor standards) to achieve equalization of working conditions.

The Single European Act, signed in February 1986 and effective January 1, 1993, seems to remove the remaining barriers to a single European market by relying on a combination of competitive and regulatory mechanisms in the labor market. For the original six EC members plus Denmark, Ireland, and the United Kingdom, who joined the community in 1973, removal of remaining labor market barriers is of limited importance. The main issues for these countries are likely to be the nature of the regulatory standards that are developed. On the other hand, competitive mechanisms may be more important for the three countries that most recently entered the community—Greece in 1981, and Spain and

The author gratefully acknowledges research support from the project on the labor market implications of European integration, coordinated by the Institute for Industrial Relations, University of California, Berkeley, and from the Netherlands Institute for Advanced Study in the Humanities and Social Science, where much of this chapter was prepared.

Portugal in 1986. Workers in the last two countries will not receive full freedom of movement within the EC until January 1, 1993.

As the EC moves into the next stage of integration, remarkably little is known about the effect of a more integrated market on the inequality of pay across EC countries and indeed on whether the benefits of open markets have mainly accrued within the Community or have flowed to workers from less developed countries outside the EC boundaries. The experience of the first thirty years following the Treaty of Rome is relevant in assessing the likely effects a further reduction of labor market barriers following 1992 will have, most notably on the wages of the newer members from southern Europe.

Much of this chapter assesses the extent to which an equalization of wages across EC countries ensued from the Treaty of Rome and how much of this effect resulted from the removal of legal barriers to labor mobility. The chapter begins by reviewing the main EC developments influencing labor flows across national borders. Next, it discusses the effect of market integration in the United States on geographic wage differentials and contrasts this with the changes in wage dispersion between European countries since the Treaty of Rome. The chapter concludes with a discussion of the implications this analysis holds for the future of the EC common market and of the effects a shift to a regulatory strategy would have on achieving greater wage equality within the Community.

Institutional Developments since the Treaty of Rome

One of the original aims of the Treaty of Rome was to spread the benefits derived from intra-Community trade as widely as possible among the populations of the member states. The principal means of achieving this objective was the free movement of goods and factors of production among member countries, through which factor price equalization would eventually be reached.

Articles 48 and 49 of the treaty guarantee citizens of each member country the right to work in any member state without discrimination on the grounds of nationality. In fact, the elimination of barriers to labor mobility occurred gradually during the first decade of the treaty. Until 1968 workers had to obtain permits to work and reside in other countries, and they had to accept job offers made through a national employment agency in their home country in order to obtain those permits. During phase one of the removal of legal barriers to labor mobility within the Community (September 1961 through May 1964) national workers had an informational advantage in that vacancies in their home markets were advertised there for three weeks before being transmitted to other member states.[1] Workers who obtained permits to work in other EC countries had to renew them for the same occupation after one year of employment; only after another three years could they be renewed for any occupation, thereby placing home country and foreign EC workers on an equal footing in the labor market. EC countries dropped the preferential notification of job vacancies at the beginning of phase two (May 1964), and for the next four years, EC migrants could achieve the same status as nationals after two years.

The final phase began in June 1968 with the abolition of work permits, and since July 1968, EC nationals have been entitled to employment on equal terms with nationals of any other member country. EC workers retained employment priority over workers from outside the EC.[2] The right to free movement was not immediately extended to Portugal and Spain when they entered the Community in 1986, but freedom of movement for all workers throughout all twelve member nations should exist beginning January 1, 1993.

Other changes were implemented to reduce the costs of migrating within the Community. The European Commission, the executive branch of the EC charged with applying the Treaty of Rome provisions, developed a uniform system of classifying jobs to help consistently list job vacancies across countries. A treaty on social security rights entitled national and EC migrant workers to the same social security benefits and permitted the transfer of benefits between member states. Articles 123 to 128 of the Treaty of Rome were intended to supplement lowered barriers to mobility with a social fund, meant to "increase the geographical and occupational mobility of workers within the Community." This fund could subsidize half the vocational retraining or resettlement allowance individual countries provided. Political action cannot remove all costs of moving to and working in another country, however. Unlike the development and integration of markets in the United States, language and cultural differences between EC countries pose significant barriers to employment and wage equalization.[3]

1. Swann (1988, p. 160).
2. Swann (1988, p. 161).
3. Where language barriers arise, they also remain a significant source of wage differentials in the United States (McManus, Gould, and Welch, 1983).

Wage Equalization

These institutional developments during the first decade of the European Community seem to indicate that integration contributes to wage equalization through a simple labor market mechanism. To the extent that legal restrictions prevented worker mobility between EC countries, removal of the barriers should increase relative labor supply to countries with high wages. The movement of workers from countries with low levels of productivity to those with high levels would reduce intra-Community allocational inefficiencies by narrowing internal differences in marginal product and wages.[4] This analysis assumes that migrants are substitutes for workers in the host country. If migrants and host-country workers are complements, intra-Community wage equalization is less certain. If migrants with low skill levels are complements to highly skilled workers in host countries, the wages of the latter group should increase, while the wages of host country workers with low skill levels (who are substitutes for the migrants) would fall.

Economic theory stresses that flows of goods can also influence wage dispersion. The Heckscher-Ohlin model of trade, for instance, maintains a radically different labor market assumption: no factor mobility. If there are no barriers to trade in goods, trade flows effectively compensate for the absence of factor flows, bidding up wages in low-wage countries and conversely. Wage equalization occurs by means of relative demand adjustments rather than through the relative supply adjustments of the simple labor market model. In economies with unrestricted trade, removal of barriers to factor mobility would have no effect on wage dispersion. In short, barriers to factor mobility can only be important sources of wage dispersion where there are parallel barriers to trade.

Robert Mundell's 1957 analysis permits some factor mobility in a world of trade restrictions and finds that factor mobility circumvents these trade barriers in allocating resources and equalizing factor incomes.[5] When all countries have the same levels of technology—a primary assumption of both the Heckscher-Ohlin and Mundell models—factor price equalization can occur through either flows of goods or

4. It is notable that in removing the main institutional impediments to factor movements between EC countries, the Treaty of Rome provides no mechanism for narrowing geographic wage differentials within member countries. Domestic institutional forces, such as collective bargaining and the legal extension of collective agreements, often maintain such differentials even in the face of geographic unemployment differentials.

5. Mundell (1957).

flows of factors, and the level of each depends on the relative importance of restrictions on mobility and on trade. Without detailed information on the relative strength of prior barriers to trade and mobility, no clear prediction of the mix of trade and factor flows associated with economic integration is possible, nor of the mechanisms influencing intra-Community wage dispersion.

How have wage dispersions changed following episodes of economic integration? The remainder of this section contrasts the historical behavior of geographic wage differentials in the United States and Europe in response to market integration. The data describe the extent to which equalization has occurred, and, in the case of Europe, the relationship between intra-Community wage dispersion and the removal of legal barriers to labor mobility.

Antecedents

The United States provides an example of the potential importance of internal migration in narrowing regional wage differentials. Immobility in the early history of the United States was not associated with political barriers as in the EC, but rather with the costs posed by great distances and significant physical barriers between some regions; these were only gradually overcome by the development of an internal transportation system. Geographic economic inequality peaked around 1880, when personal per capita income ranged from 45 percent of the national average in the south Atlantic states to 204 percent on the Pacific coast.[6] Thereafter, regional differences declined rapidly, and by 1950, per capita income on the Pacific coast was only 121 percent of the national average, while income in the poorest region (the east south central states) was 62 percent of the average. An analysis of regional differences in average hourly earnings in manufacturing over the first half of this century likewise found a decline in regional wage dispersion, though the results were somewhat contradicted by apparent countercyclical movements in wage dispersion.[7]

These developments occurred during a period of U.S. history when institutional forces that might have helped narrow interregional wage differentials were weak or nonexistent. Union representation was sparse until the 1930s, and even afterward, it never spread as widely as in most European countries. Federal statutory regulation of wages did not begin

6. Easterlin (1961, table 1).
7. Bloch (1948).

until the 1930s with the passage of minimum wage and prevailing wage laws, but in each case the initial statutory coverage was small and increased slowly. On the other hand, there is evidence that labor market mechanisms contributed to the interregional income equalization. Interregional differences in the rate of net labor influx were positively related to differences in relative per capita income.[8] Evidence from the United States therefore supports a link between labor market mechanisms (migration) and factor price equalization.

Wage Equalization in the European Community

This section examines trends in intra-Community wage dispersion since the Treaty of Rome for two groups of "integrated" countries: the original six nations who signed the treaty in 1958, the EC6, and the nine EC members since 1973 (when Denmark, Ireland, and the United Kingdom joined), or the EC9. In the 1950s and 1960s, most migrants were employed in manufacturing or construction, so evidence of pay equalization from labor market mechanisms should appear first in these sectors.

Two sources of comparative wage data are used, one produced by the Office of Productivity and Technology, U.S. Bureau of Labor Statistics (BLS), and the other by the research department of the Swedish Employers' Confederation (SAF).[9] The Bureau of Labor Statistics publishes comparative data on hourly compensation costs (including employer contributions to fringe benefits) for production workers in manufacturing.[10] The Swedish Employers' Confederation publishes comparative data on direct and total wage costs for manufacturing, construction, and mining. The SAF definition of direct labor costs corresponds to the definition of

8. Easterlin (1961, table 5).

9. Bureau of Labor Statistics (1991); Swedish Employers' Confederation (1989).

10. The Bureau of Labor Statistics defines hourly compensation as "(1) all payments made directly to the worker—pay for time worked (basic time and piece rates plus overtime premiums, shift differentials, other bonuses and premiums paid regularly each pay period, and cost-of-living adjustments), pay for time not worked (vacation, holidays, and other leave), all bonuses and other special payments, and the cost of payments in kind—before payroll deductions of any kind and (2) employer contributions to legallly required insurance programs and contractual and private benefit plans. In addition, for some countries, compensation is adjusted for other taxes on payrolls or employment (or reduced to reflect subsidies), even if they are not for the direct benefit of workers, because such taxes are regarded as labor costs" (Bureau of Labor Statistics, 1990).

average hourly earnings used in most countries, but it excludes employers' social insurance contributions and the like.[11]

Pay data from both sources were adjusted first to a common currency basis and then to account for comparative price developments not reflected in exchange rate changes. Data from the Penn World Table were used to adjust wages and labor costs into units of comparable purchasing power.[12] Certain limitations on the availability of the pay data restrict the scope of the analysis. Neither the Bureau of Labor Statistics nor the Swedish Employers' Confederation publishes data for Luxembourg. The BLS series for Belgium begins in 1960. The SAF series for Italy and Ireland begin in 1964 and 1978 respectively. The SAF dispersion measures therefore exclude Ireland and both dispersion measures exclude Luxembourg.[13]

Figures 7-1 and 7-2 show the basic trends in intra-Community dispersion (coefficient of variation) of hourly labor costs (using BLS data) and hourly wage costs (from SAF data) in manufacturing for the EC6 and EC9 countries (SAF-EC6' excludes data on both Luxembourg and Italy in order to obtain a time series from 1957). Vertical lines indicate years in which major legal barriers to intra-Community labor mobility were removed (1961, 1964, and 1968) and in which the Community was expanded to nine members (1973). Figure 7-3 provides similar information for construction using SAF data only.

The raw data give little evidence of a major decline in intra-

11. The Swedish Employers' Confederation defines direct wage costs as wages for time worked, which "denotes time rates, piece rates, shift supplements, overtime supplements, and regularly paid bonuses and premiums. . . . Payments for leave, public holidays, and other paid individual absences, are included, insofar as the corresponding days or hours are also taken into account to calculate earnings per unit of time." Regarding the treatment of payments for leave, the SAF notes that "in certain countries, payments relating to leave and other individual absences would not appreciably influence the level of the average hourly payment, given that these paid absences are taken into account in both the numerator (amounts paid) and the denominator (number of hours)" (Swedish Employers' Confederation, 1989, p. 5).

12. The Penn World Table project develops a common set of prices in a common currency (the U.S. dollar) for some 130 countries. In the present study, the BLS and SAF estimates of wages in national currency units were converted to dollar equivalents using the relevant dollar exchange rates and then multiplied by each country's purchasing power parity (PPP) price index for gross domestic product (GDP) (expressed relative to the U.S. dollar price). The price index for GDP was used because of its broad availability. In countries where the index could be compared to a PPP price index for consumption expenditures, the correlation between the two series exceeded .99. For further details on the construction of the price indexes, see Summers and Heston (1988, 1991).

13. Including Ireland in computations for 1978 and beyond produced no change in the coefficient of variation for the EC9.

Figure 7-1. *Dispersion of Hourly Labor Costs in Manufacturing (BLS Data), 1957-89*

Coefficient of variation

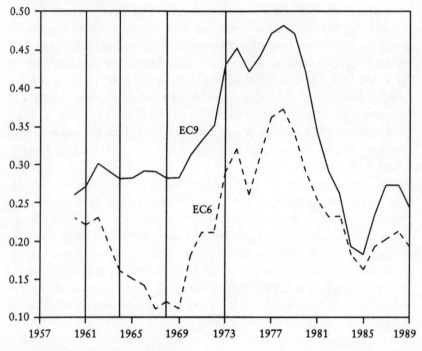

Source: Bureau of Labor Statistics (1991a).

Community wage dispersion since the Treaty of Rome. Indeed, a large increase in dispersion following the last reduction of legal barriers to mobility between EC countries in 1968 dominates the figures. The dispersion of labor costs and wages eventually falls dramatically in the late 1970s, only to rise again in the last half of the 1980s.[14] By the end of the period, the dispersion of hourly *labor costs* in manufacturing among the original EC6 is only slightly less than dispersion in 1960. The same is true of the data for the EC9, although dispersion at the end of the period is less than when Denmark, Ireland, and the United Kingdom joined the Community. Much the same may be said of the SAF measures of hourly wages in manufacturing (figure 7-2) and construction (figure 7-3), which

14. Using the same BLS data used in the computations in figure 7-1, Neven erroneously concludes that intra-Community wage dispersion has declined significantly and that few opportunities for equalization between the EC countries remain (Neven, 1990). Neven concludes his analysis in 1986 and makes no effort to connect it to institutional developments associated with European integration.

Figure 7-2. *Dispersion of Hourly Wage Costs in Manufacturing (SAF Data), 1957-89*

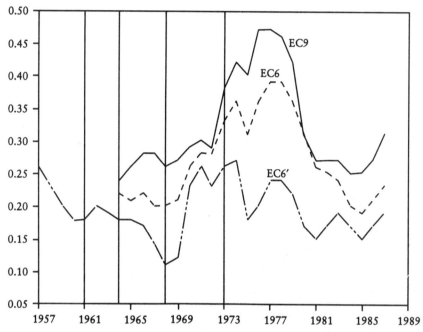

Coefficient of variation

Source: Swedish Employers' Confederation (1989).

exclude employer payments for social insurance and certain fringe benefits. In manufacturing, the SAF EC6' series, which excludes Italy, shows somewhat lower dispersion in 1987 than in 1957. Calibrated against 1964 when data for Italy become available, both this series and the SAF EC6, which includes Italy, show slightly higher dispersion at the end of the time period. The pattern in construction is similar. Generally speaking, intra-Community wage dispersion is rather similar at the beginning and end of the period.

On closer examination, the figures provide little support for a simple relationship between the removal of legal barriers to intra-Community mobility in 1961, 1964, and 1968 and intra-Community wage dispersion. For the dispersion of hourly *wage* costs, a reasonably comprehensive time series (SAF EC6) begins in 1964. This series shows a slight reduction in intra-Community wage dispersion between 1964 and 1968 for both manufacturing (figure 7-2) and construction (figure 7-3), but in both areas dispersion increases sharply following the final reduction in

Figure 7-3. *Dispersion of Hourly Wage Costs in Construction (SAF Data), 1957-89*

Coefficient of variation

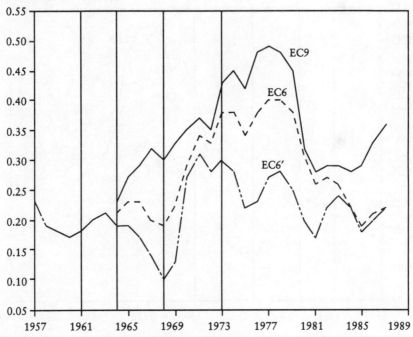

Source: Swedish Employers' Confederation (1989).

legal barriers to mobility in 1968. Stronger evidence of wage equalization following the Treaty of Rome appears in the longer but less comprehensive time series (SAF EC6'). But in this series the decreasing dispersion in manufacturing and construction following the Treaty of Rome is interrupted and for a time reversed during the period in which legal barriers to mobility began to be removed.

The dispersion of hourly *labor* costs in manufacturing (EC6 in figure 7-1) hardly changes during the first two stages of opening up EC labor markets and then increases following the last stage in 1968. Since these data include employer social insurance contributions, they are influenced by both statutory and labor market developments. All in all, a review of the data in these figures indicates no systematic reduction in wage or labor cost dispersion following the three phases of lowering legal barriers to labor mobility.

The data likewise do not indicate that the entry of Denmark, Ireland, and the United Kingdom into the European Community in 1973 narrowed wage dispersion in the expanded community. Because three of the EC9 countries could not benefit until 1973 from the reduced legal barriers to mobility, one would predict a decrease in EC6 measures of dispersion relative to EC9 measures before 1973 and the reverse following 1973, to the extent that labor mobility was a significant source of equalization. For 1964–67, patterns of wage cost dispersion in manufacturing and construction are consistent with this prediction. From 1968 to 1972, however, wage dispersion in the EC9 decreases relative to dispersion in the EC6. After 1973 the trend reverses. These patterns are the opposite of those predicted, that is, that reduction of labor market barriers and membership in the Community produce wage equalization.

The dramatic changes in intra-Community wage dispersions beginning about 1970 largely reflect the effect of exchange rate developments in the EC countries following the demise of the Bretton Woods system. When wages are expressed in real national currency units rather than in terms of a common currency, the intra-Community coefficient of variation increases only from 1.44 in 1969–71 to 1.48 in 1974–76. Moreover, dispersion in the early 1980s was the same as dispersion in the late 1950s before the legal barriers to mobility were reduced. The increased dispersion of the SAF EC6 sample in real national currency units was also slight in the 1970s.

In summary, figures 7-1, 7-2, and 7-3 cast doubts on the efficacy of any of the mechanisms unleashed by economic integration at narrowing wage differences between countries during the three decades following the Treaty of Rome. The most comprehensive data on wage and labor cost dispersion show no reduction in intra-Community wage dispersion associated with the removals of major legal barriers to mobility between countries, although there evidently was a considerable reduction in wage dispersion among EC members during the 1950s before the common labor market was developed. This is suggested both by the behavior of the more limited SAF EC9 series and trends in the dispersion of a much rougher index of the price of labor—per capita income.[15]

15. Ben-David (1991). Ben-David's data show that most of the fall in the standard deviation of logarithms of national per capita incomes occurred by 1963. Per capita income dispersion increased in 1964 when the second stage of the reduction of labor market barriers occurred, the again in 1968 following the completion of the common labor market, before declining gradually in the early 1980s. There are many conceptual differences between economywide per capita income data and the hourly earnings data used in this study as well as a difference in country coverage. (Per capita income data are available for Luxembourg.) Nevertheless, it is not clear why the per capita income data fail to show the increased dispersion during the 1970s that dominates the earnings series from two different

Migration

The impact of labor market factors can be explored more directly by analyzing the behavior of intra-Community migration flows. Removal of important institutional impediments to mobility is a necessary but not sufficient condition for migration. The act of changing one's job location is an investment decision that involves balancing the benefits and costs of moving to determine whether working in another location will produce positive net benefits. This model of migration receives considerable empirical support in settings in which migration flows are not tightly regulated by institutional rules. For example, a great many studies document the importance of these incentives in internal migration within the United States.[16] Similar results emerge from studies of the integrated Nordic labor market.[17]

Recent work indicates that migrants to European countries respond to similar incentives. Willem Molle and Aad van Mourik developed an empirical model of the 1980 stocks of migrants from nine sending countries (including some outside the EC) working in seven host countries (Austria, Belgium, France, Germany, the Netherlands, Sweden, and Switzerland).[18] The independent variables, defined as differences between pairs of sending and receiving countries, are income, distance, imports as a fraction of national income, central bank discount rates, and indexes of cultural and political obstacles to migration. With the exception of the effects of relative unemployment, the authors obtain the expected signs at conventional levels of significance.

A more subtle analysis of the German *Gastarbeiter* system in the 1960s and early 1970s emphasizes the role of demand-driven variations in institutional barriers in certain periods.[19] During this period, German employers could recruit labor from abroad if no German workers were available (labor shortage situations) and the migrants were paid the same wages as German workers in the same jobs. The second provision addressed the concern of German unions that migration might undermine German labor standards. Migration under this system departs from the

---

sources. A review of changes in European employment to population ratios for the period does not reconcile the differences. No inverse relationship between wage levels and changes in this ratio emerges.

16. The literature is reviewed in Greenwood (1975).
17. Lundborg (1991).
18. Molle and Van Mourik (1988).
19. Bhagwati, Schatz, and Wong (1984).

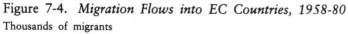

Figure 7-4. *Migration Flows into EC Countries, 1958-80*

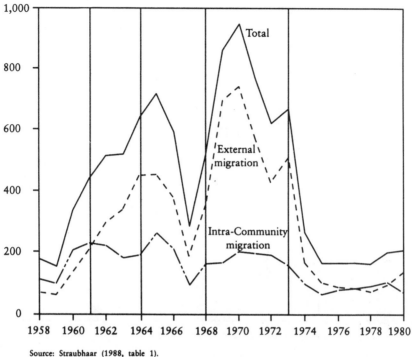

Source: Straubhaar (1988, table 1).

classical migration mechanism in two ways. First, employer recruiting rather than labor supply decisions determines the volume of migration at a given intercountry wage differential. Second, migration does not reduce wages in the host country, although it may mitigate wage increases in periods of labor shortage. Institutional rules in the host country weaken the connection between migration and wage equalization. Migration patterns clearly can depart from classical predictions depending on the specific institutional rules in force, a point of some importance in interpreting the data on European migration following the Treaty of Rome.

Total European migration flows clearly increased following the Treaty of Rome (figure 7-4). Migration quadrupled between 1959 and 1965 and following a brief decline, it peaked again in 1970 at five times the 1959 level. After a precipitous decrease in the first half of the 1970s, migration stabilized during the second half at its level at the time of the Treaty of Rome.

Figure 7-5. *Relative Internal and External Migration Shares, 1958-80*

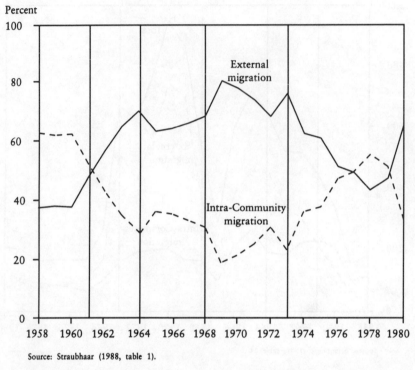

Source: Straubhaar (1988, table 1).

There are three notable points about the composition and timing of migration into EC countries. First, internal migration flows between EC countries were small in comparison to external flows from nonmember countries into the Community (see figure 7-4). The creation of a common labor market did not stimulate considerable intra-Community migration. In no year "did the immigration flows from other EC–6 members increase more quickly than immigration flows from non-EC–6 countries. . . . Bilateral intra-EC–6 migration flows grew more slowly than the bilateral immigration flows from Northern European countries not members of the EC–6 (Austria, Denmark, Finland, Norway, Sweden, Switzerland, and the United Kingdom)."[20] Figure 7-5 illustrates the relative shares of intra-Community and external migration. Clearly, European integration did not produce a burst of internal migration.

Second, such changes in internal migration as did occur were not correlated with the removal of legal impediments to crossing national bor-

20. Straubhaar (1988, p. 54).

ders. This is apparent in both figures 7-4 and 7-5. The most notable increase in internal migration flows (1959–61) predated the removal of legal barriers to mobility between EC countries.

Third, the modest changes in internal migration that did occur are not closely correlated with changes in intra-Community wage dispersion. Indeed, migration flows had returned to preintegration levels at the end of the 1970s when the rapid decrease in intra-Community wage dispersion occurred. Instead, the large increases in migration following the Treaty of Rome came mostly from outside the European Community, and both the increase and later decrease in these flows reflected to an important extent changes in the migration policies of receiving countries.

Migration Incentives

Why did internal EC migration fail to respond to the reduction of legal barriers to mobility? The institutional considerations that qualify the applicability of the classical migration model to flows from outside the EC should be of minimal importance within the common labor market. Instead, failure of internal migration to respond to the removal of legal barriers to mobility may imply that existing economic incentives were insufficient to overcome nonlegal barriers (language, culture, and so forth).

How large were the wage incentives when the Treaty of Rome was implemented? Table 7-1 provides matrices of relative wages in manufacturing and construction in 1964, the first year for which data are available for the five largest countries of the original six members. Each entry expresses the wage of the country on the horizontal axis relative to the wage of the country on the vertical axis. The table shows relative wages based on both dollar exchange rates and purchasing power parity (PPP) adjusted wage rates. (For example, the average wage of manufacturing workers in West Germany is 118 percent of the comparable wage in Belgium when based on dollar exchange rates and 127 percent when based on PPP-adjusted exchange rates). Viewing the data by column provides a quick impression of whether a country (column) generally has a high or low level of wages. West Germany, whose manufacturing wages ranged from 118 to 161 percent of other EC countries is at one extreme, and Italy, whose manufacturing wages range from 62 to 85 percent of other EC countries is at the other. Similar conclusions emerge from the construction data. By row, the data indicate how much more or less qualified workers from each country (row) could earn by moving to the var-

Table 7-1. Relative Wage between EC Countries, 1964

Percent

Country	Belgium		France		West Germany		Italy		Netherlands	
	Dollars[a]	PPP[a]	Dollars[a]	PPP[a]	Dollars[a]	PPP[a]	Dollars[a]	PPP[a]	Dollars[a]	PPP[a]
Manufacturing wage										
Belgium	100	100	86	98	118	127	74	71	91	82
France	116	102	100	100	137	129	85	72	105	83
West Germany	84	79	73	77	100	100	62	56	75	64
Italy	136	140	117	138	161	178	100	100	123	115
Netherlands	110	122	95	120	130	156	81	87	100	100
Construction wage										
Belgium	100	100	86	97	127	136	81	80	102	92
France	120	103	100	100	152	140	97	82	123	95
West Germany	79	74	66	71	100	100	64	59	81	68
Italy	123	125	103	122	157	171	100	100	126	115
Netherlands	98	108	82	105	124	147	79	86	100	100

Source: Swedish Employers' Confederation (1989).

a. Dollar exchange rate as base for comparison.

b. Purchasing power parity adjusted wage rates as base for comparison.

Table 7-2. *Relative Wage between EC Countries, Manufacturing, 1988*
Percent

Country	Italy	Greece	Portugal	Spain
Belgium				
Dollars[a]	124	250	513	172
PPP[b]	134	364	898	195
France				
Dollars[a]	96	193	397	133
PPP[b]	109	294	725	157
West Germany				
Dollars[a]	152	305	627	210
PPP[b]	186	503	1240	269
Italy				
Dollars[a]	100	201	412	138
PPP[b]	100	271	668	145
Netherlands				
Dollars[a]	132	265	545	182
PPP[b]	145	394	971	210

Source: Bureau of Labor Statistics (1991b).
a. Dollar exchange rate as base for comparison.
b. Purchasing power parity adjusted wage rate as base for comparison.

ious other countries (columns). As of 1964, for example, migrating Italian manufacturing workers could have earned between 17 percent (in France) and 61 percent (in Germany) more than in their home country.

If relative wages were all that mattered, every other EC country looked attractive to Italian workers, and Germany looked attractive to workers in all EC countries.[21] But Germany was the only attractive alternative for Belgian, Dutch, and perhaps French workers. For virtually all workers, migration within the EC entailed significant costs associated with change of language, change of culture, and loss of customary social relationships. In summary, the Treaty of Rome failed to stimulate extensive migration within the EC common labor market because the relevant net benefits of working in other EC countries were small for all except Italian workers.

What are the prospects for internal migration following the integration of southern European countries into the EC in 1993? Table 7-2 shows relative wage comparisons for 1988 between the new southern European members of the EC (Greece, Portugal, and Spain) and the original members of the Community. With the exception of Spanish workers contemplating jobs in France and Italy, manufacturing workers in south-

21. Studies of labor mobility have noted the importance of job availability as well as wages in attracting workers (Flanagan, 1987; Pissarides, 1978). Relative unemployment data for EC nations in the 1960s indicate that Italian workers also had the strongest incentives to move on grounds of job availability.

ern Europe clearly have far more to gain from working in northern Europe in the early 1990s than Italian workers did in the early 1960s. The potential for downward pressure on wages in the original EC countries because of internal migration from southern Europe seems substantial. (When compared with table 7-1, table 7-2 also indicates the extent to which the wage incentive for Italian workers to migrate north has diminished.)

Conclusions and Prospects

The evidence reviewed in this paper indicates that the institutional restrictions on labor mobility eliminated by the Treaty of Rome did not markedly increase internal migration or wage equalization across EC countries. With the exception of Italian workers, no notable increase in internal migration accompanied the reduction of legal barriers to mobility. These conclusions seem puzzling when juxtaposed with historical experience in the United States and research showing that differences in the stock of migrants in EC countries reflect the relative benefits and costs between source and host countries.[22] In fact, the net benefits of internal EC migration were modest. Significant nonpecuniary migration costs (particularly those associated with language) appear to have overwhelmed the potential wage benefits of moving between EC member countries. (Molle and van Mourik's findings appear to be influenced by the inclusion of external migrants, for whom economic differences were much greater.) As a result, total immigration was very much controlled by EC policies toward migrants from outside the Community.

If the competitive labor market mechanism proved to be a weak engine of economic equality within the European Community in the past, is there any reason to expect it to be more powerful in the future? Most of the important legal barriers to internal mobility were eliminated long ago, so that the comparatively modest changes to be completed by the end of 1992 should have little impact on migration and wage differences among the original members of the community. On the other hand, wage differentials between the nine EC members as of 1973 and Greece, Portugal, and Spain generally exceed several times over the differentials that have existed between other Community members since the Treaty of Rome. Considering the migration of Italian workers in the first decade

22. Molle and van Mourik (1988).

of the European community, the differentials between the three new and nine older members seem ample to compensate for the nonlegal barriers to working in other countries. This incentive along with the significant migration from these countries to the EC in periods in which the demand for foreign workers by EC countries was relatively unconstrained provides good reason to believe that labor market responses can produce greater equality between the north and the south of Europe than they have among the original EC members.

In contrast to the emphasis on market mechanisms during the first thirty years of the EC, the Commission began to emphasize regulatory approaches to equalization during the late 1980s.[23] Through the Social Charter the Commission may attempt to standardize wages and working conditions "among Member States, between full-time and part-time workers, and between unionized and nonunionized workplaces. The chosen instrument to this end is the directive to firms, mandating them to offer contracts that satisfy certain minimum requirements."[24] Will directing that minimum standards be met produce greater equalization among the EC's nine 1973 members where market forces have failed?

Placing a floor under wages and other employment conditions carries with it the potential for increasing unemployment in members of the Community with lower levels of productivity. The extent to which this occurs depends on the level of the floor, which in turn is likely to depend on the voting rule adopted for this issue within the EC. Under simple majority rule, the minimum standard for the Community is likely to approximate the median standard among the member nations—so that most would not have to alter their social policies. In fact, unanimity is required for most regulations on employment conditions. Standards requiring unanimous consent are likely to approximate conditions in countries with the lowest productivity, thereby having little direct impact on employment conditions in those with high productivity. In summary, neither market mechanisms nor employment regulations are likely to alter wage differentials among the EC's nine 1973 members following 1992. At the same time, without a change in EC voting rules pertaining to minimum employment standards, labor market mechanisms are more likely than regulation to raise the relative wages of workers in the new member countries.

23. The commission's shift from a unanimity voting rule (which would have permitted a veto by any adversely affected low-wage country) to majority rule facilitated this development.
24. Addison and Siebert (1991, p. 617).

References

Addison, John T., and W. Stanley Siebert. 1991. "The Social Charter of the European Community." *Industrial and Labor Relations Review* 44 (July): 597–625.

Bhagwati, Jagdish N., Klaus-Werner Schatz, and Kar-yiu Wong. 1984. "The West German Gastarbeiter System of Immigration." *European Economic Review* 26 (December): 277–94.

Ben-David, Dan. 1991. "Equalizing Exchange: A Study of the Effects of Trade Liberalization," working paper 3706. Cambridge, Mass.: National Bureau of Economic Research.

Bloch, Joseph W. 1948. "Regional Wage Differentials, 1907–46." *Monthly Labor Review* 66 (April): 371–77.

Bureau of Labor Statistics, Office of Productivity and Technology. 1990. "Hourly Compensation Costs for Production Workers." September.

———. 1991. "International Comparisons of Hourly Compensation Costs for Production Workers in Manufacturing, 1975, 1980, and 1984–90." May.

Easterlin, Richard A. 1961. "Regional Income Trends, 1840–1950." In Seymour Harris, ed., *American Economic History*. McGraw-Hill.

Flanagan, Robert J. 1987. "Labor Market Behavior and European Economic Growth." In Robert Z. Lawrence and Charles L. Schultze, eds., *Barriers to European Growth: A Transatlantic View*. Brookings.

Greenwood, Michael J. 1975. "Research in Internal Migration in the United States: A Survey." *Journal of Economic Literature* 13 (June): 397–433.

Lundborg, Per. 1991. "Determinants of Migration in the Nordic Labor Market." *Scandinavian Journal of Economics* 93 (3): 363–75.

McManus, Walter, William Gould, and Finis Welch. 1983. "Earnings of Hispanic Men: The Role of English Language Proficiency." *Journal of Labor Economics* 1 (April): 101–30.

Molle, Willem, and Aad Van Mourik. 1988. "International Movements of Labour under Conditions of Economic Integration: The Case of Western Europe." *Journal of Common Market Studies* 26 (March): 318–39.

Mundell, Robert A. 1957. "International Trade and Factor Mobility." *American Economic Review* 47 (June): 321–35.

Neven, Damien J. 1990. "EEC Integration Towards 1992: Some Distributional Aspects." *Economic Policy* (April): 13–62.

OECD. 1988. *Historical Statistics, 1960–86*. Paris.

Pissarides, Christopher. 1978. "The Role of Relative Wages and Excess Demand in the Sectoral Flow of Labour." *Review of Economic Studies* 45 (October): 453–67.

Straubhaar, Thomas. 1988. "International Labour Migration within a Common Market: Some Aspects of EC Experience." *Journal of Common Market Studies* 27 (September): 45–62.

Summers, Robert, and Alan Heston. 1988. "A New Set of International

Comparisons of Real Product and Price Levels: Estimates for 130 Countries, 1950–1985." *Review of Income and Wealth*, series 34 (March): 1–25.

Summers, Robert, and Alan Heston. 1991. "The Penn World Table (Mark 5): An Expanded Set of International Comparisons, 1950–1988." *Quarterly Journal of Economics* 106 (May): 327–68.

Swann, Dennis. 1988. *The Economics of the Common Market*, 6th ed. Penguin.

Swedish Employers' Confederation (SAF). 1989. *Wages and Total Labor Costs for Workers*. Stockholm.

CHAPTER EIGHT

European Monetary Unification and Regional Unemployment

Barry Eichengreen

M ONETARY UNIFICATION IS regarded in Brussels as an integral part of the Single Market Project. If the European Community adheres to the schedule implicit in the Delors report, by the end of the century national monies and national central banks will have been replaced by a single European currency and a European central bank.[1] Resistance to monetary unification is motivated by two concerns. The first is that the European central bank, lacking independence from political pressure, will exhibit an inflationary bias.[2] The second is that monetary unification will result in a loss of national economic policy instruments that are useful for dealing with autonomous disturbances emanating from abroad.[3]

This chapter examines the implications of monetary unification for regional unemployment differentials within EC member states. Why should monetary unification have implications for unemployment differentials within EC member states? Consider for example the effects of an

Financial support for this research was provided by the University of California's Center for German and European Studies. I thank Quaser Hussain and Carolyn Werley for research assistance; Tim Hatton, Carol Heim, Richard Layard, and Gianni Toniolo for advice; and George Akerlof, David Levine, and other project participants for their comments.

1. Committee for the Study of Economic and Monetary Union (1989).
2. For an assessment of the realism of such fears, see Fratianni, von Hagen, and Waller (1992).
3. The extent to which monetary unification implies a loss of fiscal autonomy is taken up later. No such controversy attends the issue of monetary autonomy: with the removal of capital controls and the permanent fixing of exchange rates, an individual European country will be no more able to implement an independent monetary policy or sustain a level of interest rates significantly different from those prevailing elsewhere in the European Community than can the state of California pursue a policy significantly different from the rest of the United States. See Eichengreen (1991, 1992a).

autonomous appreciation of the real exchange rate.[4] As imported goods become increasingly cheap and domestic producers of the traded goods for which imports are substitutes reduce prices to compete, the relative price of traded goods falls. Unemployment consequently increases in regions specializing in the production of tradables. As the relative price of nontraded goods rises, their output expands, and unemployment should decrease in regions specializing in the production of nontradables. The traditional policy response to such imbalances is monetary expansion, which lowers the nominal and real exchange rates.[5] Monetary unification eliminates this policy instrument.

The chapter focuses on regional unemployment problems that have arisen in Great Britain and Italy as a result of changes in the real exchange rate. Both countries have had checkered records of nominal and real exchange rate stability. In the first half of the 1980s, Italy repeatedly devalued the lira against the other European Monetary System (EMS) currencies to address inflation and lack of competitiveness; the September 1992 crisis then drove the country out of the EMS, leading to a radical depreciation of the lira. Britain remained outside the Exchange Rate Mechanism (ERM) for many years, permitting sterling to fluctuate against the other European currencies. Having entered the EMS in 1990, Britain, like Italy, was driven out of the system by the September 1992 crisis. Their experiences thus provide considerable evidence of the effects of exchange rate changes.

Assessing the seriousness of unemployment disparities within Britain and Italy requires a standard of comparison. Here U.S. experience provides an obvious standard. The United States has experienced dramatic fluctuations in its real exchange rate: the real trade-weighted value of the dollar has risen and fallen by more than 15 percent in the past fifteen years.[6] This has given rise to pronounced regional unemployment prob-

4. I define the real exchange rate as the price of goods produced abroad expressed in domestic currency units relative to the price of goods produced at home; hence a decline in the ratio signifies an appreciation.

5. Assuming some inertia in domestic wages and prices, monetary expansion lowers the real exchange rate by depreciating the nominal rate. This makes domestic goods more attractive to foreign purchasers, helping restore demand for them. The monetary expansion might be accompanied by some fiscal restraint to keep the level of aggregate demand constant. According to most models, fiscal contraction will only reinforce the depreciation of the real exchange rate occasioned by monetary expansion, assuming a high degree of international capital mobility and of substitutability between domestic and foreign assets. See Sachs and Wyplosz (1983).

6. This is the trade-weighted ratio of domestic to foreign consumer price indexes the construction of which is described in the data appendix.

lems in the United States, although not on a scale sufficient to force significant reform of U.S. international monetary policy.

In present circumstances when, as a result of the Single Market Project, market structures in Europe are changing rapidly, care must be taken in using historical data to project future trends. Historical relationships between real exchange rates and unemployment may be altered once labor mobility is increased by the continued integration of the European economy and the regional distribution of industrial activities is reorganized.[7] Fortunately, the exceptionally long time series on regional unemployment differentials that are available for Great Britain can shed some light on changes in the sensitivity of regional unemployment differentials to real exchange rate shocks. The historical relationship between British unemployment and real exchange rates in the 1920s and 1930s is therefore compared with that for the 1970s and 1980s to gauge the speed with which the relationship is likely to change.

Before proceeding, three assumptions should be made explicit. First, this paper is concerned with the implications of monetary unification for regional unemployment differentials, not for national unemployment rates. I consider the impact of real exchange rate shocks on the dispersion of regional unemployment rates, assuming the national unemployment rate is constant.[8] Second, I assume that changes in monetary policy are capable of altering the real exchange rate, that is, monetary policy has real effects, at least in the short run. Third, I assume that shocks to the real exchange rate are autonomous from the viewpoint of policymakers.

7. Many official impediments to the movement of European labor within the Community have already been eliminated. But time and completion of the internal market will be required before labor mobility between European countries reaches the levels that prevail between regions of the United States. See Eichengreen (1992, 1993).

8. Glick and Hutchison (1990) have criticized studies analyzing the relationship between the real exchange rate and aggregate manufacturing employment for failing to distinguish different reasons why the real exchange rate may change. If, for example, the real rate appreciates because of an increase in domestic demand due to expansionary fiscal policy, appreciation may be associated with a rise in aggregate manufacturing employment. But if it appreciates because of a fall in the demand for traded goods abroad due to a foreign recession, aggregate manufacturing employment may fall instead. Here I hold aggregate demand and employment constant and focus on the intersectoral reallocation of resources due to a change in relative prices. In effect, I assume that if appreciation of the real exchange rate threatens to increase national unemployment, domestic officials can still respond with an increase in deficit spending to keep the overall unemployment rate unchanged. In models such as that of Sachs and Wyplosz (1983), this fiscal expansion will reinforce the appreciation of the exchange rate, exacerbating any regional disparities produced by the autonomous change in the real rate. This assumes, of course, that national authorities retain autonomy over the conduct of fiscal policy following currency unification.

Monetary unification, in removing monetary policy instruments and limiting the tools of fiscal policy, tightens the constraints on policymakers, therefore increasing countries' vulnerability to foreign disturbances. Some observers have expressed a contrary opinion of the role of pegged exchange rates in Europe, maintaining that erratic domestic policies, not foreign disturbances, were an important source of real exchange rate variability in the 1970s and 1980s. According to this argument, countries are better off committing to pegged exchange rates, which restrain domestic monetary policymakers from acting erratically.[9]

In fact, there is no real inconsistency between the two positions. The pegged exchange rates of the EMS have already imposed increasingly tight constraints on European policymakers. By disciplining erratic national policies, the commitment to pegged rates has reduced the variability of nominal exchange rates and contributed to a reduction in the short-term volatility of real exchange rates as well. The convergence of domestic and foreign interest rates in the 1980s suggests that the commitment to pegged rates is increasingly credible.[10] But with pegged rates, policymakers retain the option of changing the exchange rate to recover policy autonomy in the event of a major disturbance. It is this further option that will be lost in the event of monetary unification.

The argument for a commitment to pegged exchange rates to discipline erratic policymakers is an argument for the EMS as it existed in the later 1980s, when realignments became infrequent. The argument for monetary unification is different: unification achieves a reduction in transactions costs and encourages other forms of market integration. These benefits should be weighed against the costs. One potential cost is associated with the problem considered in this chapter: the increase in regional unemployment differentials due to loss of insulation from foreign disturbances.

The Debate over Monetary Unification

To the casual observer, it is not obvious that monetary unification is a necessary concomitant of completing the internal European market. The

9. Giavazzi and Giovannini (1989) present evidence that for a number of European countries the shift to more stable nominal exchange rates under the EMS has also stabilized real rates, presumably by constraining the policies pursued by the domestic authorities.

10. This generalization does not apply equally to all countries, as the September 1992 EMS crisis made clear. For evidence, see Giavazzi and Spaventa (1990) and Frankel and Phillips (1993).

argument that it is runs as follows. Europe's traditional means of stabilizing its exchange rates, the EMS, used controls on short-term capital movements to reconcile national monetary autonomy with exchange rate stability. Interest rates were permitted to vary across European countries at the same time as exchange rates were pegged because controls raised the cost of shifting financial capital from countries with low interest rates to others with higher ones. To liberalize intra-European financial flows as part of the Single Market Project, it was necessary to remove those controls. Consequently, EC members must either submit to the loss of monetary autonomy or revert to floating exchange rates. A floating regime is unacceptable because exchange rate fluctuations would disrupt the intra-European commodity and factor flows that the Single Market Project is designed to promote.[11] Loss of monetary independence is therefore a necessary corollary of the Single Market. Since European nations will no longer possess autonomy in monetary policy, they may as well benefit from the efficiency, convenience, and credibility of a single currency.

The necessity of monetary unification for the liberalization of trade and factor flows can be disputed. The United States and Canada, two countries that enjoy extensive cross-border capital and labor mobility, do not regard monetary unification as a necessary element of their free trade negotiations. Their currencies continue to float against one another without seriously disrupting trade and factor mobility. Mexico and the United States have initiated negotiations for establishing a free trade area without even considering exchange rate stabilization, much less monetary unification.[12]

Skepticism of monetary unification is reinforced by concerns that loss of monetary autonomy may have significant costs. Monetary policy may be useful for combating domestic unemployment. Consider for example an autonomous appreciation of a country's exchange rate. This leads to a decline in the prices of traded goods. As import prices fall the demand curve for domestically produced importables shifts to the left, and their prices will fall as well. As domestic producers begin to be priced out of

11. The public reponse to Italy's and Britain's forced departures from the EMS in September 1992 is an illustration. Floating would also create other problems—for example, increasing the cost of the Common Agricultural Policy. See Giavazzi (1990). In addition, it is often argued that Europeans oppose floating because of their unsatisfactory experience with it in the past. See, for example, Giavazzi and Giovannini (1989).

12. Virtually the only discussions of these questions in the literature are McLeod and Welch (1991a, 1991b). Whether this situation is sustainable is discussed by Eichengreen and Wyplosz (1993).

export markets, they move back down their supply curves, and export prices (denominated in domestic currency) fall. The prices of nontraded goods rise relative to those of tradables. If wages and other nominally denominated costs are slow to adjust, unemployment increases in sectors specializing in the production of tradable goods. The problem can be ameliorated by an expansionary monetary policy that raises domestic prices relative to costs and, by depreciating the exchange rate, switches demand back toward tradable goods produced locally. With monetary unification, this policy response is no longer feasible. The implication is that European nations prepared to sacrifice their monetary autonomy in the name of monetary unification run the risk of making regional unemployment problems worse.

There are standard rebuttals to these objections. Many of the shocks to which EMS members are subject are the same for all participating countries.[13] Asymmetric monetary policies are necessary where asymmetric shocks prevail; otherwise a common European monetary policy will suffice. If all members of the exchange rate union experience a simultaneous decline in domestic demand, a simultaneous coordinated expansion of domestic money supplies will ameliorate the unemployment problem without threatening exchange rate stability.

Even if shocks are asymmetric and monetary policy instruments are no longer available, other macroeconomic tools may be used to address domestic unemployment—fiscal policy, for instance. A country experiencing an autonomous contraction in the demand for its exports can offset the impact on aggregate demand with an increase in deficit spending. Of course, this raises the question of whether individual nations will retain much fiscal autonomy once factor markets are fully integrated.[14] Governments will be required to harmonize their tax rates to prevent capital from fleeing relatively high levels of taxation. This does not mean

13. So it is argued, for example, by Bini-Smaghi and Vori (1992). Two empirical analyses of the cross-country incidence of shocks are Cohen and Wyplosz (1989) and Bayoumi and Eichengreen (1993).

14. Another problem is that this response is likely to worsen the uneven sectoral impact of the shock. Fiscal expansion generally leads to further exchange rate appreciation. By driving up domestic interest rates, fiscal deficits strengthen the nominal exchange rate even while pushing up commodity prices measured in domestic currency; this combination is the definition of a real appreciation. The relative price of traded goods declines further insofar as government spending falls disproportionately on nontraded goods. Unemployment rises further in sectors producing tradables and falls in sectors specializing in the production of nontradables. Even if the impact of the real exchange rate shock on aggregate unemployment is neutralized, sectors and regions specializing in the production of nontradables will benefit at the expense of those specializing in the production of tradables.

that tax rates will have to be equalized; the costs of capital mobility will not disappear even after the completion of the internal market. Still, greater capital mobility implies pressure for tax convergence, perhaps to the point where the variability of tax rates across European countries falls to the levels that prevail within the United States.[15]

Capital mobility therefore limits the scope for deficit spending. Running a government budget deficit requires the issue of debt, and the debt that governments can market today is limited by the present value of the taxes they can collect tomorrow (taxes that will be used to service accumulated debt obligations). This is evident in the experience of U.S. states, which find their bond ratings are downgraded and the interest rates they pay increased when they increase their borrowing.[16] Given the high mobility of capital within the United States, individual states cannot credibly promise to raise future taxes significantly above those prevailing elsewhere in the currency and customs union because capital will flee to jurisdictions with lower taxes if they attempt to do so. Deficit spending, though not ruled out, will be constrained.

Proponents of monetary unification point out that regions of the United States already functioning under these constraints do not lobby to secede from the U.S. monetary union in order to reduce regional unemployment. In the last fifteen years, the United States has experienced pronounced real exchange rate swings, with an extremely uneven regional incidence. They would seem to imply that the regional unemployment problems so worrying to critics of monetary unification are in fact entirely tolerable. Those skeptical of unification respond that the smooth operation of the U.S. currency union reflects special factors not present in Europe. The United States possesses an exceptionally mobile labor force. Compared to their European counterparts, U.S. workers exhibit a greater propensity to relocate in response to asymmetric regional shocks.[17] Although state governments in the United States may be able to do relatively little to stem the rise in unemployment due to deteriorating conditions in the local market, the labor force itself can do a lot to bring it back down.

15. Eichengreen (1990a) computes total state tax revenue as a share of state personal income for nine U.S. census regions and twelve EC member states. Its coefficient of variation is 52 percent as large in the United States as in Europe.

16. Eichengreen (1990a) provides evidence using regression analysis of the positive relationship between the required rate of return on state debt and the size of the debt burden.

17. For evidence on the importance of labor mobility for regional adjustment in the United States, see Blanchard and Katz (1992). Eichengreen (1993) presents evidence that the responsiveness of migration to interregional wage and unemployment differentials is much lower in Europe. The raw data also indicate this. See OECD (1986).

Also contributing to the U.S. economy's tolerance of region-specific shocks is the country's highly developed system of fiscal federalism. According to Xavier Sala-i-Martin and Jeffrey Sachs, when incomes in a U.S. census region decline by one dollar, federal tax payments by residents of that region decline by nearly 30 cents.[18] Transfers to that region from Washington, D.C., increase by nearly 10 cents. The impact of regional shocks on interregional income disparities is thereby attenuated. Insofar as the locus of regional shocks shifts over time, all regions are rendered better off through the risk sharing achieved by means of the federal fiscal system.[19] No comparable mechanism currently exists for fiscal redistribution between EC member states.

Regional Unemployment Disparities in Britain and Italy

The last decade and a half in Britain and Italy has been characterized by volatile fluctuations in unemployment at both the national and regional levels. In addition, Britain experienced a rise in the average level of unemployment after 1974 (figure 8-1). The real exchange rate appreciated steadily during the first half of the period, except in 1975–76, an episode of rapid depreciation of the nominal rate. Real appreciation in 1979–81 reflected the policy of monetary stringency initiated by the Thatcher government to curb inflation; since the exchange rate strengthened more quickly than domestic inflation slowed, a dramatic real appreciation resulted. As inflation subsequently decelerated, bringing prices and exchange rates back into balance, the real exchange rate gave up some of the ground it had gained.

Italy experienced a dramatic increase in unemployment in the mid-1970s, followed by a further increase through the first half of the 1980s (figure 8-2). Italy's real exchange rate depreciated with the breakdown of the Bretton Woods system and the first OPEC shock but recovered after 1979 as the lira was pegged increasingly tightly to other European currencies, leading in the popular view to a growing problem of exchange rate overvaluation.

Figure 8-3 shows the very different rates of unemployment prevailing

18. Sala-i-Martin and Sachs (1992). Some observers dispute Sala-i-Martin and Sachs's results (see, for example, von Hagen, 1991). For supportive evidence drawn from the Canadian experience, see Bayoumi and Masson (1991).

19. There are caveats to this argument for fiscal federalism. See Eichengreen (1992).

Figure 8-1. *British Unemployment and Real Exchange Rate, 1974-87*

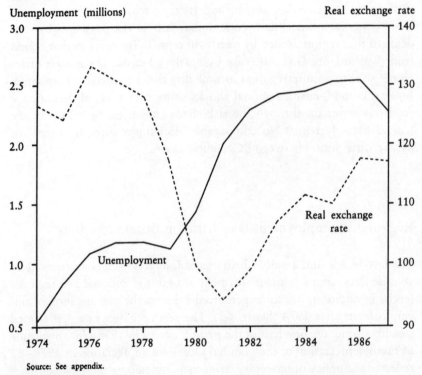

Unemployment (millions)   Real exchange rate

Source: See appendix.

in different British regions in 1988. Their standard deviation is 3.46. A prominent feature of the figure is the north-south divide, with unemployment well below the national average in the Southeast, Southwest, and East Anglia, slightly below average in the East Midlands, and above average in the West Midlands, Northwest, Wales and Scotland.

In part, the different fortunes of the regions reflect the composition of economic activity. Wales relies for much of its income and employment on metal manufacturing and on coal mining and oil refining, which fell on hard times in the 1980s. The North and Yorkshire-Humberside are similarly oriented toward energy and heavy manufacturing, particularly minerals, metals, and chemicals. Unemployment in the West Midlands is associated with a higher share of employment in manufacturing than any other British region and its dependence on a relatively narrow range of industries focusing on engineering and motor vehicles, both of which were depressed throughout most of the 1980s.

Areas dependent on light manufacturing and services were less se-

Figure 8-2. *Italian Unemployment and Real Exchange Rate, 1960-84*

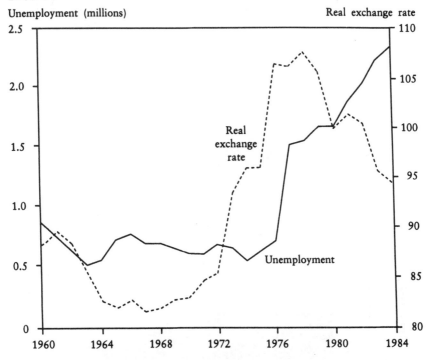

Source: See appendix. Pre- and post-1976 categories combined.

verely affected by the post–1979 slump. Employment in the Southeast, dominated by London, is concentrated in banking, insurance, finance, business services, and leasing. The Southwest relies on public administration, agriculture, and defense. In the East Midlands, the share of regional GDP generated by manufacturing is higher than average (31 percent in 1986 compared to a U.K. average of 25 percent); those industries are predominantly engaged in light manufacturing of such products as textiles, clothing, and footwear. East Anglia was similarly insulated by its specialization in light manufacturing (primarily food and beverages) and agriculture.

Figure 8-4 shows the cyclical responsiveness of unemployment in the post–1979 slump. Among regions with low unemployment the Southwest stands out for its exceptionally low elasticity. At the national average in 1979, unemployment in the southwest rose very slowly. The West Midlands and Yorkshire-Humberside show the opposite pattern: starting from the national average, unemployment rates rose exceptionally fast

Figure 8-3. *British Regional Unemployment Rates, April 1988*

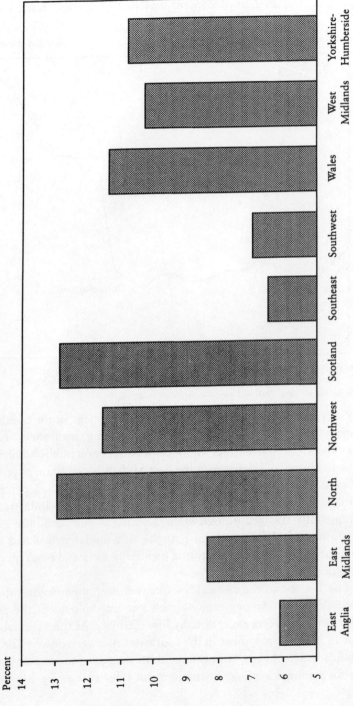

Source: See appendix.

over the 1980s. In regions with high unemployment, unemployment increased at roughly the same rate as elsewhere in Britain.

Figure 8-5 shows the different levels of unemployment in Italian regions in 1988. Their standard deviation is 6.40, or nearly twice the comparable figure for Britain, even though the countries had average unemployment rates for 1988 that were almost the same. The dominant feature in Italy was the north-south divide: unemployment was above 15 percent in Sardinia, Campania, Sicily, and the rest of the south; at roughly the national average of 11 percent in Lazio (which includes Rome) and Abruzzi; but less than 10 percent elsewhere in the center and the north.

As in Britain, differences among the sectoral compositions of employment contribute to regional unemployment disparities in Italy. The north, defined here to include Piedmont, Liguria, Veneto, and Emilia-Romagna, accounts for 70 percent of Italy's manufacturing employment.[20] Piedmont and Liguria specialize in such heavy industries as motor vehicles, iron and steel, and shipbuilding; Veneto in such light industries as footwear and apparel. Small and medium-sized firms producing labor-intensive products with high value added, such as ceramics, furniture, scientific instruments and automotive parts, are increasingly evident in Emilia-Romagna.[21] Lombardy has the most broadly based industrial structure, with traditional staples such as textiles, food processing, metalworking, and engineering as well as newer light industries such as electronics. Its capital, Milan, has a highly developed service sector: it is the seat of the Italian stock exchange, the site of the country's leading trade fair, and home to the head offices of most important Italian corporations.

The situation in Campania, Sicily, Sardinia and the rest of southern Italy is very different. Along with agriculture, these regions rely on heavy industries such as oil, petrochemicals, and steel, whose location in the south and whose capital intensity are the result of regional economic policy. These industries operated at only a fraction of capacity for much of the 1980s.

Central Italy (Marche, Umbria, Tuscany, and Lazio) combines elements of the north and south. The region relies heavily on the tertiary sector. Textiles, chemicals, metallurgy, and motor vehicles are all represented in Lazio. The Emilian model of light industry characterized by

20. Following King (1985), I include as part of northern Italy Val d'Aosta, Trentino-Alto Adige, and Friuli-Venezia Giulia.
21. See Bianchi and Gualtieri (1990).

Figure 8-4. *British Regional and National Unemployment Rates, 1979-87*

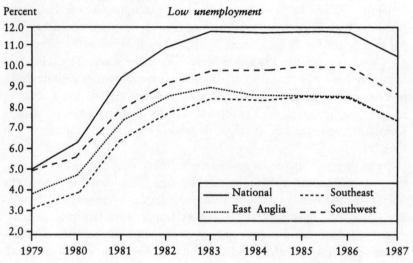

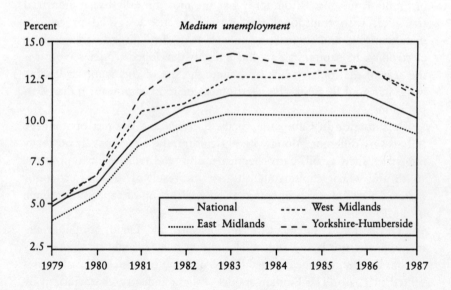

Figure 8-4. *Continued*

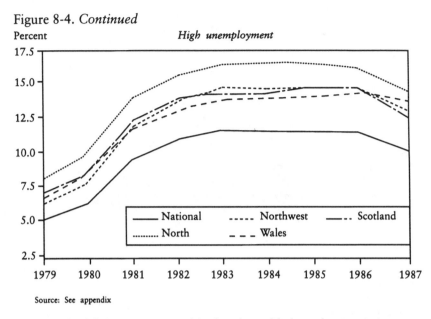

Source: See appendix

small scale, labor intensity, and high-value-added production is increasingly evident as well.

This discussion has been intended to show regional patterns of industrial specialization. Their implications for the dispersion of regional responses to real exchange rate shocks is the subject of remaining sections.

Econometric Evidence

To analyze the impact of real exchange rate changes on regional unemployment, I use a variant of the model applied by William Branson and James Love to data for the United States. I regress regional unemployment on unemployment nationwide, on the real exchange rate, and on the real price of energy.[22] Following Branson and Love's approach, a time trend is included where necessary to pick up long-term trends not captured by the other variables. Regressions are estimated using ordinary least squares.[23]

22. Branson and Love (1988).
23. Endogeneity of the explanatory variables, notably the real exchange rate, is unlikely to be a problem insofar as these are measured for the entire economy while the dependent variables are for relatively small regions. For example, any one region's unemployment is

Figure 8-5. *Italian Regional Unemployment Rates, 1988*

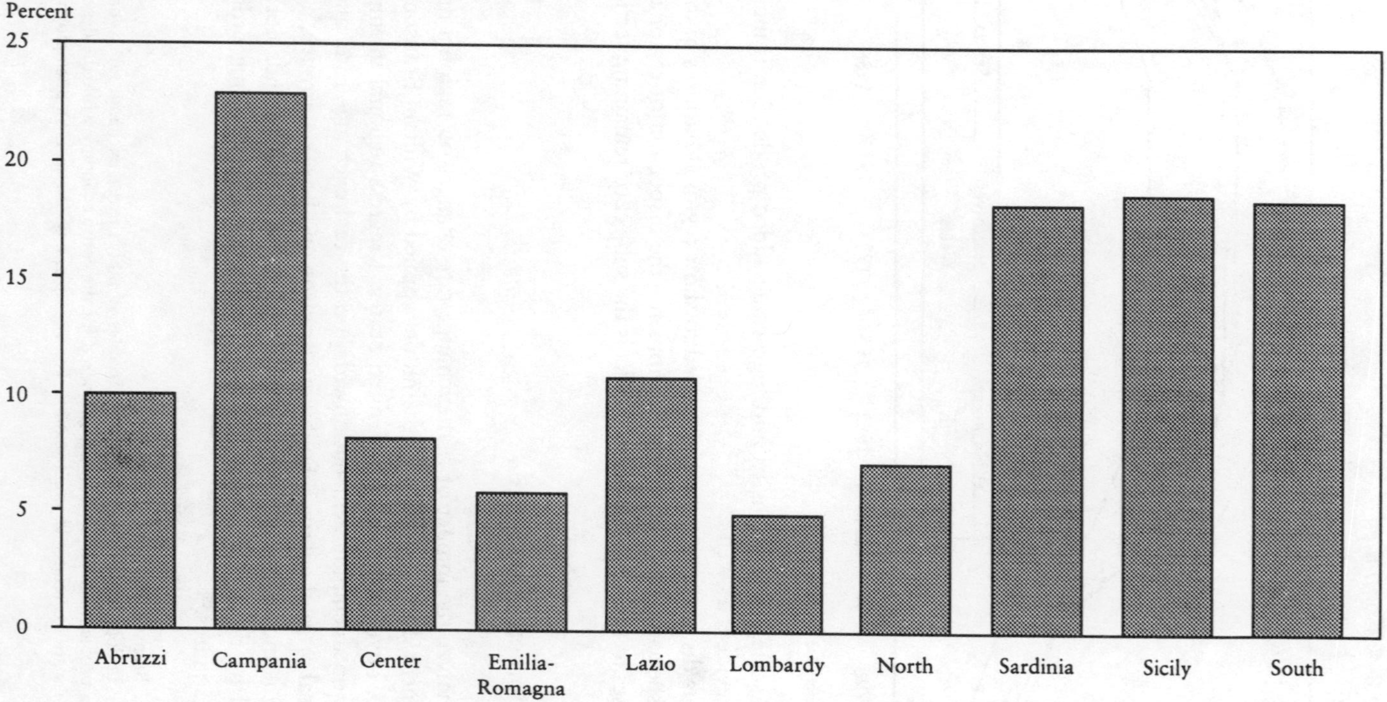

Percent

Source: See appendix.

Because of the difficulty of measuring the labor force accurately, the number of workers unemployed (in thousands) is used instead of the unemployment rate. Regional and national unemployment are expressed in logarithms. Insofar as the cyclical sensitivity of regional unemployment exceeds (or falls short of) the cyclical sensitivity of national unemployment, the coefficient on the log of national unemployment should exceed (or fall short of) unity. The coefficient on the real exchange rate should be positive for regions specializing in the production of nontraded goods, since a decline in the real rate signals an appreciation. The coefficient on the real energy price should be positive for regions that consume energy and negative for regions that produce it.

Table 8-1 shows regression results for Britain starting in 1974.[24] The elasticity of regional unemployment with respect to national unemployment varies from 0.85 in the North to 1.21 in the Southeast. Scotland has a relatively low cyclical sensitivity, the East Midlands and West Midlands relatively high ones. Once again, industrial composition helps explain these regional characteristics. The tendency for employment to hold up relatively well in Scotland, for instance, reflects the economy's diversification out of traditional staples (textiles, shipbuilding, and metals) into electronics and services.[25] The cyclical sensitivity of unemployment in the Midlands reflects the importance of manufacturing industries (motor vehicles and engineering in the West Midlands, textiles in the East Midlands).[26] The standard deviation of the ten table 8-1 coefficients on national unemployment for British regions is 0.13.[27]

---

unlikely to have a discernible impact on real wages economywide and hence on the nation's real exchange rate. One exception to this statement occurs when workers in the industries that dominate economic activity in a particular region set the tone for wage negotiations in the whole economy. I return to this issue below.

24. Standard definitions of regions used by the Ministry of Labour were revised in 1974, rendering any attempts to use pre- and post-1974 data together difficult. There were also a variety of procedural changes in the measurement of British unemployment in the 1980s, which inevitably complicate the interpretation of the time series behavior of the variable.

25. North Sea oil provided an additional boost to Scottish unemployment in the early 1980s. Townsend (1983, p. 98).

26. Townsend (1983, pp. 118–19).

27. All subsequent comparisons across countries refer to estimates for Britain found in table 8-1. These results differ from previous studies of cyclical sensitivity. For example, Armstrong and Taylor (1985) found by regressing regional unemployment on national unemployment that cyclical sensitivity was lowest in the Northwest, Southeast, and East Anglia; highest in the North, Wales, and the West Midlands. Whereas previous studies failed to control for determinants of regional unemployment other than unemployment nation-

Table 8-1. *Covariates of Regional Unemployment in Britain, 1974–87*

Region	Constant	National unemployment	Real exchange rate	Real energy price	R^2
East Anglia	−5.299	1.147	0.003	0.001	.99
	(16.68)	(44.39)	(2.87)	(0.13)	
East Midlands	−3.800	1.146	−0.001	−0.001	.99
	(13.54)	(50.25)	(1.06)	(0.96)	
West Midlands	−3.652	1.186	−0.002	0.001	.99
	(7.51)	(29.98)	(1.40)	(0.24)	
North	−0.719	0.849	−0.002	0.001	.99
	(1.98)	(28.73)	(1.43)	(0.31)	
Northwest	−1.293	0.946	0.001	0.001	.99
	(12.22)	(109.87)	(0.07)	(1.98)	
Yorkshire-Humberside	−2.899	1.112	−0.002	−0.002	.99
	(9.15)	(43.44)	(1.71)	(1.61)	
Southeast	−4.036	1.206	0.005	0.001	.99
	(13.60)	(49.96)	(5.17)	(1.13)	
Southwest	−2.912	0.971	0.005	0.001	.99
	(5.62)	(23.02)	(2.86)	(0.45)	
Wales	−1.740	0.914	−0.001	0.001	.99
	(7.07)	(45.68)	(1.27)	(0.62)	
Scotland	−0.830	0.910	−0.001	−0.001	.99
	(1.63)	(21.95)	(0.45)	(0.60)	

Source: Author's calculations using sources discussed in the appendix. Unemployment in logarithms; *t*-statistics in parentheses.

Only one of the ten coefficients on the real price of energy, that for the Northwest, differs significantly from zero at the 90 percent level. Although it is plausible that this reflects the energy-consuming character of the region's industries, it is not clear why the same relationship is not evident for other industrial areas, Yorkshire and the Midlands for instance.

Most important, three of the ten coefficients on the real exchange rate in table 8-1 differ significantly from zero at the 90 percent confidence level, and a fourth, that for Yorkshire and Humberside, comes close to significance at that level. Six of the ten coefficients are negative, and four are positive, indicating considerable regional heterogeneity in the unemployment response to real exchange rate shocks. Thus, even after controlling for the business cycle and the relative price of energy, the real exchange rate significantly affects regional unemployment differentials in Britain.

The signs of the coefficients on the real exchange rate can be inter-

wide, the results in table 8-1 are partial correlations controlling for the real exchange rate and the real price of energy.

Table 8-2. *Covariates of Regional Unemployment in Britain, Including Time Trend, 1974–87*

Region	Constant	National unemployment	Real exchange rate	Real energy price	Time	R^2
East Anglia	−6.187	1.335	0.003	−0.002	0.021	.99
	(33.55)	(45.71)	(6.09)	(3.23)	(6.94)	
East Midlands	−3.427	1.067	−0.001	−0.001	0.009	.99
	(9.26)	(18.21)	(0.96)	(0.15)	(1.44)	
West Midlands	−4.564	1.379	−0.003	0.002	0.021	.99
	(8.13)	(15.51)	(1.92)	(0.92)	(2.34)	
North	0.171	0.660	−0.001	0.003	0.021	.99
	(0.54)	(13.20)	(1.84)	(2.47)	(4.02)	
Northwest	−1.192	0.924	0.001	0.001	0.002	.99
	(8.11)	(39.68)	(0.17)	(2.21)	(1.00)	
Yorkshire-Humberside	2.195	0.970	−0.002	−0.001	0.016	.99
	(6.91)	(19.28)	(2.02)	(0.32)	(3.19)	
Southeast	4.688	1.344	0.005	−0.001	−0.015	.99
	(15.57)	(28.20)	(6.71)	(0.24)	(3.12)	
Southwest	−4.25	1.255	0.005	−0.002	−0.031	.99
	(10.51)	(19.58)	(4.57)	(1.71)	(4.76)	
Wales	−1.800	0.927	−0.001	0.001	−0.001	.99
	(5.01)	(16.29)	(1.23)	(0.39)	(0.24)	
Scotland	0.086	0.716	−0.001	0.001	0.021	.99
	(0.14)	(7.50)	(0.30)	(0.50)	(2.19)	

Source: Author's calculations using sources discussed in the appendix. Unemployment in logarithms; *t*-statistics in parentheses.

preted in terms of sectoral composition: employment in the regions with positive coefficients is concentrated disproportionately in sheltered sectors (services in the Southeast, public administration and defense in the Southwest, agriculture and light manufacturing in East Anglia). The positive coefficient for the Northwest is an anomaly, but unlike the other three positive coefficients it differs insignificantly from zero.

Table 8-2 adds a time trend to the basic regression. Six of the ten coefficients on the real exchange rate now differ from zero at standard confidence levels. Their magnitude remains basically unchanged from what it was in table 8-1. The positive coefficient for the Northwest turns reassuringly negative, although that for Scotland turns positive, albeit to an insignificant degree.

For Italy, there exist separate definitions of unemployment for the pre– and post–1976 periods. Surveys for the post–1976 period added a third category of unemployed workers to the two categories reported previously.[28] The results of the two definitions are distinguished in figure 8-6. Insofar as the national unemployment rate included as an explanatory

28. See the data appendix for further discussion.

Figure 8-6. *Italian Unemployment, Pre- and Post–1976 Definitions, 1960-84*

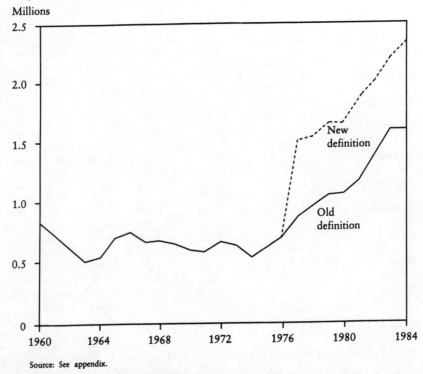

Source: See appendix.

variable in the regressions is an aggregation of the dependent variables for the individual regions, the coefficient on unemployment nationwide may capture any implications of the shift. This is not true, of course, to the extent that the change in definition had different effects on measured unemployment in individual regions. Therefore, two variants of the basic equation have been estimated, one that included among the unemployed only the two categories of workers considered before 1976, the other that also included the third category of unemployed workers for the post–1976 years.

The variation across regions in the cyclical sensitivity of local unemployment to national unemployment is almost exactly the same for Italy as for Britain. In table 8-3, which uses only pre–1976 categories of unemployment, the elasticity of regional unemployment with respect to national unemployment ranges from 1.28 for Lombardy to 0.80 for Abruzzi and Molise, with a standard deviation for the nine regions of 0.16. In table 8-4, which uses the alternative definition of unemploy-

Table 8-3. *Covariates of Regional Unemployment in Italy Using Pre-1976 Definitions of Unemployment, 1960–84*

Region	Constant	National unemployment	Real exchange rate	Real energy price	R^2
Piedmont,	−4.067	1.182	0.005	−0.001	.97
Val d'Aosta, Liguria	(6.67)	(14.33)	(1.76)	(0.74)	
Lombardy	−3.215	1.275	−0.009	0.001	.86
	(2.41)	(7.09)	(1.45)	(0.003)	
Veneto	−1.476	1.095	−0.011	−0.001	.77
	(1.03)	(5.67)	(2.36)	(0.02)	
Emilia-Romagna,	−0.049	0.889	−0.012	−0.001	.87
Marches	(0.61)	(8.19)	(2.98)	(0.34)	
Tuscany, Umbria,	−1.732	0.990	0.007	−0.001	.97
Alto Lazio, Lazio	(3.07)	(12.98)	(2.60)	(0.65)	
Meridionale,					
Campania					
Abruzzi, Molise	−2.389	0.800	0.004	−0.001	.92
	(3.96)	(9.28)	(1.45)	(1.52)	
Puglia, Basilicata,	−1.259	0.817	0.006	−0.001	.88
Calabria	(1.28)	(6.14)	(1.25)	(0.008)	
Sicily	−1.596	0.828	0.001	0.003	.97
	(2.72)	(10.47)	(0.27)	(3.33)	
Sardinia	−5.459	1.231	0.005	0.002	.94
	(5.07)	(8.46)	(0.87)	(1.11)	

Sources: Author's calculations using sources discussed in the appendix. Unemployment in logarithms; *t*-statistics in parentheses.

ment, this elasticity ranges from 1.23 (again for Lombardy) to 0.83 (this time for Puglia, Basilicata and Calabria), with a standard deviation of 0.14.[29] Recall that for Britain the comparable high and low values of this elasticity were 1.21 and 0.85, with a standard deviation of 0.13. Thus the variability in regional responses to the business cycle is almost the same in the two countries.

Only for Sicily and for Abruzzi and Molise is there evidence of a differential response to real energy prices. In contrast, four of the nine coefficients on the real exchange rate in table 8-3 differ significantly from zero at the 90 percent level; in table 8-4, six of the nine are statistically significant. (The pattern of signs is identical across the two tables.) Of the six significant coefficients in table 8-4, three are positive and three negative, again suggesting considerable regional heterogeneity in responses of unemployment levels to changes in the real exchange rate.

29. The relatively low coefficients for Abruzzi, Calabria, and the rest of the south are consistent with the results of Caroleo (1990), who regressed unemployment in the Italian south on national unemployment and a time trend, obtaining coefficients on national unemployment of about 0.8.

Table 8-4. Covariates of Regional Unemployment in Italy Using
Post-1976 Definitions of Unemployment, 1960–84

Region	Constant	National unemployment	Real exchange rate	Real energy price	R^2
Piedmont,	−3.880	1.148	0.006	−0.001	.98
Val d'Aosta, Liguria	(8.69)	(18.71)	(1.90)	(1.06)	
Lombardy	−2.692	1.228	−0.012	−0.001	.94
	(3.02)	(10.01)	(1.94)	(0.06)	
Veneto	−1.214	1.041	−0.016	0.001	.89
	(1.25)	(7.77)	(2.34)	(0.22)	
Emilia-Romagna,	−1.176	0.940	−0.007	−0.001	.95
Marche	(2.19)	(12.75)	(1.94)	(1.03)	
Tuscany, Umbria,	−1.533	0.978	0.006	−0.001	.98
Alto Lazio, Lazio	(4.04)	(18.73)	(2.19)	(0.66)	
Meriodionale,					
Campania					
Abruzzi, Molise	−3.452	0.937	0.007	−0.002	.97
	(7.45)	(14.71)	(2.07)	(1.93)	
Puglia, Basilicata,	−1.353	0.827	0.006	0.001	.94
Calabria	(2.04)	(9.08)	(1.32)	(0.47)	
Sicily	−2.301	0.907	0.003	0.003	.99
	(5.77)	(16.53)	(1.17)	(3.27)	
Sardinia	−5.114	1.198	0.003	0.001	.97
	(6.88)	(11.71)	(0.65)	(0.91)	

Sources: Author's calculations using sources discussed in the appendix. Unemployment in logarithms; *t*-statistics in parentheses.

The signs of the coefficients are generally plausible, although there are anomalies. The negative real exchange rate coefficients are for Lombardy, Veneto, and Emilia-Romagna, which produce a variety of manufactures and thus should be adversely affected by a real appreciation.[30]

The regional responses of unemployment levels to real exchange rate shocks differs between Italy and Britain in that regional disparities are more important for Italy. The standard deviation of the regional regression coefficients for the real exchange rate is 0.0028 for Britain but 0.0074 for Italy when table 8-3 data are used and 0.0087 for Italy when table 8-4 data are used. Thus although there are roughly comparable regional unemployment disparities in the two countries in response to

30. Insofar as workers in these manufacturing industries set the tone for wage negotiations nationwide, an increase in their unemployment rate may put downward pressure on real wages, leading to real exchange rate depreciation. This positive correlation between unemployment and the real exchange rate is the opposite of the sign of the estimated coefficient on the real exchange rate, suggesting that the estimated effect represents a lower bound on the real exchange rate effect. However, reverse causation may help explain the positive coefficient for Piedmont-Liguria, the home of much of Italy's heavy industry.

business cycle fluctuations (holding the real exchange rate constant), larger regional unemployment differentials emerge in Italy in response to real exchange rate fluctuations (holding aggregate unemployment constant). If monetary unification reduces insulation to real exchange rate disturbances, then Italy's regional unemployment problem will become worse to a greater extent than Britain's.

Comparisons with the United States

One way to gauge the seriousness of the regional problems in Britain and Italy in response to real exchange rate disturbances is to view the results through the lens provided by U.S. experience. Unemployment rates among U.S. regions show a surprisingly weak tendency to move together.[31] Regional disparities in unemployment are a subject of long-standing concern.[32] Although swings in real exchange rates cause regional problems in the United States, these are not sufficiently severe to lead to a reform of U.S. international monetary policy.

Real exchange rate fluctuations are as important for the United States as for Britain and Italy. Figure 8-7 shows the steady real depreciation of the 1970s and the dramatic reversal brought on by the tight monetary policy initiated in 1979 in combination with growing fiscal deficits once the Reagan administration took office in 1981. After 1974, unemployment seems to have risen when the real exchange rate appreciated, but no clear relationship is evident for the earlier period.

Table 8-5 summarizes the results of estimating the same equation as reported for Italy and Britain in the previous section. The dispersion of regional unemployment responses to national unemployment is remarkably similar to those for Britain and Italy. The elasticity of regional unemployment with respect to national unemployment ranges from 1.12 for the East North Central region (home of the cyclically sensitive motor vehicle complex) to 0.81 for the Mountain states. These findings are consistent with the conclusions of Christopher Gellner, who emphasized the cyclical sensitivity of unemployment in the North Central and Northeast regions for the first half of the period.[33] The standard deviation for the nine regions is 0.12. Recall that the analogous estimates for Britain and Italy were 0.13 and 0.14–0.16, respectively. The similar range is surpris-

---

31. See Eichengreen (1990a).
32. See, for instance, Sum and Rush (1975).
33. Getliner (1974).

Figure 8-7. U.S. Unemployment and Real Exchange Rate, 1960-89

Source: See appendix.

ing given the presumption of high labor mobility among U.S. regions. The similarity of results across countries may reflect two offsetting effects. On one hand, differences in the cyclical sensitivity of the demand for labor across regions may be greater in the United States than in Britain or Italy. On the other hand, greater labor mobility within the United States may dampen the regional unemployment disparities that would otherwise emerge.

There is evidence of a tendency for higher energy prices to increase regional unemployment only in the East North Central region (again reflecting the importance of motor vehicle production) and the East South Central region (which traditionally relies on the energy-using steel sector and other industries that supply the automotive complex). The negative coefficient for the West South Central United States has some significance, reflecting the tendency for higher energy prices to reduce unemployment in oil-producing states such as Texas and Oklahoma.

Six of the nine coefficients on the real exchange rate differ significantly from zero at the 95 percent level or better. Three of the six significant coefficients are positive and three negative, again indicating considerable

Table 8-5. *Covariates of Regional Unemployment in the United States,*
1960–89

Region	Constant	National unemployment	Real exchange rate	Real energy price	Time	R^2
New England	−4.073	1.104	0.014	−0.572	−0.032	.78
	(3.50)	(6.70)	(3.26)	(1.46)	(5.46)	
East North	−2.931	1.119	−0.002	0.330	0.001	.98
Central	(5.91)	(16.22)	(0.97)	(1.98)	(0.22)	
East South	−1.379	0.849	−0.011	0.882	0.012	.95
Central	(1.59)	(6.90)	(3.42)	(3.03)	(2.69)	
Middle Atlantic	−2.389	1.034	0.008	0.189	−0.027	.96
	(4.97)	(15.20)	(4.25)	(1.17)	(11.06)	
South Atlantic	−2.691	1.021	0.005	0.184	−0.001	.99
	(7.33)	(19.64)	(3.42)	(1.49)	(0.17)	
West North	−0.726	0.816	−0.008	0.212	0.007	.98
Central	(1.99)	(15.80)	(6.22)	(1.73)	(3.85)	
West South	−0.783	0.942	−0.013	−0.566	0.028	.93
Central	(0.74)	(6.31)	(3.19)	(1.61)	(5.19)	
Mountain	−1.700	0.807	−0.002	−0.057	0.025	.98
	(3.08)	(10.33)	(0.75)	(0.31)	(8.94)	
Pacific	−0.800	0.874	0.002	−0.345	0.009	.94
	(1.02)	(7.86)	(0.64)	(1.30)	(2.13)	

Sources: Author's calculations using sources discussed in the appendix. Unemployment in logarithms; *t*-statistics in parentheses.

diversity of regional responses to real exchange rate shocks. Of all nine coefficients, five are positive.

The standard deviation of the nine estimated coefficients for the real exchange rate is 0.0089, matching almost precisely the estimate in table 8-4 for Italy. Thus, holding constant the overall level of unemployment, a real exchange rate shock has the same tendency to create regional unemployment disparities in Italy as it does in the United States. Britain is less vulnerable than the United States to regional problems caused by real exchange rate disturbances.

Because of the relatively low levels of European labor mobility, observers sometimes suggest that regional unemployment differentials within European countries are more likely to be aggravated by the loss of insulation from real exchange rate shocks associated with monetary unification than regional disparities in the United States would be affected by a comparable increase in real exchange rate volatility. The findings of this section suggest otherwise. Regions of the United States differ more from one another than do regions of Britain or Italy in terms of the sensitivity of regional economic activity to the real exchange rate. Greater labor mobility among U.S. regions does not free the United

States from this problem, although it reduces the impact on regional unemployment differentials to the same extent as in Italy and to a slightly smaller degree than in Britain.

Charting the Future with Evidence from the Past

Any implications these findings hold for policy must be qualified to the extent that labor mobility and regional specialization change over time. There seems to be a long-term tendency for transportation costs to fall and for cultural impediments to relocation to diminish. By removing obstacles to migration among European countries, the Single Market Project may provide an additional safety valve for unemployed labor in depressed regions. To the extent that the importance of natural resources in many forms of economic activity has decreased, the sectoral specialization of regions may fade. Thus inferences drawn from the experience of recent years may overstate prospective regional disparities.

How do regional unemployment differentials in recent decades compare with those from the past? This section replicates the preceding analysis using data for Britain from the 1920s and 1930s.[34] Britain's regional differentials were prominent in the 1920s and 1930s and attracted considerable attention. The major policy-related impediments to interregional mobility characteristic of the 1980s (housing restrictions, residence-based unemployment insurance) were already in place between the wars.[35]

The significance of regional unemployment differentials in interwar Britain is evident in table 8-6. Between 1923 and 1938 unemployment averaged only 8.5 percent in London but 23.5 percent in Wales. Averages for the period were 9 percent in the Southeast, 10 percent in the Southwest, and 12 percent in the Midlands but more than 17 percent in the

---

34. Analysis of regional unemployment between the wars has been undertaken by Hatton (1986), who regressed regional unemployment rates on the national unemployment rate and on other measures of economic performance. Though his results are broadly consistent with those reported here, his implementation differed. He included data from after 1935, despite a revision of the Ministry of Labour's geographical definition of regions. He used estimated unemployment rates rather than number of persons unemployed; the difficulty with the former is that while monthly counts are available of persons unemployed, counts of persons in the labor force are available for only one month of the year. Finally, rather than the real exchange rate and real energy prices, he examined the impact of the shares of exports and investment in national income on regional unemployment disparities.

35. See Baines (1991).

Table 8-6. *British Insured Unemployment Rate, by Administrative Division, 1923–38*

Year	London	Southeast	Southwest	Midlands	Northeast	Northwest	Scotland	Wales
1923	10.1	9.2	10.6	10.7	12.2	14.5	14.3	6.4
1924	9.0	7.5	9.1	9.0	10.9	12.9	12.4	8.6
1925	7.8	5.9	8.5	9.1	15.0	11.4	15.2	16.5
1926	6.9	5.4	8.4	11.0	17.2	14.7	16.4	18.0
1927	5.8	5.0	7.2	8.4	13.7	10.7	10.6	19.5
1928	5.6	5.4	8.1	9.9	15.1	12.4	11.7	23.0
1929	5.6	5.6	8.1	9.3	13.7	13.3	12.1	19.3
1930	8.1	8.0	10.4	14.7	20.2	23.8	18.5	25.9
1931	12.2	12.0	14.5	20.3	27.4	28.2	26.6	32.4
1932	13.5	14.3	17.1	20.1	28.5	25.8	27.7	36.5
1933	11.8	11.5	15.7	17.4	26.0	23.5	26.1	34.6
1934[a]	9.2	8.7	13.1	12.9	22.1	20.8	23.1	32.3
1935[a]	8.5	8.1	11.6	11.2	20.7	19.7	21.3	31.2
1936[a]	7.2	7.3	9.4	9.2	16.8	17.1	18.7	29.4
1937[a]	6.4	6.7	7.8	7.3	11.1	14.0 (17.9)[b]	16.0	23.3
1938[a]	8.0	8.0	8.2	10.3	13.6	17.9 (18.4)[b]	16.4	24.8

Source: *Ministry of Labour Gazette*, 31 (January 1923), various pages.
a. The figures exclude juveniles younger than age 16 and persons insured under the agriculture scheme, who first became insurable in September 1934 and May 1936 respectively.
b. Figures for the new Northern division created on August 1, 1936. This consisted of Northumberland (except Berwick district), Durham, and the Cleveland district of Yorkshire (previously part of the Northeastern division) and Cumberland and Westmorland (previously parts of the Northwestern division). Details of the areas contained in all administrative divisions can be found in Department of Employment and Productivity (1971, appendix E).

Northeast, Northwest, and Scotland.[36] Hence the distinction between inner Britain and the outer regions made by Ministry of Labour officials and other contemporary commentators.

A striking aspect of this dichotomy was the reversal of the regional incidence of unemployment between the prewar and interwar eras. Before World War I, unemployment was consistently lower in the north than in the south.[37] The unemployment problem of the outer regions between the wars seemed to be associated with the difficulties of Britain's staple exports (coal, iron, and steel, shipbuilding, textiles, and mechanical engineering). Contemporary observers attributed lagging exports to the exchange rate overvaluation brought on by the decision in 1925 to return to the gold standard at the prewar parity, exacerbating the difficulties of industries producing traded goods and giving rise to the regional differences.[38]

Yet as figure 8-8 shows, the evolution of the real exchange rate and unemployment after 1925 suggests no simple pattern. Although the real rate strengthened dramatically starting in 1929 as commodity prices fell more rapidly overseas than at home, British unemployment increased. Starting in 1931, despite a depreciation of the real rate brought about by the devaluation of sterling, unemployment continued to rise. It fell only after 1932, coinciding with a period of renewed real appreciation reflecting the devaluations of the dollar and the currencies of the European gold bloc.

Regression results are reported in table 8-7. The elasticity of regional unemployment with respect to national unemployment ranges from 0.79 to 1.17, with a standard deviation of 0.13. These values are strikingly similar to those for the postwar period. The real energy price shows up as statistically significant at the 90 percent level for Wales, Scotland, and London. Higher energy prices reduced unemployment in Welsh coal mining but increased unemployment slightly in Scotland, where the shipbuilding industry and its suppliers depended on coal. The explanation for London's positive coefficient is not clear.

Three of the eight coefficients on the real exchange rate are statistically significant at the 90 percent level, and two others have *t*-statistics of

36. All references here are to the official unemployment statistics as described by Hatton (1986). The official statistics are likely to have overstated the actual situation by neglecting workers in agriculture, government, and domestic service, whose unemployment rates were relatively low. See Garside (1980).

37. Royal Commission on the Poor Laws (1909); Beveridge (1944, pp. 73-75).

38. See, for example, Bowley (1930).

Figure 8-8. *British Unemployment and Real Exchange Rate, 1923-35*

Unemployment (millions)   Real exchange rate

Source: See appendix.

about 1.5. Three of the eight coefficients are positive and five are negative. All are large, ranging from −0.012 to 0.025, with a standard deviation of 0.0121. This is about four times as large as the comparable standard deviation of the estimated real exchange rate coefficients for post-1973 Britain, suggesting that the interwar economy was more vulnerable to real exchange rate shocks than its postwar counterpart.

These large real exchange rate coefficients may reflect the effects of shocks to regional labor markets correlated with real exchange rate movements but not attributable to them. An example of such a shock is the 1926 coal strike, which idled part of the labor force of Wales but not of other regions and coincided with the continued real appreciation of sterling in the wake of Britain's 1925 return to the gold standard (figure 8-8.) Table 8-8 therefore adds to the equation a strike dummy for 1926. Its inclusion slightly reduces the size and range of real exchange rate coefficients; the standard deviation falls from to 0.0121 to 0.0118, still considerably larger than the analogous figure for post-1973 Britain.

Thus the comparison of interwar and contemporary Britain suggests

Table 8-7. Covariates of Regional Unemployment in Britain, 1923–38

Region	Constant	National unemployment	Real exchange rate	Real energy price	R^2
London	−0.999	0.795	−0.009	0.010	.85
	(0.89)	(6.29)	(1.44)	(2.58)	
Midlands	−4.887	1.139	0.025	−0.004	.88
	(3.42)	(7.07)	(3.17)	(0.76)	
Northeast	−1.133	0.960	0.002	−0.002	.94
	(1.51)	(11.35)	(0.40)	(0.93)	
Northwest	−1.346	1.013	−0.006	0.002	.96
	(2.32)	(15.46)	(1.78)	(1.09)	
Southeast	−3.702	1.120	−0.009	0.004	.87
	(2.91)	(7.78)	(1.29)	(0.96)	
Southwest	−1.911	0.953	−0.009	0.001	.93
	(2.35)	(10.39)	(1.94)	(0.44)	
Wales	−2.288	1.174	0.007	−0.021	.82
	(1.24)	(5.63)	(0.70)	(3.16)	
Scotland	−1.675	1.028	−0.012	0.005	.96
	(2.49)	(13.54)	(3.15)	(2.21)	

Sources: Author's calculations using sources discussed in the appendix. Unemployment in logarithms; t-statistics in parentheses.

Table 8-8. Covariates of Regional Unemployment in Britain, Including the Effects of the 1926 General Strike, 1923–38

Region	Constant	National unemployment	Real exchange rate	Real energy price	Strike dummy	R^2
London	−1.110	0.738	−0.007	0.014	−0.347	.91
	(1.21)	(6.94)	(1.33)	(3.82)	(2.33)	
Midlands	−4.935	1.114	0.025	−0.002	−0.152	.89
	(3.34)	(6.50)	(3.12)	(0.41)	(0.63)	
Northeast	−1.065	0.994	0.004	−0.004	0.212	.96
	(1.65)	(13.24)	(0.10)	(1.79)	(2.01)	
Northwest	−1.342	1.015	−0.006	0.002	0.13	.96
	(2.18)	(14.23)	(1.68)	(0.89)	(0.13)	
Southeast	−3.837	1.052	−0.006	0.008	−0.421	.93
	(3.85)	(9.09)	(1.18)	(2.18)	(2.59)	
Southwest	−1.970	0.924	−0.007	0.003	−0.184	.94
	(2.57)	(10.42)	(1.77)	(1.03)	(1.48)	
Wales	−2.124	1.258	0.004	−0.025	0.510	.88
	(1.31)	(6.71)	(0.45)	(4.08)	(1.94)	
Scotland	−1.637	1.047	−0.012	0.004	0.118	.96
	(2.46)	(13.56)	(3.32)	(1.61)	(1.09)	

Sources: Author's calculations using sources discussed in the appendix. Unemployment in logarithms; t-statistics in parentheses.

a decrease over time in the sensitivity of regional unemployment differentials to real exchange rate shocks. Increasing labor mobility and long-term declines in the importance of natural resource availability for the location decisions of industries may have combined to attenuate the dispersion of regional responses to real exchange rate changes. This tendency is important to bear in mind when pondering the regional effects of the Single Market Project.

Conclusion

Although there is considerable variation in the response of unemployment levels in Italian and British regions to changes in the real exchange rate, there is no evidence that the range of responses is greater than in the United States. The range of regional responses is virtually identical in Italy and the United States, and Britain's is even smaller than that of the United States. Insofar as monetary unification implies a loss of insulation from real exchange rate shocks, Britain and Italy thus appear no more vulnerable than the United States to regional problems arising from this source.

The analysis is predicated on the assumption that the national unemployment rate can be held constant, presumably through the use of fiscal policy, which is a matter of dispute. To the extent that monetary unification implies constraints on fiscal policy, real exchange rate shocks may raise the overall national level of unemployment. But the resulting problem is likely to be one of depressed countries, not of depressed regions within otherwise prosperous nations.

How other aspects of the Single Market will affect these patterns remains unclear. The removal of barriers to labor mobility is likely to further attenuate regional unemployment differentials. Workers in regions of high unemployment will have the opportunity to relocate to regions of lower unemployment not only within their native countries but elsewhere in the European Community. Most observers are skeptical, however, that labor mobility across national borders will increase significantly in the foreseeable future. Completion of the internal market could heighten regional specialization within countries, magnifying regional disparities, as European industries attempt to exploit economies of agglomeration made feasible by the opportunity to sell standardized products throughout the Community. The removal of economic barriers between countries, however, suggests most obviously that countries will become more specialized.[39] The impact on the specialization of different regions within countries is less straightforward.

Appendix: Description of Data

Postwar Britain

Data on British unemployment were drawn from Department of Employment and Productivity (1971) supplemented by various issues of the Department of Employment *Gazette*. The standard English regions distinguished by the department are the Southeast, East Anglia, Southwest, West Midlands, East Midlands, Yorkshire and Humberside, Northwest, and North. Data for Wales and Scotland were also used. Northern Ireland is excluded on the grounds that its labor market is imperfectly integrated with that of Great Britain.

To construct the real exchange rate, exchange rates and consumer price indexes were first gathered for Britain's ten leading trading partners. Trade was measured as the sum of imports and exports in 1980. A consumer price index for Saudi Arabia is not available for the early part of the period; Saudi Arabia was therefore omitted from the sample. (Because British imports from Saudi Arabia consist almost entirely of oil, the impact of conditions there on the British economy should be captured by real energy prices.) The real exchange rate was computed as the trade-weighted arithmetic average of foreign consumer prices, converted into sterling using the spot exchange rate, relative to the British consumer price index.

Energy prices were drawn from the prices of fuel purchased by the manufacturing industry and given in the *Annual Statistical Abstract of the United Kingdom* deflated by consumer prices drawn from C. H. Feinstein (1972) for years through 1965, from B. R. Mitchell (1988, pp. 714–71) for 1966–70, and from *International Financial Statistics* (various years) thereafter.

Italy

The surveys used to gather unemployment statistics for Italy were revised in 1977 to reflect new definitions. In previous years, two categories

39. This is the conclusion, for example, of Krugman (1991) and Bayoumi and Eichengreen (1993). Giersch (1949–50, p. 91) seems to have been the first to suggest this effect.

of unemployed persons were distinguished: people separated from a previous position and new entrants to the labor force. Much of the rise in Italian unemployment in the 1970s was concentrated in the second category, reflecting legally mandated severance pay that discouraged layoffs and made it more difficult for those seeking a first position. The revised surveys after 1976 distinguish persons recently separated from a previous position, new entrants in search of a first position, and other persons in search of work. These data are drawn from Istituto Centrale di Statistica, *Annuario Statistico del Lavoro*. An attempt to reconcile problems of comparability between pre- and post-1976 data is made by Guido Massarotto and Ugo Trivellato (1983).

The Italian real exchange rate was calculated the same way Britain's was, except that both Saudi Arabia and Libya were excluded from the initial list of leading trade partners due to the absence of continuous consumer price indexes. An energy price index for the period was created from the following series: the price of fuel oil in Turin for 1958–62, the arithmetic average of indexes for crude petroleum and for petroleum products for 1963–74, and the published index for crude oil and petroleum products for 1975–84. All series were taken from the *Annuario Statistico Italiano* (various years). The resulting index was deflated by Italian consumer prices as published in *International Financial Statistics*.

United States

Data for the United States on unemployment by state based on the Current Population Survey are published by the Department of Labor beginning in the early to mid-1970s (depending on the state and the size of the survey sample). These data appear in the Labor Department's *Geographic Profile of Employment and Unemployment* (various years). Data for earlier years were drawn from estimates of the number of unemployed workers gathered by individual state agencies and tabulated in the *Manpower Report of the President* (various years).

The real exchange rate for the United States was calculated to be comparable to those for Britain and Italy. Consumer price indexes and exchange rates for the country's ten leading trade partners in 1980 (excluding Saudi Arabia) were aggregated using trade weights. The real price of energy was computed as the consumer price index for energy relative to the consumer price index for all items, both from Council of Economic Advisors (1991).

Interwar Britain

The data used in the interwar analysis were drawn primarily from Department of Employment and Productivity (1971). The number of unemployed workers by region is provided on a monthly basis; arithmetic averages of monthly totals were taken. These figures derive from counts of unemployed persons on the registers of the Ministry of Labour Employment Exchanges, Branch Employment Offices and Juvenile Employment Bureaux. Before October 1924, workers on systematic short time are excluded; thereafter those on systematic short time actually unemployed on the dates of the counts are included. I calculated the number of unemployed persons in Britain as the sum of the figures for the six English regions (London, Southeast, Southwest, Midlands, Northeast, Northwest), Scotland, and Wales. In contrast to the procedure followed by the British authorities after World War II, London was distinguished from the rest of the Southeast.

The time series for real energy prices is the annual average price of best (Yorkshire house) coal in London given in Mitchell (1988, p. 748), deflated by Feinstein's consumer price index. The real exchange rate was calculated by deflating British wholesale prices by a trade-weighted average of the wholesale prices of Britain's principal trading partners, each converted to sterling using the relevant bilateral exchange rate. Wholesale prices for Britain's ten leading trade partners other than Germany were used.[40]

---

40. Germany is excluded because the figures for 1923 would otherwise be dominated by the country's 1923 hyperinflation. On the construction of this series, see Eichengreen (1990b).

References

Armstrong, Harvey, and Jim Taylor. 1985. *Regional Economics and Policy*. London: Philip Allan.

Baines, Dudley. 1993. "Population, Migration and Regional Development, 1870–1939." In Roderick Floud and Donald McCloskey, eds., *The Economic History of Britain Since 1700*. 2d ed. Cambridge University Press.

Bayoumi, Tamim, and Barry Eichengreen. 1993. "Shocking Aspects of European Monetary Unification." In Francesco Giavazzi and Francesco Torres, eds., *The Transition to Economic and Monetary Unification in Europe*. Cambridge University Press. Forthcoming.

Bayoumi, Tamim, and Paul R. Masson. 1991. "Fiscal Flows in the United States and Canada: Lessons for Monetary Union in Europe." International Monetary Fund. November.

Beveridge, William H. 1944. *Full Employment in a Free Society*. London: Allen and Unwin.

Bianchi, Patrizio, and Guiseppina Gualtieri. 1990. "Emilia-Romagna and its Industrial Districts: The Evolution of a Model." In Robert Leonardi and Raffaella Y. Nanetti, eds., *The Regions and European Integration: The Case of Emilia-Romagna*. London: Pinter.

Bini-Smaghi, Lorenzo, and Silvia Vori. 1992. "Rating the EC as an Optimal Currency Area: Is It Worse than the U.S.?" Bank of Italy. July.

Blanchard, Olivier, and Lawrence Katz. 1992. "Regional Evolutions." *Brookings Papers on Economic Activity 2.*

Bowley, Arthur L. 1930. *Some Economic Consequences of the Great War*. London: Butterworth.

Branson, William H., and James P. Love. 1988. "U.S. Manufacturing and the Real Exchange Rate." In Richard Marston, ed., *Misalignment of Exchange Rates: Effects on Trade and Industry*. University of Chicago Press.

Caroleo, Floro E. 1989. "Le Cause Economiche nei Differenziali Regionali del Tasso di Disoccupazione." *Economia & Lavoro* 23 (July-September): 41–53.

Cohen, Daniel, and Charles Wyplosz. 1989. "The European Monetary Union: An Agnostic Evaluation." In Ralph Bryant and others, eds., *Macroeconomic Policies in an Interdependent World*. Brookings.

Committee for the Study of Economic and Monetary Union. 1989. *Report on Monetary Union in the European Community*. Brussels: Office for Official Publications of the European Community.

Council of Economic Advisors. 1991. *Economic Report of the President*. Washington.

Department of Employment and Productivity. 1971. *British Labour Statistics: Historical Abstract 1886–1968*. London: Her Majesty's Stationers Office.

Eichengreen, Barry. 1990a. "One Money for Europe? Lessons from the U.S. Currency Union." *Economic Policy* 10 (April): 117–87.

————. 1990b. "The Comparative Performance of Fixed and Flexible Exchange Rate Regimes: Interwar Evidence." In K. Villipilai and N. Thygesen, eds., *Recent Developments in Business Cycle Analysis*. London: Macmillan.

————. 1991. "Couts et avantages de l'unification monetaire de l'Europe." In Pierre Beregovoy, ed., *Vers l'Union Economique et Monetaire Europeenne*. Paris: Ministry of Finance.

————. 1992. "Is Europe an Optimum Currency Area?" In Herbert G. Grubel and Silvio Borner, eds., *The European Community after 1992: Perspectives from the Outside*. London: Macmillan.

————. 1993. "Labor Markets and European Monetary Unification." In Paul Masson and Mark Taylor, eds., *Policy Issues in the Operation of Currency Unions*. Cambridge University Press.

Eichengreen, Barry, and Charles Wyplosz. 1993. "The Unstable EMS." *Brookings Papers on Economic Activity*. Forthcoming.

Frankel, Jeffrey A., and Steven Phillips. 1993. "The European Monetary System: Credible at Last?" In Francesco Giavazzi and Francisco Torres, eds., *The Transition to Economic and Monetary Union in Europe*. Cambridge University Press. Forthcoming.

Fratianni, Michele, Jurgen von Hagen, and Christopher Waller. 1992. "The Maastricht Way to EMU." *Princeton Studies in International Finance*.

Garside, W. R. 1980. *The Measurement of Unemployment: Methods and Sources in Great Britain, 1850–1979*. Oxford: Blackwell.

Gellner, Christopher G. 1974. "Regional Differences in Employment and Unemployment, 1957–72." *Monthly Labor Review* 97 (March): 15–24.

Glick, Reuven, and Michael Hutchison. 1990. "Does Exchange Rate Appreciation 'Deindustrialize' the Open Economy? A Critique of U.S. Evidence." *Economic Inquiry* 28 (January): 19–38.

Giavazzi, Francesco. 1990. "The EMS Experience." In Yoshio Suzuki, Junichi Miyake, and Mitsuaki Okabe, eds., *The Evolution of the International Monetary System: How Can Efficiency and Stability Be Attained?* University of Tokyo Press.

Giavazzi, Francesco, and Alberto Giovannini. 1989. *Limiting Exchange Rate Flexibility: The European Monetary System*. MIT Press.

Giersch, Herbert. 1949–50. "Economic Union between Nations and the Location of Industries." *Review of Economic Studies* 17 (2): 87–97.

Hatton, T. J. 1986. "Structural Aspects of Unemployment between the World Wars." *Research in Economic History* 10: 55–92.

International Monetary Fund. Various years. *International Financial Statistics*.

Istituto Centrale di Statistica. Annual. *Annuario Statistico del Lavoro*. Rome.

Istituto Centrale di Statistica. Annual. *Annuario Statistico Italiano*. Rome.

King, Russell. 1985. *The Industrial Geography of Italy.* London: Croom Helm.

Krugman, Paul R. 1991. *Geography and Trade.* MIT Press.

Massarotto, Guido, and Ugo Trivellato. 1983. "Un Metodo per il Raccordo delle Serie Regionali Sulle Forze di Lavoro Senza Informazioni Estranee." *Economia & Lavoro* 4 (October-December): 67–77.

McLeod, Darryl, and John H. Welch. 1991a. "The Case for a Peso Target Zone." *Business Mexico* 1 (November): 19–22.

McLeod, Darryl, and John H. Welch. 1991b. "Free Trade and the Peso." Fordham University and Federal Reserve Bank of Dallas.

Mitchell, B. R. 1988. *British Historical Statistics.* Cambridge University Press.

OECD. 1986. *Flexibility in the Labor Market: The Current Debate.* Paris.

Royal Commission on the Poor Laws and Relief of Distress. 1909. *Report,* Cd. 4499. London: HMSO.

Sachs, Jeffrey, and Charles Wyplosz. 1983. "Real Exchange Rate Effects of Fiscal Policy," Harvard Institute of Economic Research discussion paper 1050 (April).

Sala-i-Martin, Xavier, and Jeffrey Sachs. 1992. "Fiscal Federalism and Optimum Currency Areas: Evidence for Europe from the United States." In Matthew B. Canzoneri, Vittorio Grilli, and Paul Masson, eds., *Establishing a Central Bank: Issues in Europe and Lessons from the U.S.* Cambridge University Press.

Sum, Andrew M., and Thomas P. Rush. 1975. "The Geographic Structure of Unemployment Rates." *Monthly Labor Review* 98 (March): 3–9.

Townsend, Alan R. 1983. *The Impact of Recession.* London: Croom Helm.

von Hagen, Jurgen. 1992. "Fiscal Arrangements in a Monetary Union: Evidence from the U.S." In Donald E. Fair and Christian de Boisseau, eds., *Fiscal Policy, Taxation, and the Financial System in an Increasingly Integrated Europe.* Kluwer.

CHAPTER NINE

Immigration Policies in Fortress Europe

Bent Hansen

R ADICAL CHANGES IN postwar European immigration and policies took place around 1973.[1] The immediate impact of these changes on the total labor force was modest, but they signaled a change in the composition of immigrants, with a relative decrease in the supply of unskilled labor and construction workers that in the longer term has led to stagnation in the growth of the labor force. An examination of the political economy of the changes in immigration policies suggests that noneconomic factors dominated national decisionmaking in this matter. The present analysis applies the Beveridge curve to immigration policy to describe and analyze maladjustments and mismatches between aggregate demand and supply as indicated in national vacancy and unemployment rates. The analysis finds that the Beveridge curve seems to have shifted outward since the mid–1970s, suggesting increased mismatch associated with the immigration ban. Attempts to specify these effects with greater precision by using fixed-weight mismatch indexes based on disaggregated data have not yielded convincing results, and these indexes are not applied in this chapter. However, a leading model of the Beveridge curve (by Blanchard and Diamond) suggests that while so-called spontaneous immigration from developing countries may give rise to increased stagflation, systematic recruitment of foreign labor to fill vacancies combined with strict rotation of foreign workers will diminish stagflation.[2] On the basis of this analysis such an immigration policy is recommended to be compulsory in the EC single market.

1. For descriptive surveys of postwar European immigration and policies, see Böhning (1984) and Hammar (1985). OECD (1985) provides an analytical survey.
2. Blanchard and Diamond (1989).

From Liberal to Protectionist Immigration Policies

Two decades of virtual laissez-faire policies toward foreign workers were inaugurated in the 1950s with the establishment of two common labor markets, the Nordic in 1954 and the EC in 1956. Each provided free internal mobility to the citizens of member countries and lax admission policies to nonmember citizens.[3] In the early 1970s, the major destination countries of immigration to Europe suddenly imposed a near total ban on the entrance and settlement of new foreign workers. This was accompanied, however, by liberalized rules for the entrance of dependents and relatives. Of course, member-state citizens within the EC and the Nordic area were exempted from the ban. Although the pretext for this policy reversal was the first oil shock of 1973–74 and the accompanying economic crisis, both the timing and political economy of the policy reversal suggest more complex reasons for the actions.

The legal stock of foreign workers in the nine most important destinations for immigrants to Europe increased from 2.5 million in 1960 to 6.3 million in 1975, remained almost constant until 1980, and then seems to have declined to 5.8 million in 1987 (table 9-1).[4] The annual rate of increase of foreign workers thus fell from 8.7 percent for 1960–70 to 3.1 percent for 1970–75, turned slightly negative for 1975–80, and declined to –1.1 percent for 1980–87. Individual European countries shifted from net immigration to net emigration, even after the emigration of natives to countries outside the EC was disregarded.

The inflow of foreign workers before 1967 coincided with the postwar reconstruction and recovery of the European economy and with the Ger-

---

3. A British-Irish common labor market had in effect existed since the independence of the Irish Republic in 1921 and even earlier as part of British colonial policies (Foster, 1989, chap. 15). With the entrance into the EC of both Ireland and the United Kingdom in 1973, this market became part of the EC common labor market. A similar outcome may be expected for the Nordic common labor market with the eventual accession of Sweden (and possibly Finland, Iceland, and Norway) into the EC. Negotiations between the European Free Trade Association and the EC are yet another factor to monitor vis-à-vis common labor markets.

4. A detailed survey of incomplete, and partly uncertain data on foreign workers in Europe since World War II, categorized by country of origin, sex, age, activity, occupation, and earnings can be found in Hansen (1990b). U.S. information about immigrant earnings appears inadequate (Chiswick, 1992). Recent studies (Borjas and Trejo, 1991; Funkhouser and Trejo, 1992) are beginning to remedy the situation but the findings, which suggest improved education and earnings for U.S. immigrants during the 1980s, hardly apply to European immigrants.

Table 9-1. Foreign Workers in Nine European Countries and West Germany Only, Selected Years, 1961–87[a]

Percent unless otherwise specified

| | Nine European countries | | West Germany | | | |
| | | | | | Share of foreign workers in total workers | |
Year	Foreign workers (millions)	Annual rate of increase	Foreign workers (millions)	Annual rate of increase	Percent	Annual increase of share[b]
1961	2.54[c]	...	0.47	...	2.3	...
1966	n.a.	n.a.	1.24	21.4	5.7	0.7
1970	5.40[d]	8.7	1.80	9.7	8.7	0.7
1974	n.a.	n.a.	2.40	7.5	11.2	0.6
1975	6.31	3.1	2.22	−7.4	10.3	−0.9
1980	6.28	−0.1	2.18	−0.9	9.8	−0.1
1987	5.80[e]	−1.1	1.85	−2.3	7.5	−0.3

Sources: column 1: *1960–80*, Böhning (1984, table 2-1); *1985* (United Kingdom only) EUROSTAT (1989, 3.c, table III/6); *1987*, SOPEMI (1988, table A.7).

Columns 3, 4, 5: *Statistisches Jahrbuch* (1988 and earlier years, table 6.8.1).

n.a. Not available.

a. The countries are Austria, Belgium, France, Luxembourg, Netherlands, Sweden, Switzerland, United Kingdom, and West Germany. Illegal immigrants, seasonal workers, and commuters are not included.

b. Simple average over previous year, ignoring 1974.

c. Early 1960s.

d. Early 1970s.

e. Includes data from the United Kingdom for 1985, not including unemployed.

man economic miracle. Kindleberger regarded the high growth rates of early postwar Europe as an example of surplus labor-driven growth, the sort described by the Arthur Lewis model, and he considered the tapering off of growth rates after the mid–1960s to be a consequence of dwindling surplus labor.[5] Certain things are not explained in this scenario, however. Of course, the ample supply of foreign labor was a sine qua non of early high growth rates. After 1967, however, Europe's early massive general labor shortage was replaced by growing cyclical partial labor surpluses. With the recession of 1966–67, moreover, many immigrants migrated back to their countries of origin or migrated to third countries. After 1968, when expansion resumed on a modest scale, Turkish, North African and, after 1971, Egyptian laborers became available in essentially unlimited numbers, and vacancies for skilled labor fluctuated at a low level.[6] Rather than labor shortages, the end of reconstruction and recovery was marked by the return of the business cycle inherent in the capitalist system at an increasingly unsatisfactory aggregate level.

Although the major features of the growth of the foreign work force

5. Kindleberger (1967).
6. In 1971 Sadat's constitutional reforms introduced emigration rights to Egypt.

are well known, the impact of immigration policies on the growth in the periods before and following 1973–74 is less well understood. Because of data problems, estimates of the share of foreign workers in total private sector employees in West Germany are used. That share increased from 2.3 percent in 1961 to 11.2 percent in 1974, then declined to 7.5 percent in 1987 (table 9-1). Given a relatively constant number of native employees in the private sector, these shares indicate a decline in the annual growth rate of the total private sector labor force from about 0.7 percent before 1974 to about − 0.2 percent from 1975 to 1987, amounting to a 1 percentage point decline each year after 1974. For other European immigration destinations, the change in net immigration was probably smaller. In any case, a decline of this order in the growth rate of the labor supply would introduce a dramatic shock into the growth process. These figures, however, do not adequately represent the size of the impact of the immigration policy reversal in West Germany; such endogenous factors as relative earnings, unemployment, and cumulated stocks of foreign workers must be considered as well.

Wolfgang Franz's 1981 econometric study details the determinants of quarterly in- and out-migration of foreign workers to and from West Germany.[7] The study gives a breakdown of internal EC and foreign migrants and distinguishes between the periods before and after November 1973. Despite its data problems, this study attempts to model and quantify the effects of the change in immigration policies. Its specification is largely noncontroversial, reflecting consensus views. The quarterly inflow of new non-Community workers (recruitment abroad) is specified as a function of the stock of unfilled vacancies in West Germany, while the inflow of workers' relatives and dependents is explained by the stock of non-Community workers. Before November 1973 only recruitment abroad matters; after that date, only the inflow of relatives. The effects of other determinants were not influenced by the changes in immigration policy. The outflow of foreign migrants, or remigration, is explained by the diminished stock of such migrants and by other variables. Remigration, which played an important role in 1967, declined with the restrictions on in-migration after November 1973, which made reentry almost impossible.

Franz's equations can be used to calculate the hypothetical net inflow that would have obtained in the absence of policy changes. The impact of hypothetical policy changes in 1969 and 1980 was computed to give

7. Franz (1981).

an idea of the importance of their timing. As a share of the private labor force, the computed effect for the year of the policy change, 1973, was small but significant, about −0.2 percent. The net effect was small because the relaxation in the rules for relatives combined with a decline in remigration actually diminished the effect of the recruitment ban. Had the policy changes been made in 1969, the effect would have been larger, −0.9 percent, because the inflow of relatives (based on a smaller stock of foreign workers) would have been smaller. Had the policy changes been made in 1980, the net effect would have been an increase of 0.1 percent (because banned recruitment, which is related to actual vacancies, would have been smaller).

The impact of immigration policies on wages is also important. Under well-known assumptions of neoclassical Heckscher-Ohlin-Samuelson theory, immigration has no effect on factor prices, but will shift production toward labor-intensive goods with a corresponding change in the volume of trade. Under autarky, production will also shift toward labor-intensive goods, but with a decrease in real wages and an increase in the rate of return to capital. In reality, with both traded and nontraded goods, the effect will be somewhere in between. Native labor will lose ground and capital will gain, consequences that are likely to become issues in domestic politics.

No studies appear to have been done on the impact of the 1973–74 policy changes on wages, and information about immigrants' earnings is meager. A handful of studies on legal immigrants' earnings exist.[8] A technical problem well known from aggregate studies of women and minority earnings in the United States is that the composition of such groups differs greatly from that of the labor force generally, rendering simple averages biased and misleading. Nevertheless, discrimination against legal immigrants in the sense of unequal pay for equal work does not appear to have been significant. (In some countries it was illegal.) Violation of statutory minimum wage laws and collective agreements has been strongly resisted by the authorities as well as by labor organizations, regardless of their attitudes toward immigration and immigrants. Discrimination shows up instead in the kinds of jobs available to immigrants. This is not to deny, of course, that the mere presence of a significant number of immigrants may exert downward pressure on wages, including minimum and collectively negotiated wages, but work condi-

8. A small number of studies for West Germany (Bundesministerium für Arbeit, 1986), France (Chabanas and Volkoff, 1973), the United Kingdom (Chiswick, 1980), and Sweden (Wadensjö, 1975), cover earnings for legal immigrants only.

tions do not appear to have changed significantly because of them. The matter is complicated to the extent that immigrants are often less militant than natives and have lower reservation wages.

The Political Economy of Immigration Policy Reversals

The changes in immigration policy in a number of European countries in the early 1970s were not motivated exclusively by considerations related to employment. This fact is basic to understanding the events of the time and the subsequent difficulty of changing the policies.

The period from immediately after World War II until the early 1970s was characterized by large movements and resettlement of prisoners of war, forced laborers, refugees, and so-called displaced persons. Immigration was regulated by almost as many systems as there were countries. At one extreme was the rotation system, practiced most notably in Switzerland and West Germany. At the other extreme were systems of permanent immigration, which were in effect in Sweden and the United Kingdom. Under the rotation system, residence and work permits were issued for a limited duration and could not be renewed or extended. Under the permanent system, a permanent permit was issued on admission to the country. Other countries employed mixtures of the two systems, and no country in the Nordic or EC common labor markets was open to unlimited, free nonmember immigration.[9] Nowhere did legislatures establish either open labor markets as practiced in the United States before 1921 or the rigid ceilings and quotas that were applied thereafter. European systems seem to have developed pragmatically in different ways in various countries.

A combined policy of recruitment and rotation was adopted in West Germany in the late 1950s to fill temporary gaps in the labor force. These gaps were perceived as related to the distorted distribution of ages and sexes in the postwar population and to a general labor shortage accompanying West German reconstruction and recovery particularly after the erection of the Berlin Wall in 1961. The policy was intended to avoid polluting society permanently with *Fremden* (outsiders) and depriving developing countries of needed labor. Developing countries, it was argued, benefited from the return of their migrants with improved skills and from a flow of hard currency remittances. The rotation policy failed

---

9. The laissez-faire policies mentioned early in this chapter refer to the lax attitudes and admission practices of national administrations toward immigrants.

miserably, however, at least from West Germany's point of view. The policy irrationally linked the possibility of the renewal or extension of visas to actual length of stay. The high turnover associated with rotation discouraged training. Nor did the policy advance the interests of the immigrants themselves; a solid majority seemed to prefer to establish themselves more permanently and actually succeeded in doing so as time passed. Thus recruitment-rotation became increasingly difficult to administer.[10]

Systems of permanent immigration generally aim to assimilate potential immigrants into the native population. Sweden's parliament adopted such a system in declarations of 1968 and 1975. In keeping with the politically prominent egalitarian ideology, it made economic equality, freedom of choice, and political partnership the pillars of Swedish immigration policy. This system also foundered because of inherent contradictions. Just as the rotation system was dynamically bound to involve permanent immigration, the permanent system was bound to prevent any significant immigration at all: "To achieve the aim of equality explicit in [the Swedish] immigrant policy tougher immigration regulation was required."[11] Assimilation entails a cultural exchange, with both natives and foreigners combined into a new amalgam that is essentially similar to preimmigration society as long as the immigrant population is small. With a large body of immigrants, assimilation may either entail a new nation or may never occur. Faced with this dilemma, Swedish nationalism gained the upper hand.

The Economics of West German Policy

By 1973 the rotation system had clearly failed in West Germany and the time had come for a change in policy. The share of foreigners in the total employed work force exceeded 10 percent. Many were long-time residents of West Germany: Turks alone accounted for no less than 23 percent of all employed foreigners. Recruitment efforts abroad were halted in November 1973. Permits for spontaneous immigration (not recruited through German authorities) were reduced to nothing, although much of the effect was neutralized through the liberalized rules for relatives. West Germany's policies were ambiguous and self-contradictory. In part they were leftovers from the defeat in World War II (reflected in the

10. For constitutional reasons refugees seeking asylum have enjoyed a privileged position as immigrants to the Federal Republic of Germany. After the 1950s and until recently this problem was quantitatively unimportant, but this may change.

11. Hammar (1985, p. 41).

asylum policy laid down in the constitution imposed by the victorious powers). In part they reflected foreign labor's influence as union members on the domestic labor market and upward pressure exerted by special interest groups and international organizations. The legal basis for the 1973 decree was the Aliens Act of 1965 in conjunction with an Implementation Act of June 1972 and the Labor Promotions Act of 1969 with an accompanying decree on work permits. It was generally understood that with the recession of 1967–68, the economic miracle was over. After reaching a peak in January 1970, vacancies (seasonally adjusted) decreased through 1973. The unemployment rate, which remained at 1.0 to 1.3 percent through 1972–73, began to increase in October 1973, potentially indicating a new recession. Nevertheless, the labor minister's response to the increase in oil prices was surprisingly strong in light of the employment situation. Thus the oil price shock appears to have provided a pretext for a policy change (the recruitment ban) that was, in fact, primarily crafted in reaction to noneconomic factors.

In its economic survey of West Germany for 1973–74, the first to discuss the oil crisis, the Organization for Economic Cooperation and Development (OECD) failed to mention these policy changes even in its detailed appendix, and neither foreign workers nor immigration policies were referred to in the text.[12] At that time West Germany was already an influential member of the OECD. In fairness to the West German government, however, it should be emphasized that the structure of the country's labor market had been changing to the disadvantage of foreign migrants ever since the recession of 1967. These workers tended to compete with unskilled labor and with construction and building workers. Although unemployment rates for foreign workers are not available before 1980, unemployment was apparently not a problem for foreign workers in the 1950s and early 1960s. The situation began to change after 1967, and by the 1980s, unemployment rates for foreign workers were double those for natives. Labor shortages in occupations supplied by migrants gave way to labor surpluses.

Obtaining unemployment rates by occupation is always difficult, but the absolute difference between unfilled vacancies and unemployment is categorized by occupation, and this may serve as an index of labor shortage or surplus. Table 9-2 shows unemployment, vacancies, and labor shortages for all occupations, distinguishing unskilled laborers and

---

12. OECD (1974). Appendix 3, "Chronology of Main Economic Policy Measures," makes no mention of immigration policy shifts.

Table 9-2. *West German Unemployment, Unfilled Vacancies, and Labor Shortage, Selected Periods, 1964–89*

Percent of total civilian labor force[a]

Date	All occupations			Unskilled laborers[b]			Building and construction[c]			All other occupations		
	Unemployment	Unfilled vacancies	Labor shortage	Unemployment	Unfilled vacancies	Labor shortage	Unemployment	Unfilled vacancies	Labor shortage	Unemployment	Unfilled vacancies	Labor shortage
Source: FRG												
Oct. 1964	0.5	3.2	2.7	0.1	0.3	0.2	0.0	0.3	0.3	0.4	2.6	2.2
Feb. 1967	3.1	1.3	-1.8	0.7	0	-0.6	0.6	0.1	-0.5	1.8	1.2	-0.7
Jan. 1973	1.6	2.4	0.8	0.1	0	-0.1	0.2	0.2	0.0	1.3	2.2	0.9
Source: OECD												
Jan. 1973	1.0	2.9	1.9	n.a.	n.a.	n.a.	n.a.	n.a.	n.a.	n.a.	n.a.	n.a.
Oct. 1973	1.4	2.3	0.9	n.a.	n.a.	n.a.	n.a.	n.a.	n.a.	n.a.	n.a.	n.a.
Jan. 1974	1.9	1.6	-0.3	n.a.	n.a.	n.a.	n.a.	n.a.	n.a.	n.a.	n.a.	n.a.
Source: FRG												
Jan. 1974	2.8	1.4	-1.4	0.1	0	-0.1	0.4	0.1	-0.3	2.3	1.3	-1.0
Jan. 1976	5.9	0.8	-5.0	0.2	0	-0.2	0.5	0.1	-0.5	5.2	0.9	-4.3
Sept. 1983	8.6	0.3	-8.3	0.2	0	-0.2	0.4	0	-0.4	8.0	0.3	-7.7
Sept. 1989	7.3	1.1	-6.2	0.1	0	-0.1	0.3	0.1	-0.2	6.9	1.0	-5.9

Sources: FRG: *Statistisches Jahrbuch* (annual); numbers unadjusted. OECD: *Main Economic Indicators* (1964–83, 1989); adjusted seasonally.

n.a. Not available.

a. Abhängigen Erwerbspersonen (ohne Soldaten), percents partly inferred.

b. Ungelernte Hilfskräfte (after 1974: Hilfsarbeitern ohne nähere Tätigkeitsangaben).

c. Bauberufe.

building and construction occupations, all normalized by total civilian labor force. In 1964 West Germany experienced a general labor shortage for all occupations (2.7 percent) including unskilled laborers (0.2 percent) and building and construction laborers (0.3 percent). During the 1967 recession a 1.8 percent net surplus of labor emerged for all occupations. More than half the surplus was unskilled labor in these three occupational groups. In January 1973 a shortage of labor for all occupations reappeared. This, however, was reduced to 0.8 percent, with a surplus for unskilled laborers and near balance in building and construction occupations. Politically, the case for limiting immigration appears to have been weaker than in 1964.

Tracing developments through the critical year 1973 is possible using the OECD's seasonally adjusted monthly data for all occupations. These show that in October 1973 there was still an overall labor shortage, but it was half the size it had been in January 1973. By January 1974 a general labor surplus of 1.4 percent had emerged. Thus, internal labor market predictions immediately before the oil embargo may well have been unduly pessimistic, with the oil situation contributing to the ban. However, an economically rational immigration policy should be based on vacancy data rather than labor shortage, surplus, or unemployment data.

Table 9-2 shows data for January 1974 to September 1989 that are roughly comparable to data for September 1964 to January 1973. While unemployment for all occupations increased from 2.8 percent to 7.3 percent (reaching 8.6 percent in 1983), vacancies fell from 1.4 to 1.1 percent (dipping as low as 0.3 percent in 1983). For unskilled laborers and building and construction occupations, however, unemployment decreased while vacancies remained unchanged at a very low level. Thus, for the two groups together labor surplus decreased slightly, while for all other occupations it increased to a level six times higher than before, a striking difference.

A different classification of labor force by skilled and unskilled labor, the latter defined as having an "incomplete vocational education," shows a roughly similar development of surplus labor among all skilled and unskilled workers from 1976 to 1989 (table 9-3). The broader definition of unskilled may account for the difference, in particular since the emphasis is on education without mentioning experience and training. Though not directly relevant, it is a useful reminder of the ambiguity of conceptions such as skill, a problem well known to both labor economists and demographers.

Table 9-3. *West German Average Unemployment, Unfilled Vacancies, and Labor Shortage Rates, 1976, 1983, 1989*
Percent of total labor force

Item	1976	1983	1989
Total labor force			
Unemployment	4.6	9.1	7.9
Unfilled vacancies	1.0	0.3	1.0
Labor shortage	−3.6	−8.8	−6.9
All unskilled			
Unemployment	2.4	4.6	4.0
Unfilled vacancies	0.5	0.1	0.3
Labor shortage	−1.9	−4.5	−3.7
All skilled			
Unemployment	2.2	4.5	3.9
Unfilled vacancies	0.5	0.2	0.7
Labor shortage	−1.7	−4.3	−3.2

Source: Franz (1991, table 3.3 and notes 25 and 26).
a. Incomplete vocational education.

These figures should be considered in the context of dramatic changes in the composition of production. From 1974 to 1984, real GDP in construction was unchanged while GDP in other activities increased by 21.4 percent. This development tended to increase labor surpluses in construction relative to the rest of the economy. Employment in construction fell by 12.9 percent, while employment in other activities fell by only 1.5 percent, something that should also, all else being equal, tend to increase the relative labor surplus in construction. In addition, activities employing unskilled labor shifted toward capital-intensive technologies, further tending to increase labor surplus in sectors such as construction. Immigration policies seem to have been the only major factor pulling in the other direction, assuming that immigration of construction labor before the ban had largely been spontaneous and noncomplementary, a likely possibility (see figure 9-1). Indeed, this factor must have been very strong, considering the absolute as well as relative decrease in surplus labor in construction. The possibility even occurs that the stagflation of the 1980s initially started in the 1970s as a supply side phenomenon with construction choked by a shortage of immigrants.

Restrictions in Other European Destinations

In France the so-called Fontanet circular of January 1972 attempted to tighten the rules for hiring foreign labor and regularization of the widespread employment of illegal immigrants. The Fontanet circular failed because employers opposed it, and it was suspended during the summer of 1973. Legislation to prevent illegal entry was enacted in July 1973, although the definitive policy move against immigration came only in 1974.[13]

The Swedish government, urged by the central federation of labor unions, halted recruitment of foreign labor and reduced non-Nordic immigration to a minimum in 1972.[14] Denmark and Norway concurred.

Based on the Federal Law on Abode and Settlement of Foreigners of 1931, Switzerland liberally issued combined residence and work permits until 1970. Administration of the law became very restrictive after a narrowly defeated referendum in 1970. A ceiling was established allowing for only 10,000-odd residence and work permits annually, on a nonpermanent basis if not a strictly rotating one.

In the United Kingdom the policies of successive governments after 1962 increasingly tightened controls on nonwhite immigration from the new Commonwealth, especially through the Commonwealth Immigration Acts of 1962 and 1968. Although the legal situation is very complex, under the Immigration Act of 1971 non-Community immigration is mostly limited to dependents of previous immigrants.

The Netherlands did not definitively change its immigration policies until the late 1970s.

This brief survey of increased restrictions in European immigration policies in the early 1970s suggests that their relationship to the oil embargo and price hikes and the accompanying economic shock was fortuitous, tenuous, or even nonexistent. Although the moderate increase in unemployment and the declines in vacancies and growth before 1974 may have influenced immigration policies, these were principally features of the European postwar business cycle that had reemerged before the oil embargo. Moreover the subsequent high unemployment and low growth rates of the 1980s may not have been the paramount factors in maintaining restrictive immigration policies after 1974.

Three Aspects of Immigration

Three special aspects of the political economy of immigration have been apparent everywhere: ethnic concerns, infrastructure problems, and labor union policies.

"Ethnic concerns" is a U.S. euphemism for any adverse attitude or behavior toward groups of human beings (other than one's own) based on genetic, linguistic, cultural, national, or regional differences, real or

13. Kennedy-Brenner (1979, p. 28).
14. Hammar (1985, pp. 18, 285).

imagined, and covering anything from organized, aggressive intolerance to mild-mannered, individual uneasiness in dealing with members of such groups. Skin color, religion, and language are the immigrant characteristics that have most often stirred up ethnic concerns with immigration policies in Europe after World War II and have been responsible to varying degrees for changing them. There is hardly a country in Europe that has not experienced ethnic incidents or seen political action directed against immigration, immigrants, or both. There is no doubt that ethnic problems will be a factor in future attempts to reverse European immigration policies.

The limited capacity of infrastructure, a finite supply of public goods and transfers, and the need to increase tax financing have been highly visible sources of irritation with immigration of any kind, even domestic migration at the local level, in most countries. Educational services faced with the problems of children with foreign mother tongues and functional illiteracy among parents become strained and tend to discriminate against immigrants. In response immigrants self-segregate into closed communities. Housing capacity and policy are also affected by immigration, the French "bidonville" providing the classical example.

The immigration of foreign workers also confronts national labor unions and their central organizations with special and difficult problems. Although traditions of international solidarity and egalitarianism may theoretically dictate free immigration and equal rights for disadvantaged brethren and sisters abroad, potentially depressive effects on real wages and employment are obvious union concerns. Along with concerns about ethnic differences and reduced public goods, these effects stir up deep feelings among the rank and file. The distinction between member countries' policies governing foreign immigrants and the rights guaranteed by the EC under the Treaty of Rome and subsequent court decisions has created equal rights dilemmas for the unions. They have tended to solve such dilemmas by applying EC regulations to non-Community immigrants. However, both official and rank and file responses are often confused by populist views on the effects of immigration, for instance, that employing a foreign worker means that a native worker will be unemployed or that all the costs of public goods and transfers delivered to foreign workers are paid by natives. It was no accident that unions in all European immigration destinations strongly supported or even played instrumental roles in establishing tighter restrictions on in-migration of workers in the early 1970s. They offered lukewarm and often divided support for easier acquisition of permanent residence permits and naturalization and for liberalization of in-migration for dependents and relatives.[15] The changing structure of labor markets (mentioned in the context of West Germany) may have contributed to the restrictive position adopted by individual unions. Moreover, unions have at times even welcomed immigration in order to make policies of wage restraint more effective and supportable; West Germany in the 1960s is again a good example.[16]

Both the OECD and the EC have begun to face the problem of immigration policy for Europe for the 1990s. The OECD has called attention to demographic projections that suggest the need for immigration of young people. The EC is confronted by applications for membership, especially from Turkey, that imply a radical extension of the single labor market. Within the framework of its Social Charter, the EC Commission has recently called for rules to guarantee minimum social conditions and remuneration to temporary foreign workers in EC member countries. The proposed legislation (which reflects a traditional union stance) covers cross-border subcontracting (in which workers are hired or transferred between EC countries) but applies as well to workers hired from outside the EC through labor recruitment. Such subcontracting is especially important in construction. "Without EC legislation, companies could use subcontracting to undercut wage levels and conditions set by law or collective bargaining agreements in EC nations. Such so-called social dumping could give companies an unfair advantage over rivals and undermine the EC's aim of creating a single market that benefits workers as well as industry."[17] These seem to be preliminary steps toward a common protectionist EC immigration policy, which would make the EC's internally free, albeit regulated, common labor market subject to heavy external protection.

The Maastricht Treaty's designs for a European Union have, so far, done little to settle the situation. In eleven (or without Denmark, ten) EC countries "laws on third-country nationals working in the Community . . . will require unanimity. . . . Asylum seekers and immigrants will face simpler—perhaps tougher—rules when they try to enter the Community. They are committed, by 1993, to common policies on how to deal with asylum requests. Community rules will determine who needs a visa to get into the EC."[18] With the Danish rejection of Maastricht in 1992, immigration policies remain in the hands of national governments, and

15. Edye (1987); Hammar (1985).
16. Ulman and Flanagan (1971).
17. *Wall Street Journal*, June 21, 1991, p. 10. See also *Economist*, June 29, 1991, p. 64.
18. *Economist*, December 14, 1991, p. 53.

the future of a European Union immigration policy appears difficult to predict, with "subsidiarity" a factor of great ambiguity.[19]

Immigration and the Beveridge Curve

It is often assumed that immigrants are employed in occupations unattractive to native workers because they involve heavy, dirty, or boring work and low security and status, although not necessarily low pay.[20] Thus immigrant labor does not directly substitute for but may even complement native labor. If so, a cutoff of immigration will tend to increase maladjustment or mismatch in the demand and supply of labor. In the aggregate the mismatch will show up as a shift, upward and to the right, of the Beveridge curve, which is obtained by plotting rates or, alternatively, durations of unemployment against those of vacancies.[21]

Without mentioning the Beveridge curve, the OECD clearly assumes mismatches to have been created by the immigration ban after 1973.[22] In addition, it suggests that the long period of liberal immigration policies in Europe, by equilibrating labor markets with in-migration or out-migration, may have served to make wages less flexible and domestic labor markets more imperfect. Switzerland is the classic example of this. Predicted demographic developments (aging native labor forces that are stagnant or even declining in number) bode a worsened situation during the 1990s. In the longer run these may make the problem worse, reinforcing the need to fill vacancies with young, relatively unskilled workers from countries outside the EC and Nordic common markets.[23]

The debate over the causes of high unemployment and stagflation in Europe during the 1980s and possibly extending into the 1990s has

19. "Survey: European Community," *Economist,* July 11, 1992, p. 52.

20. See Böhning (1984); Piore (1979). This is not unchallenged; see Greenwood (1975); Greenwood and McDowell (1986); OECD (1985, p. 95).

21. Dow and Dicks-Mireaux (1958); Dicks-Mireaux and Dow (1959); Jackman, Layard, and Pissarides (1989). Operating with durations rather than rates of unemployment and vacancies is not just a matter of convenience. The theory of the former is more complex than that of the latter (the conventional Beveridge curve). Not only does it require more restrictive assumptions (constant returns to scale in the matching function), measurements of durations are also fraught with conceptual and data difficulties, and typically steady-state substitutes have to be used (Akerlof and Main, 1980; Franz, 1991; Schettkat, 1991). Moreover, the analytical properties of the duration curve differ from those of the Beveridge curve.

22. OECD (1985).

23. OECD (1991, chap. 1).

drawn much attention to the possibility that increased mismatch in the labor markets is the root of the phenomena. Although not specifically oriented toward immigration problems, recent mismatch studies are relevant. Important works generated by two conferences sponsored by the EC at Chelwood Gate in 1985 and 1988 have recently appeared; unfortunately they yield no unambiguous answer to the mismatch problem. Participants in the conferences were apparently divided over the proper approach to the issue. Hence, there now exist two serious, conflicting attempts to corroborate or set aside the hypothesis of increasing labor market mismatch in Europe and the United States. Since neither side has come up with strong conclusive evidence, a brief examination of them is in order.

It is generally acknowledged that the national Beveridge curves have in fact shifted outward during the 1970s and 1980s. But dissatisfied with the aggregate Beveridge curve as an indicator of structural labor market problems, some British labor economists have developed a family of special mismatch indexes based on adjusted neoclassical theory with so-called matching functions and disaggregated vacancy data, unemployment data, or both. One such index does not suggest pronounced general tendencies for increased mismatch to have developed during the 1980s.[24] It is, however, based exclusively on unemployment dispersion with very crude classifications. The other approach is based on the Barro-Grossman-Benassi macroeconomic disequilibrium theory using a different data set. It seems to indicate a significant increase in labor market mismatch in major European countries and the United States from 1960 to 1984. However, this approach is confined as well by the use of special and very crude information about effective market constraints.[25]

As far as my analysis is concerned, it would be important if shifts in the Beveridge curve occurred in the years around 1973 because this would imply that the change in immigration policy was responsible. There seems to be little doubt that both British and German data support the idea that the immigration ban created such a shift in those two countries.[26] However, in other countries such as Sweden, no such shift is observable, either because policies were not sharply articulated, data are not available or reliable, or simply because no shift occurred.[27]

24. Jackman, Layard and Savouri (1991, chap. 1, tables 2.4, 2.9).
25. Drèze and Bean (1990).
26. For British data, see Jackman, Layard, and Pissarides (1989); for German, see Franz (1991).
27. For Swedish data, see Karlson and Löfgren (1990).

Although neither side has presented strong evidence in favor of its own position, there appears to be sufficient evidence to consider the hypothesis that the labor market in Europe has become increasingly mismatched. I now turn to the question of whether the change in immigration policy could be responsible.

Theories of Stagflation and Immigration

There is a decided lack of consensus in contemporary macroeconomic analysis on the causes of unemployment and stagflation. Most immigration analysis has been pursued in terms of neoclassical general equilibrium, either in the form of simplistic demand and supply curves for labor with both native and foreign workers or of the highly aggregated general equilibrium theory (the Heckscher-Ohlin-Samuelson theory) applied to international trade and factor mobility.[28] Whatever the relevance of such theory for long-term problems under perfect competition, economists acknowledge that it is not adequate for dealing with problems of unemployment and stagflation. The so-called new trade theory has revised the theory, taking into account economies of scale and imperfect competition in both factor and commodity markets, but a general discussion of immigration in terms of it would be too great a divergence for my purpose here. To concentrate on the possibility of mismatch as the cause of European stagflation I shall analyze immigration in the context of the Beveridge curve theory developed by Blanchard and Diamond, who followed and simplified the work of Pissarides.[29]

The centerpiece of these models is a matching function explaining new hires, H, as an increasing function with possible constant returns in vacancies, V, and unemployment, U:

$$H = am(V, U), a > 0, m'_V, m'_U \geq 0, m(0, U) = m(V, 0), = 0.$$

The matching function assumes that both vacant jobs and unemployed workers are heterogeneous (in education, training, experience, and other characteristics and requirements) and that both employer and worker are involved in search processes to find counterparts that are sufficiently similar to make an employment contract profitable to both sides. When the process is successful, hiring will take place. Wage rates

28. Greenwood and McDowell (1986, figure 1 and text) is a typical example of the first sort of analysis.
29. Blanchard and Diamond (1989); Pissarides (1986).

are assumed to be given. Thus, given the number of unemployed, the larger the number of vacancies, the higher the probability that a new hiring will take place. Conversely, given the number of vacancies, the larger the number of unemployed the higher the probability that a new hiring will take place.[30] Constant returns to scale may be assumed and have been postulated to produce neat mismatch indexes, but such assumptions are probably little more than wishful thinking.

Two easily understood dynamic relations can then be obtained from the definitional relations:

$$\dot{U} = -am + (q + \pi_0)(L - U)$$
$$\dot{V} = -am + (q - \pi_1)(L - U) + \pi_1\hat{L} - (\pi_0 + \pi_1)V$$

where L denotes the labor force and $\hat{L}$, the total number of productive jobs, q denotes the quit rate, and π_0 and π_1, respectively, are the probabilities of the elimination and the creation of productive jobs, that is, jobs that would be profitable if labor were available. The steady-state values of U and V have then to satisfy $\dot{U} = 0$ and $\dot{V} = 0$. Their intersection is a stable equilibrium in U and V and is interpreted as a point on the Beveridge curve. Now define $c = \pi_1/(\pi_0 + \pi_1)$, the proportion of productive jobs filled in the steady state, as an indicator of aggregate activity. Let $s = \hat{L}\pi_0 c$, the instantaneous flow of jobs changing between profitability and unprofitability in a steady state, indicate the degree of sectoral shifts and mismatch in the economy. Changes in c can be thought of as aggregate shocks (including aggregate policies and wage bargains) and s as sectoral shocks (including sectoral policies and wage bargains). Letting c vary, one can trace a Beveridge curve, *BB*, as shown in figure 9-1. Increasing or decreasing c results in a movement up or down the curve. Varying s, one generates shifts of the curve, proportional along rays through the origin, outward or inward with increasing or decreasing s, that is, mismatch.[31] Macroeconomic modeling now means modeling the determinants of c and s; this is the point at which, for instance, wage flexibility might be entered into the model.

Now consider immigration within the framework of this model. An increase in the labor force leads instantaneously to a corresponding increase in unemployment, given number of vacancies, from, say B_0 to B'.

30. An earlier attempt to build a joint theory of Beveridge and Phillips curves based on Dow and Dicks-Mireaux (1958) assuming homogeneous submarkets with disequilibrium was presented in Hansen (1970).

31. This is the conventional way of operating with the Beveridge curve in the tradition of Dow and Dicks-Mireaux. See Gordon (1967).

Figure 9-1. *Immigration and the Beveridge Curve*

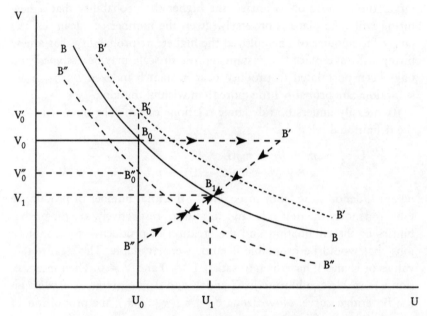

By virtue of the matching function, hirings increase, and both vacancies and unemployment decrease. The labor market's temporary equilibrium moves downward to the left from B' to B_1, where a new steady state is reached with higher unemployment and fewer vacancies. With a larger labor force the steady-state Beveridge curve may shift outward (to $B'B'$, for instance).[32] An expansionary policy to bring about the same level of unemployment as initially prevailed will result in more vacancies (V'_0) with the consequence that stagflation increases.

Now introduce immigration. Assume that for immigrants to find employment, work and residence permits are required (illegal immigration is disregarded). What effects does the model show between spontaneous immigration versus recruitment of foreign workers?

In the case of spontaneous immigration, foreign workers individually obtain work and residence permits, enter the country, and instantaneously augment the pool of the unemployed. From then on the process is the same as with the internal labor market shock analyzed above. If, however, the foreign workers line up to take the jobs native workers are unwilling to fill, then the matching function shifts up and the Beveridge

32. Blanchard and Diamond (1989) at least implies this plausible though unproven assumption.

curve shifts down to $B''B''$, with less mismatch as a result. However, it is not clear whether this common assumption is realistic. Much depends on the characteristics of the immigrants, the heterogeneity of the native work force, and the possible existence of segregated labor markets. Increased mismatch and stagflation is possible (in the case of educated, older foreigners), but improved matching and stagflation cannot be ruled out (as with unskilled, young foreigners).

Assume instead that selective recruitment of foreign workers to fill vacancies is permitted and that this is the only source of immigration. The dynamic path is now radically different. The temporary equilibrium shifts downward vertically from B_0 to B''. The subsequent development depends entirely on the legal situation of the recruited workers and the vigor of enforcement. With a rigorously implemented system of recruitment and rotation, the situation would be locked in B''. Otherwise the regulated, temporary equilibrium would shift upward to the right, ending on a possibly shifted Beveridge curve, $B''B''$ or $B'B'$, for instance, depending on the nature of immigrants and administration. In the short term stagflation clearly improves; in the long term it may improve or worsen as indicated.

Another body of labor market theory useful for analyzing policies and effects of immigration is the Lindbeck-Snower insider-outsider model of wage formation and unemployment.[33] In its extreme form this model assumes that all wage earners can be classified as insiders or as outsiders. Insiders participate in wage negotiations and agreements with employers (enterprises), their counterparts. They are assumed to pay no attention to the consequences for outsiders of the wage agreements reached. They only consider the consequences for insiders. If until this time insiders have been correctly informed and have negotiated wages to the precise level that the market can bear without loss of employment, so far so good. If mistakes have been made and wages are pushed too high, some insiders will become unemployed and will be outsiders. On balance the system therefore may generate increasingly excessive wages and increasing unemployment, increasing stagflation.

For the present analysis, the place of foreign workers in the insider-outsider hierarchy is crucial. The distinction between spontaneous immigration and foreign worker recruitment is again a good starting point. Spontaneous immigrants, even when they are legal, are the classic outsiders. Such labor may move up in the hierarchy, but the movement may

33. Lindbeck and Snower (1988).

take generations. With officially sponsored recruitment, however, foreign workers immediately become insiders, possibly even union members with a vote and social security, for the period of their contract. In this case, the effects on stagflation chiefly depend on the foreign workers' militancy and reservation wages.

Immigration and the Single Market

The Maastricht Treaty did little to clarify the future of immigration for the European Community. For the sake of argument, assume that the EC is a perfect customs union with common external tariffs as the only obstacle to trade with nonmembers, with free internal mobility for citizens and capital of member countries but without any common labor market policies regarding wages, employment, social security, and so forth. Even if common aggregate monetary and fiscal policies are assumed, the imperfections of labor mobility within the EC are sure to remain significant (due to such considerations as language, religion, ethnicity, and the availability of public goods). Hence, a common matching function and Beveridge curve may not exist, and average unemployment and vacancy rates as well as their regional dispersions may differ significantly among member countries.[34] What are the prospects of a common immigration policy in this setting?

The definition of a "common" immigration policy is by no means self-evident. Numerous alternatives can be visualized, ranging from totally free migration of labor (as will soon exist for capital) to a rigid immigration ban. Quota arrangements, with quotas distributed among member countries and prohibitions against immigrants' moving between member countries, are but one example of the various possible compromises. Because a recruitment-rotation policy might be attractive from an individual country's point of view, it is natural to first consider a common immigration policy that leaves each member country to pursue a rigorous version of such a policy (the subsidiarity problem thus being solved in favor of decentralization). Individual member countries might be strongly but very differently affected by this particular common policy; moreover no country was actually pursuing this policy in 1992. Would

---

34. Comparisons with U.S. internal migration and immigration policies might here be rewarding (Blanchard and Katz, 1992; Borjas and Trejo, 1991; Funkhouser and Trejo, 1992) but are beyond the scope of the present analysis.

this policy be attractive from a narrow EC point of view?[35] It is not clear, in any case, why any member country should adopt a policy of recruitment and rotation simply because it is permitted. Let us assume therefore that such a policy, decentralized with respect to implementation and administration, is imposed upon all member countries.

Assume that firms are permitted to hire labor from outside the Community solely to fill vacancies that are not expected to be filled by EC labor. "Rotation" signifies that foreign workers will be hired for a limited time without any possibility of contract renewal. Thus while recruitment will not directly create domestic unemployment, it may create complementary domestic employment and increase profits. With fewer vacancies and without more unemployment, money wages will tend to fall and some aggregate expansion (through monetary or fiscal policy, for example) should be possible without increased inflation. Possible income adjustments with efficient lump-sum transfers will only strengthen this effect. Finally, it can be assumed that labor from developing countries will prefer recruitment-rotation to no legal immigration at all.

A number of caveats should be noted. First, given the existence of several layers of government and administration, the meaning of the words centralization and decentralization needs to be carefully specified. Recruitment may be implemented by individual enterprises with permission from and oversight by the appropriate member country or the European Commission. Alternatively, it may be implemented and controlled by the member country or EC administrators directly. Joint implementaion is, of course, also possible.

Second, the steady-state assumptions of Blanchard and Diamond and of Pissarides applied to an economy with full employment might mean that recruitment-rotation immigration causes hiring of domestic labor to decrease and vacancies and unemployment for the domestic labor force to increase. However, the reduced inflationary pressures would permit a corresponding monetary or fiscal expansion, and the steady-state assumption accordingly does not upset the conclusion.

Third, a recruitment-rotation policy depends for its success on strict administration and control of recruitment. Recruited workers who quit would lose their residence visas, be deported, and replaced through new recruitment. Both employers and recruited foreign workers, however, have an incentive to evade these regulations—the worker for self-evident reasons, the employer because of the investment in training. Moreover,

---

35. The question has been raised by *Economist*, August 17, 1991, pp. 12–13.

if employers underreport vacancies, they may easily replace native employees with foreigners. Is compulsory vacancy reporting then necessary? This leads to the problem of foreign dumping of labor to which both the Community bureaucracy and unions adamantly object, instead favoring protectionism of both goods and labor.

Fourth, the extent to which vacancies in the EC may be filled by foreign labor depends on the quantity and composition of unfilled EC vacancies as well as the available supplies and composition of foreign labor. As early as the 1960s when European growth rates fell from very high to moderate, Kindleberger suggested that immigrants no longer provided the appropriate mix of skills formerly supplied by eastern European expellees and refugees, who had dominated the additions to the labor force. In his opinion, they "constituted one of the finest sources of additional labor in all of Europe. They were skilled in much higher proportions than foreign workers" generally.[36] Instead non-European "foreign workers" predominated during the 1960s and early 1970s and mismatch resulted. With stagflation in the 1980s this mismatch became even more pronounced. Hence, vacancies for other than unskilled and construction labor may not be easily filled by labor from countries such as Turkey, Egypt, and North Africa, rendering the scope of recruitment-rotation policies limited.

The breakup of the Soviet Union does not seem to have improved the situation for western Europe, although Soviet immigrants to Israel are a possible exception. It should be noted, however, that demographic predictions suggest an increasing shortage of younger workers in Europe during the 1990s and more so in the longer run.[37] Even so, for the 1990s the prospects for increasing vacancies seem slight, and a successful recruitment-rotation policy per se may at best make only a small impact on stagflation in the EC, to say nothing of unemployment in developing countries.

Conclusions

A detailed survey of immigration policies in Europe since World War II with an evaluation of alternative policies within the EC or EU, as the case may be, has not been possible in this short chapter. Political and administrative feasibility need to be balanced against economic effi-

36. Kindleberger (1967, p. 31).
37. OECD (1991, charts 5-2 and 5-4 and pp. 7, 62).

ciency. Available, reliable information about these matters is far from sufficient to reach definitive conclusions. Tentative analysis suggests that decentralized recruitment-rotation policy may be economically beneficial for both Community and member country, but the scope for such policy appears limited even in the long run and economic rationality may not be decisive in future immigration policies whatever the subsidiarity situation becomes.

References

Akerlof, George A., and Brian G. M. Main. 1980. "Unemployment Spells and Unemployment Experience." *American Economic Review* 70 (December): 885–93.

Blanchard, Oliver J., and Peter Diamond. 1989. "The Beveridge Curve." *Brookings Papers on Economic Activity* 1: 1–60.

Blanchard, Oliver J., and L. F. Katz. 1992. "Regional Evolutions." *Brookings Papers on Economic Activity* 1: 1–61.

Böhning, W. R. 1984. *Studies in International Labour Migration.* MacMillan.

Borjas, George J., and Stephen J. Trejo. 1991. "Immigrant Participation in the Welfare System." *Industrial and Labor Relations Review* 44 (January): 195–211.

Bundesministerium für Arbeit und Sozialordnung. 1986. *Situation der ausländischen Arbeitnehmer und ihrer Familienangehörigen in der Bundesrepublik Deutschland—Repräsentativuntersuchung '85.* Bonn.

Chabanas, N., and S. Volkoff. 1973. "Les Salaires dans l'Industrie, le Commerce et les Services en 1970." *Collections de l'INSEC Serie M,* no. 29 (December). Paris.

Chiswick, Barry R. 1980. "The Earnings of White and Coloured Male Immigrants in Britain." *Economica* (February): 81–87.

———. 1992. "Review of 1991." John M. Abowd and Richard B. Freeman, eds., Immigration, Trade and the Labor Market. *Journal of Economic Literature* 30 (March): 212–13.

Dicks-Mireaux, L. A., and Christopher R. Dow. 1959. "The Determinants of Wage Inflation: United Kingdom, 1946–56." *Journal of the Royal Statistical Society,* series A (General), pt. 2.

Dow, Christopher R., and Leslie A. Dicks-Mireaux. 1958. "The Excess Demand for Labour: A Study of Conditions in Great Britain, 1946–1956." *Oxford Economic Papers* (February).

Drèze, Jacques H., and Charles R. Bean. 1990. "Europe's Unemployment Problem: Introduction and Synthesis." In Jacques H. Drèze and Charles R. Bean, eds., *Europe's Unemployment Problem.* MIT Press.

Edye, Dave. 1987. *Immigrant Labour and Government Policy: The Cases of the Federal Republic and France.* Brookfield, Vt.: Gower.

Franz, Wolfgang. 1981. "Employment Policy and Labour Supply of Foreign Workers in the Federal Republic of Germany: A Theoretical and Empirical Analysis." *Zeitschrift für die gesamte Staatswissenschaft* 137.

———. 1991. "Match and Mismatch in the German Labor Market." In Fiorella P. Schioppa, ed., *Mismatch and Labour Mobility.* Cambridge University Press.

Funkhouser, Edward, and Stephen J. Trejo. 1992. "The Decline in Immigrant Labor Market Skills: Did It Continue in the 1980s?" University of California at Santa Barbara, Department of Economics.

Gordon, Robert A. 1967. *The Goal of Full Employment.* Wiley.

Greenwood, Michael J. 1975. "Research on Internal Migration in the United States: A Survey." *Journal of Economic Literature* (December).

Greenwood, Michael J., and John M. McDowell. 1986. "The Factor Market Consequences of U.S. Immigration." *Journal of Economic Literature* (December).

Hammar, Tomas. 1985. *European Immigration Policy.* Cambridge University Press.

Hansen, Bent. 1970. "Excess Demand, Unemployment, Vacancies, and Wages." *Quarterly Journal of Economics* 74 (February): 1–23.

———. 1990. "European Labor Immigration: Its Past, Present, and Future," working paper. University of California at Berkeley, Department of Economics.

Jackman, Richard, Richard Layard, and Christopher Pissarides. 1989. "On Vacancies." *Oxford Bulletin of Economics and Statistics* 51 (November): 377–94.

Jackman, Richard, Richard Layard, and Savvas Savouri. 1991. "Mismatch: A Framework for Thought." In Fiorella P. Schioppa, ed., *Mismatch and Labour Mobility.* Cambridge University Press.

Karlson, T., and Karl Gustaf Löfgren. 1990. "Comments on J. Dreze and C. Bean, European Unemployment." *Scandinavian Journal of Economics* 92 (no. 2):135–65.

Kennedy-Brenner, Carliene. 1979. *Foreign Workers and Immigration Policy: The Case of France.* Paris: OECD.

Kindleberger, Charles P. 1967. *Europe's Postwar Growth—The Role of Labor Supply.* Harvard University Press.

Lindbeck, A., and D. J. Snower. 1988. *The Insider Outsider Theory of Employment and Unemployment.* Cambridge, England: Cambridge University Press.

OECD. 1985. "The Labour Market Implications of International Migration in Selected O.E.C.D. Countries." *Employment Outlook.* Paris.

———. 1987. *The Future of Migration.* Paris.

———. 1991. *Migration: The Demographic Aspects.* Paris.

10a Piore, Michael J. 1979. *Birds of Passage: Migrant Labor and Industrial Societies.* Cambridge University Press.

Pissarides, Christopher. 1986. "Unemployment and Vacancies in Britain." *Economic Policy, A European Forum* 3 (October): 499–541.

Schettkat, Ronald. 1992. *The Labor Market Dynamics of Economic Restructuring: The United States and Germany in Transition.* Praeger.

Ulman, L., and R. J. Flanagan. 1971. *Wage Restraint: A Study of Incomes Policies in Western Europe.* University of California Press.

Wadensjö, Eskil. 1975. "Remuneration of Migrant Workers in Sweden." *International Labour Review* 112 (July): 1–14.

CHAPTER TEN

European Economic Integration and U.S. Wages and Employment

William T. Dickens

In 1985 A white paper drafted by the European Community Commission under the leadership of Lord Cockfield identified 300 legislative changes necessary to complete the integration of the economies of the EC.[1] The Single European Act adopted by the European Parliament in February 1986 put in place the machinery to accomplish this agenda and set Europe on the course for complete economic integration, with the target year being 1992. Although the totality of the changes needed to accomplish this end are overwhelmingly complex, most can be summarized under four broad headings:

—Eliminating differences in regulatory and technical standards.

—Eliminating nontariff barriers to trade—mostly customs delays and related paperwork since most tariffs and quotas have already been eliminated.

—Opening up competition for government purchases in each nation to firms in all EC nations.

—Eliminating laws preventing providers of certain services (financial and transportation services, for instance) from operating across national boundaries.

The first and (to a lesser extent) the second of these changes are expected to have tremendous effects on the EC market for manufactured goods. The third can be expected to increase competitive pressures on many firms, and the import of the fourth for the affected sectors is obvious.

The research assistance of Michael Barnes, Gustavo Gonzaga, and Bryan Lincoln is gratefully acknowledged as is the generous research support of the National Commission for Employment Policy, the Institute of Industrial Relations, and the Center for Western European Studies at the University of California, Berkeley.
1. European Community Commission (1988).

What is not obvious is just how these changes will affect the EC and the rest of the world. Although considerable progress has been made toward defining how the issues raised by the 1985 white paper will be dealt with, many of the most important issues are still unresolved—we do not yet know what the single market will look like. Further, many of the most important questions about its effects depend not on the responses to the problems outlined in the white paper, but on the relations of the newly integrated EC to the rest of the world. What sort of access will other countries have and what will be the quid pro quo for that access?

Even if these uncertainties were resolved, the problem of assessing the effects of the integrated market would still be daunting. Economists are practiced at gauging the effects of quantitative changes. The analysis of the reduction of tariffs or quotas has been common practice for years—the analysis of qualitative changes is a far greater challenge. This is particularly true given that the greatest effects are expected to flow from increased market size and hence opportunities for realizing economies of scale. The relevance of such considerations for growth is something that has only recently begun to receive serious attention in economics.

Consequently, the present analysis has the status of informed speculation based on informed speculation. No independent attempt is made to assess the effects of the single market on the EC; critical readings of existing studies are presented instead. The analysis is further limited in that it concentrates exclusively on the market reforms.[2] The first section considers the impact of the planned part of the integrated market from the perspective of standard models of trade and concludes that effects are likely to be small. The subsequent section discusses several considerations that may complicate the effects of the single market for the United States, including the possibility of a major trade war with Europe resulting in prohibitive tariffs. Other authors have dubbed this the Fortress Europe disaster scenario. In this case the possibility of large macroeconomic effects is found.

These two sections mainly present a critical review and extension of existing studies. The next section considers the issue from a new perspective. It analyzes the effects of European trade, taking into account the welfare effects resulting from labor market distortions. This section briefly describes labor-rents models and presents some of the evidence for their relevance. The analysis of the effects of the planned changes is

2. Dickens (forthcoming) considers the implications of the full range of developments.

then developed in such a model. Finally the implications of some of the special considerations raised earlier in the chapter are examined in light of the labor-rents model. Despite good reason to expect otherwise, none of the analysis of the first two sections is substantially changed. However, a labor-rents analysis of some important issues in current trade relations between the Community and the United States suggests that a change in U.S. trade strategy may be appropriate.

The Standard Analyses

What impact will the single integrated market have on Europe? All studies anticipate at least some increase in productivity relying on basic features of the economic analysis of trade expansion: the elimination of distortions through the removal of barriers to trade and a reduction of monopoly power; increased gains from comparative advantage; economies of scale; and reduced costs for existing trade because of the eradication of customs barriers. European consumers are expected to be the major beneficiaries with lower priced goods resulting from increased productivity and decreased monopoly power. Some gains will certainly be realized; how large they will be is an open question.

The official estimate of the EC as reported by the Cecchini commission is a range the midpoint of which is an increase in GDP of 4.5 percent above normal growth.[3] On the low end is a study by Data Resources, Inc., predicting an increase of only 0.5 percent through 1995.[4] Richard Baldwin gives an analysis based on a model with external increasing returns to scale and argues that the present value of gains could be as large as 35 percent of GDP over the long term once the dynamics of savings and investment are taken into account.[5]

Whatever the size of the effects, repercussions are certain to be felt in the United States through any of three possible routes: immigration, capital markets, and trade in goods and services. Even the largest changes are unlikely to have a significant impact on immigration to the United States given the low responsiveness of immigration to economic incentives and U.S. immigration policy. The present study focuses on the other routes.

3. Cecchini (1988, p. 101).
4. Data Resources, Inc. (1989).
5. Baldwin (1989).

Impact on Capital Markets

The effect of the integrated European market on world capital markets is not clear. On the one hand the increased productivity of the EC should lead to increased demand for investment. On the other hand, increased income will increase private savings and, in the current climate, may reduce fiscal deficits, thereby increasing public savings. It is impossible to say a priori whether these savings effects will be larger or smaller than the effects on the demand for capital. However, since the effects on savings will not be realized until after the productivity effects, it seems likely that there will be an increase in the demand for foreign capital in the short term that will diminish and possibly be reversed in the long term.

Thus in the short term the integrated market can be expected to put further upward pressure on world interest rates, a third factor in addition to the demand for capital for the rebuilding of eastern Europe and record U.S. fiscal deficits. Some reduction in capital flows from Europe to the United States might be expected. These have been positive, though falling, in recent years. Whether these capital market effects will be discernible will depend on the size of the European demand relative to the increase in the U.S. fiscal deficit and the effect of the impending recovery on demand for capital in the United States.

To induce a capital outflow from the United States to Europe, or to reduce the current inflow, U.S. terms of trade with Europe would have to deteriorate. This should be only a short-term effect with the change abating and perhaps reversing as the enhancing effects of the single market on productivity make themselves felt and demands for foreign capital fall.

Trade Effects

In addition to the effects on capital markets, an increase in EC productivity, particularly in traded goods, can be expected to have trade-creating and positive terms-of-trade effects for the United States. However, the completion of the internal market in the EC can also be expected to have trade-diverting effects as Europeans (and perhaps others) substitute European goods, now lower priced, for U.S. imports.

In theory it is impossible to determine whether trade creation or trade diversion will dominate. Moreover, the empirical literature hardly addresses the issue of external trade creation, providing only fragmentary and inconclusive evidence.[6]

A companion piece to the Cecchini study by Michael Emerson and others estimates that trade diversion may amount to as much as 8 percent of EC imports.[7] Given the similarity of the U.S. and European economies trade diversion for imports from the United States might be larger than for imports generally, possibly twice as large. However this study does not account for the trade-creating effects of growth. With an income elasticity of EC demand for U.S. exports of approximately 2,[8] the Cecchini report's estimate of EC growth implies a trade creation effect of 9 percent. Thus the tendencies to create or divert trade seem likely to be roughly offsetting, with the sign of the effect depending mainly on the magnitude of European income growth.

Quantifying the Effects

What do existing studies say about the size of the capital and goods market effects? Only the Congressional Budget Office's study attempts to estimate the effect on interest rates.[9] Using two different world models and assuming the Cecchini estimates of the magnitudes of the productivity effects, the Congressional Budget Office finds the effect on U.S. real long-term interest rates peaking at a maximum increase of 50 basis points in 1991, then declining to nothing by 2000. Alternatively, when a high-savings fiscal policy is assumed for the EC and a different world model used, U.S. interest rates are predicted to be about 20 basis points lower than they would otherwise have been for most of the 1990s.

Assuming a Cobb-Douglas model of output and factor returns in the United States, with a capital share of 20 percent, and a real return on capital of 10 percent, an increase of 0.5 percentage points in the real return on capital might be expected to decrease the marginal product of

6. Dickens (forthcoming). One widely cited study, Yannopoulos (1988, table 7.11), incorrectly reports the results of a previous study as indicating a significant increase in trade with the United States, though the cited study instead measures total external trade creation with the rest of the world.

7. Emerson and others (1988). Hufbauer (1990) cites a figure of only 2.6 percent, but he reads table A-5 in Emerson rather than A-6. Freeman and Katz (1990) cite an estimate of 10 percent from Emerson, presumably from the macroeconomic estimates of a 1 percent deterioration in Europe's trade balance in one scenario. The 8 percent figure cited here comes from column 4 in table A-6.

8. Cline (1989).

9. Congressional Budget Office (1990).

labor by about 2.5 percent.[10] Given the study's prediction that any interest rate increase will be transitory, the effect can be expected to be significantly less than this. A smaller decline in real rates would have even smaller effects of an opposite sign—about a 1 percent increase in the real wage.

The Congressional Budget Office study also considers how the changes in demand for capital and U.S. exports affect terms of trade. Estimates of the magnitude of the effects range from an initial 1.7 percent real depreciation of the dollar over the short term to an appreciation of about 4 percent continuing into the next century. With the U.S. ratio of imports to national income running around 17 percent, a 4 percent appreciation would increase the real purchasing power of U.S. wages by about 0.7 percent. This estimate is at the high end of the range; other scenarios and models predict effects about half this size. The Congressional Budget Office study does not consider the effects of terms of trade on trade diversion. To the extent that they offset trade creation, the total effect would be smaller. Overall real U.S. labor compensation seems likely to increase less than 1 percent, with some possibility of short-term losses of about the same magnitude.

Employment Effects

How will European integration affect employment? The worst-case scenario from the Congressional Budget Office study, a 10 percent worsening in the U.S. current account, would give rise to a drag on aggregate demand of less than 1.6 percent of GNP over a period of about five years. With exports to Europe accounting for only about 15 percent of U.S. trade, the Congressional Budget Office's 10 percent estimate seems very high. Thus it seems safe to conclude that the macroeconomic effects on employment are likely to be very small. Even with a consumption mul-

---

10. This assumes a fixed supply of labor and a perfectly elastic demand for output. If labor supply is at all elastic or product demand less than perfectly elastic, the effects would be smaller. Cobb-Douglas technology implies $Y = AK^\alpha L^{1-\alpha}$, where Y is output, K is capital, L is labor, A is total factor productivity, and α is capital's share of income. Assuming perfectly inelastic supply of labor and perfectly elastic demand for output, demand for capital is $K = (0.2\ PA/i)^{1.25}L$, where P is the price of the good, i is the cost of capital, and α is assumed to be 0.2. The marginal product of labor is $0.8\ AP\ (K/L)^{0.2}$. Substituting the demand for capital into this equation yields $MPL = 0.8\ PA\ (0.2\ PA/i)^{0.25}$, or an elasticity of MPL with respect to an i of -0.25. Assuming a real return on capital of 5 percent gives this figure.

tiplier of 2, Okun's law would predict a slowing of the growth of labor demand of only 0.25 percent a year for about five years.[11]

The displacement effects caused by changes in trade demand are likely to be similarly small. If U.S. exports to Europe were to decrease by 16 percent, this would only amount to a loss of about $16 billion, or about 325,000 jobs.[12] This would be an insignificant contribution to the total displacement created by the disappearance of jobs in the United States, which is conservatively estimated to be 14 million annually.[13]

Besides the effects on labor income and employment, European integration may also affect U.S. distribution of income. Some authors have suggested that an increased demand for skilled workers in the United States because of expanding trade may have led to the increased dispersion of incomes the United States experienced in the 1980s.[14] Given that reasonable estimates of trade creation or diversion from an integrated European market place the net effect at far less than 20 percent of U.S. trade with the EC, and given that EC trade with the United States is less than 20 percent of all trade, the anticipated changes in the importance of trade for the U.S. economy amount to less than 4 percent. Compared with the near doubling in the real value of both imports and exports in the 1980s in the United States, it is clear that any effects of the European integration on income distribution in the United States will be extremely small.

Considered by any measure, the aggregate impact of the European market on U.S. employment and compensation is bound to be small. However, within particular industries or under certain circumstances, these effects may loom larger.

Special Considerations

The first special consideration of the effects of the integrated market is the planned changes in government procurement policies; these hold out

11. Okun's Law states that employment changes less than output during recessions, so that a 1 percent decline in employment will follow a 2.5 percent to 3.0 percent decline in output.

12. The job loss was computed using the input-output model described in the labor-rents section.

13. Leonard (1987), Davis and Haltiwanger (1989). The potential for a far smaller number of job losses from the creation of a North American Free Trade Area has created considerable concern and political activity. However, U.S. labor correctly views the United States as not having much say in European progress towards economic union.

14. Murphy and Welch (1988); Katz and Murphy (1990).

some hope of increased sales for U.S. companies, particularly makers of telecommunications equipment.

This liberalization of government procurement is supposed to increase intra-Community competition for government contracts in all countries. While all European firms will supposedly be on an equal footing, the EC appears to be heading toward adopting rules requiring at least 50 percent EC content in all procurement in addition to granting a 3 percent preference to domestic companies. These rules are very similar to buy-American provisions in recent U.S. trade legislation, though the EC rules are slightly less restrictive. Nonetheless, the United States is complaining. It is primarily concerned that the rules would unfairly restrict U.S. manufacturers of telecommunications equipment from competing for European business to the same extent as European firms can compete in the recently deregulated U.S. market. Most telecommunications services in Europe are provided by state-run monopolies. Should the United States be successful in negotiating with the EC on this issue, there could be a windfall for U.S. firms—though not necessarily for U.S. workers if most of the production is based in Europe.

Special circumstances may also affect the fortunes of industries besides telecommunications. There has been considerable intrigue concerning how the EC will deal with foreign firms in banking, semiconductors, electronics, automobiles, and agriculture.

Financial and Banking Services

To accomplish substantial integration and deregulation of European financial markets, barriers to intra-Community banking and investment are being eliminated, creating the largest integrated market for financial services anywhere. This is a potential boon not only to European firms, but to banks and securities firms around the world. Europeans have recognized the value of access to this market and have suggested that it will only come at a price.

Initially it was proposed that to gain access to the European market other countries would have to allow EC firms identical access to their financial markets. The United States strenuously objected; such access is considered impossible given the restrictive regulation of U.S. banking and securities firms. EC officials have since reassured the United States that it need only offer European firms the same access to its markets as U.S. firms enjoy. Europeans have insisted that the restrictions were mainly conceived with Japan in mind; European firms have been very unsuccessful in marketing financial services there. Whatever the outcome, the effects on the U.S. labor market are likely to be very small, even in the banking industry. If U.S. firms expand, most of the new employment created will be in Europe.

Electronics and Semiconductors

An area where tensions are fairly high and outcomes uncertain is semiconductors and electronics. The EC's role in producing semiconductors diminished to virtually nothing in the 1980s. It was considered sufficiently unimportant that Japan and the United States could ignore it in making an agreement on world prices for chips in the mid-1980s. This outraged the EC, which complained to the GATT and succeeded in having the agreement declared illegal. Nonetheless, the United States has indicated to Japan that it expects Japan to abide by the agreement. The potential for trilateral trouble increases as semiconductor prices fall toward the floors set in the U.S.-Japan accord.

Because of the embarrassment of falling so far behind in semiconductor technology, the EC has set up several major research programs to create semiconductor products and applications to return to the forefront in this technology.

There have also been discussions to the effect that the EC might require chips sold in its market to be diffused there. (Diffusion is the etching of the circuit onto the silicon wafer.) U.S. firms have objected to this even though they are well positioned to gain from such a move. The Japanese have many chip assembly plants in Europe but few diffusion facilities. U.S. firms have considerable diffusion capacity in place.

Although EC officials deny that plans are being made to restrict semiconductor imports, rumors to that effect are sufficiently credible that European producers have been able to garner a larger share of the market because of fears of a cutoff of supplies of foreign equipment. Such restrictions could severely harm U.S. producers, who enjoy a large market share. Even if the short-term problems of protection fail to materialize, EC support for research in high-tech electronics is strong, threatening the long-term competitive position of U.S. firms.

Agriculture

Tensions between the United States and the EC are the highest over agricultural policy. Like many others, the governments of the EC must contend with politically powerful agricultural interests that insist on protection. This is particularly true of France. U.S. agricultural exports account for a large part of total U.S. exports to the EC, and their share would be much larger if existing barriers were removed. U.S. farm interests have fought for their removal, and the most recent round of GATT negotiations have reached an impasse because of disagreements between the United States and the EC over EC member states' protection of agriculture.

If the EC were to acquiesce, trade between the United States and the EC would undoubtedly expand, and U.S. terms of trade with Europe would improve. Although the effects would be small on the aggregate level, they might well be significant in the agricultural sector. However, such a move might have negative consequences for the United States as well (see the section on labor rents).

Automotive Exports

U.S. auto exports to the EC are significant and with the lowering of European barriers their potential to grow is great. The United States is currently the beneficiary of voluntary export restriction agreements between Japan and a number of European countries. Japanese cars are viewed as the major competition for U.S. firms in many countries. The most pressing issue is whether the existing voluntary export restrictions will be extended Community-wide. The voluntary export restriction has now been extended through the end of the century. Thereafter, the future for U.S. and European automakers is uncertain.

Another aspect of this issue may be of more concern to U.S. workers. Much of the EC demand for U.S. cars is now being satisfied with production in Europe. A considerable amount of the EC demand for Japanese cars is being satisfied with production in U.S. plants. Currently, the EC treats these cars as Japanese made. The United States has complained, but is not in a strong bargaining position because of its insistence that Japanese cars produced in Canada are Japanese and therefore subject to voluntary export restriction agreements between the United States and Japan.

Except for the bailouts of a few large companies and its Byzantine system of support for agriculture, the United States has eschewed industrial targeting or industrial policy.[15] This is certainly not true of Europe, where specific industrial subsidies for employment, capital, and research

---

15. Many observers have suggested that U.S. defense procurement amounts to an unconscious industrial policy, and it is true that many industries in which the United States enjoys an advantage in world trade are beholden to defense largesse for their development.

and development are the rule. The excesses of some of these policies have been identified as causing Eurosclerosis in at least one country.[16] This difference in approach to industrial policy is unlikely to disappear with the advent of the single European market. The EC already has a huge array of Community-wide initiatives under way targeting aerospace, electronics, communications, and other industries.

From the perspective of the standard long-term trade model, there is little a country can hope to achieve by subsidizing its exports beyond improving the terms of trade of its partners. However, modern strategic trade theory has suggested that countries may be able to capture monopoly profits by subsidizing industries with increasing returns to scale. The EC seems to have embraced this theory despite a lack of empirical evidence. The few studies that have been done suggest that the little a country may gain in monopoly profits from a project such as Airbus are more than offset by the costs.[17] However, such conclusion are not definitive. In particular, the labor-rents perspective on the value of industrial targeting may yet vindicate the European perspective.

European managers have for long expressed concern that the advantages of increased economic integration may not go to their firms but to foreign producers instead. Japanese and U.S. producers already enjoy economies of scale that may allow them to beat out competition from small European producers in the newly integrated EC market. Further, many U.S. and Japanese businesses already have experience dealing with the EC market in industries, such as autos, in which each country has a dominant national firm with few sales outside the home state.

Fortress Europe

To assuage these concerns and to signal to foreign countries that they must be willing to negotiate access to the EC, Willy DeClercq, the EC commissioner for external relations, announced in 1988 that "we see no reason why the benefits of our internal liberalization should be extended unilaterally to third countries." [18] This touched off a flurry of speculation that the EC intended to bar foreign participation in its internal market unless significant trade concessions were made. This gave birth to fears of Fortress Europe, a wall of trade barriers that would close off world access.

16. Leonard and Van Audenrode (1991).
17. See Baldwin and Krugman (1988).
18. DeClercq (1988).

These original fears have abated, at least in the United States. For instance it had been feared that U.S. firms would not be allowed any say in setting EC standards. In fact, U.S. firms and the American National Standards Institute (ANSI) have had considerable say in the process. Earlier fears that U.S. banks would be shut out of the EC market have also dissipated. But this may be only the prelude to more serious problems later.

Once full integration is accomplished, pressures for protection may prove irresistible. The inevitable rationalization will mean severe displacement as previously protected national firms are beaten out by more efficient European and foreign firms. Also, tensions are high between the United States and the EC over a wide range of issues, including public procurement, agricultural policy, and semiconductor trade. These problems could flare up at any time and result in a devastating trade war.

What would be the effects of a trade war that reduced trade between the United States and the EC by one-half?[19] Obviously they would be considerably greater than the effects of liberalization described earlier. With EC trade accounting for more than 15 percent of U.S. exports, a sudden reduction by half of U.S. trade would amount to a loss of more than 1.2 percent of GNP to autonomous spending.[20] In the short term, increased autonomous import demand would be unlikely to make up for much of this. Given a multiplier of 2, the static loss of aggregate demand would amount to more than 2.5 percent. Undergoing such a loss all at once in the middle of a recovery from a recession would undoubtedly cause another serious recession. Further, with U.S. fiscal deficits at historically high levels, the political will to deal with the problem through fiscal policy would be limited. There might even be a temptation to exacerbate the problem with tax increases to balance a growing budget deficit. The ability of monetary policy to address the problem, already in question because of the current low interest rates, might be reduced further by inflationary pressures brought on by the increased prices of European goods. The possibility exists for a disaster of major proportions.

In comparison, the long-term costs of such a loss of trade from balanced increases in tariffs in the EC and the United States are very small. With the ratio of U.S. imports from the EC to U.S. GNP at less than 4 percent, if gains from trade are an unimaginably large 50 percent of the value of trade (for purposes of argument), welfare losses would be less

19. A decline of this magnitude has some precedence. Trade with Europe fell by more than this amount in the aftermath of the Smoot-Hawley tariff and the Great Depression.
20. Organization for Economic Cooperation and Development (1990).

than 1 percent of national income. Thus the great threat of a trade war with Europe lies in its immediate macroeconomic consequences.

The Labor-Rents Perspective

In basic trade theory—the source of the preference for free trade evinced by most economists and many policymakers—there is no reason for countries to change the mix of goods they import and export. International prices and the profit motive will lead firms to export those goods in whose production the country has a comparative advantage in exchange for goods in which other countries have comparative advantages. Absolute free trade leaves all countries better off.

Modern strategic trade theory suggests that this free trade prescription is not always the best medicine. However, concrete examples and analyses of strategic trade policy that suggest where it might be successful have not yet been developed. But strategic trade theory is not the only rationale for active trade policy.

Distortions in factor markets can give rise to situations in which trade policies can provide second-best solutions to the problem of maximizing social welfare. In particular, if wages are not equalized across different sectors of the economy, there are potential welfare gains to industrial or trade policies that increase employment in the high-wage sectors.[21] The welfare gains arise because the shadow cost to society of moving a worker from the low-wage to the high-wage sector is the individual's output in the low-wage sector, which is equal to the individual's wage in the low-wage sector, due to the profit-maximizing labor demand decisions of firms in that sector. However, the cost to a firm in the high-wage sector is the high wage. Consequently profit-maximizing high-wage firms hire too few workers from society's perspective. Policies that increase employment in the high-wage sector increase national income by the approximate difference in wages between the two sectors (which is equal to the difference in the marginal revenue product of labor) times the number of workers relocated.[22]

While it has long been recognized that developing countries suffer from wage dualism, mainstream economics in the United States has only recently begun to treat seriously the idea that wages typically differ sub-

21. See for example Bhagwati and Srinivasan (1983).
22. See Dickens (1992) for a discussion of these points and an evaluation of arguments against them.

stantially between industries. There have been two reasons for this growth of interest in labor market segmentation. First, the quest for an understanding of the microeconomic foundations of unemployment has led to the development of a number of models in which profit-maximizing employers set wages above the level required to clear the market despite the excess supply of labor this creates. In efficiency wage models this is done because increasing the wage increases worker productivity. It may do this by increasing the disciplinary effectiveness of the threat of firing, decreasing the likelihood that workers will quit (wasting firm-specific training), increasing the quality of the applicant pool, or decreasing the amount of time it takes to fill job vacancies.[23] Another explanation is provided by rent-extraction or insider-outsider models in which the threat of collective action by workers forces a firm to share the returns to fixed capital, worker training, or both, with workers.

These theoretical developments have given rise to a growing empirical literature that explores wage differences and attempts to distinguish possible explanations. Most important from the policymaking perspective has been the evidence on interindustry wage differences. Several studies have now established that even after controlling for many individual and geographic factors, wages differ substantially between industries. Standard deviations of log wages across industries are 10 to 20 percent. Further, the pattern of industries that pay more is stable over long periods of time, ruling out the possibility that the differences are due to transient changes in the demand for labor in some industries. Not only is the pattern stable across time, it is also stable across countries and occupations. High-wage industries are high-wage industries everywhere and for all workers in all occupations within the industry.

Because even the best data sets are limited in the individual characteristics available in them, it has often been suggested that interindustry wage differences are due to unobservable differences in worker quality. A simple test of this hypothesis is to see whether workers who change industries incur wage changes of the same size as the average wage difference between the industries. If worker quality is the reason for the interindustry differences and quality is equally valuable everywhere workers' wages should not change. Several studies have now examined this question, and all but one have concluded that wages change by nearly the full amount of the interindustry difference. Attempts to repli-

---

23. See Dickens and Lang (1993) for a review of these theories as well as the empirical evidence.

cate the one study that found otherwise (using a different data set from the original study) were unsuccessful—the replication found that the wage change for industry changers was nearly the same size as the interindustry difference.

Finally, if interindustry differences do not reflect the inherent productivity of workers employed in the industry or the compensation for job characterstics, there should be evidence that higher-wage jobs are in greater demand among workers than low-wage jobs. Such evidence exists. Several studies have shown a negative correlation between quit rates and industry wage differences. A recent study also shows that high-wage jobs receive a greater number of applications per open position than low-wage jobs.[24]

If high-wage industries are paying higher than market clearing wages, worker productivity in those industries is greater than that of other industries.[25] A country can improve the productivity of its economy by increasing employment in the high-wage industry. The most direct way to do this is with employment subsidies to that industry. However this may not be politically feasible. It may be easier to increase demand in the high-wage industry by promoting the export of high-wage goods, restricting their import, or both.[26]

But with the pattern of industry wage differences so similar around the world, all countries will want to increase employment in the same industries, setting the stage for potentially destructive trade wars. If countries attempt to pursue such policies by restricting imports, the resulting loss of trade due to balanced increases in tariffs around the world would impose welfare losses on nearly all, if not all, countries. However, if all countries attempt to press their national interest by using export subsidies (a more rational policy if high-wage industries are also industries with significant returns to scale), it is possible to reach an optimal outcome through escalation of subsidies to the Nash equilibrium level.[27]

24. This and other evidence is summarized in Dickens and Lang (forthcoming).

25. This need not be the case in rent-extraction and insider-ousider models, as Topel (1989) points out. Dickens (1989) argues that models where employment is set efficiently are unrealistic and presents an alternative rent-extraction model where the marginal revenue product of labor is nearly equal to the wage.

26. For example, Dickens (1992) redoes problematic calculations from Katz and Summers (1989) to show that EC subsidies to Airbus were productivity enhancing when the gain in employment in high-wage production is taken into account. This reverses the conclusion of Baldwin and Krugman (1987) that the Airbus subsidies failed to produce a positive return.

27. Dickens and Lang (1989). A Nash equilibrium is reached when neither party can further its interests by making unilateral changes.

Europe is actively pursuing subsidies for high-wage industries: electronics, aerospace, autos, and others. The United States has traditionally avoided such policies. Further, the United States has a large surplus in agricultural trade ($5 billion in 1984) and a deficit in automobile trade (nearly $2 billion in 1984). Agriculture is the lowest-wage industry among traded goods. Autos are among the highest. A country that exports agricultural goods and imports autos would have to have a very strong comparative advantage in agriculture to overcome the loss of welfare from the loss of productivity due to the movement of labor from the high-wage to the low-wage sector. From these figures it is possible that increased trade with Europe could be significantly less beneficial to the United States than it would be to Europe. It is even possible that an increase in agricultural exports to the EC could worsen welfare in the United States.

How does one measure the effect that the composition of a country's trade with respect to low- and high-wage industries has on its welfare? In theory the gain to a country of increasing high-wage employment is the difference between the wage and the shadow cost of labor to that sector. In the simplest models this equals the difference between the wages in the industries a worker is moving between. However, when the possibility of unemployment, changing labor supply, and differences in labor quality are taken into account, the problem becomes more complicated.

Other studies have dealt with the problem of labor quality by adjusting industry wage differences for observable variations in labor quality using regression techniques.[28] This technique is far from perfect because remaining wage differences may still reflect unobservable variations in labor quality. Alternatively, in some models workers of high ability may sort into high-wage jobs as employers attempt to regain some of their wage premium by hiring high-quality workers. However, the social return to ability may be far smaller than the individual returns in such models. Regression techniques will identify the individual returns and will therefore overstate the shadow cost of highly educated and experienced labor thus biasing downward the measured industry differences. Despite these problems this study uses the regression method.[29]

A first measure of the welfare consequences of industry wage differences is the difference in the shadow cost of domestic production of im-

28. Dickens and Lang (1989); Katz and Summers (1989); Dickens (1992).
29. The estimates of the shadow costs of production used here are developed in Dickens (1992).

port-competing goods as opposed to exports. The difference between shadow cost and price are those due to labor rents.

To compute the shadow cost of domestic production of U.S. exports to the EC, U.S. merchandise exports to the EC were multiplied by the Leontief inverse of a seventy-nine sector U.S. input-output matrix, augmented to take into account capital use as well as intermediate inputs, to obtain the implied final demand in each sector. These figures were multiplied by labor coefficients to obtain the number of worker-hours needed in each sector to produce the final demand. The inner product of the vector of hours and the vector of wage surpluses was computed and divided by the total value of U.S. exports to the EC. Wage surpluses were defined as the difference between the earnings of workers in the industry and the average worker in the economy corrected for differences in individual characteristics. Using the theory discussed earlier, this amount is an estimate of the difference between the market price and the shadow cost of our exports to the EC. Analogous computations were performed for U.S. imports originating in the EC. The computations were done for U.S. trade in 1990.

Remarkably, despite the differences in trade composition described earlier, the labor-rents contents of imports and exports are fairly close. The shadow cost of production is 95 cents for each $1.00 of exports to the EC. The shadow cost of domestic production of import-competing goods is measured as 96 cents for each $1.00 of imports. Given the uncertainty in the measurement of these figures, they can be considered equal. Thus to a reasonable approximation, balanced trade between the United States and the EC has no net welfare effects for either party due to the presence of labor rents.[30]

Although the average values of labor rents in imports and exports are nearly equal, it need not be the case that marginal changes in trade— such as those likely to be induced by the integrated European market— will bring about equal changes in flows of labor rents. However, when a simple model of the sectoral responsiveness of U.S. exports and imports to exchange rate changes is estimated and marginal changes are analyzed, the results are nearly identical.

One conclusion of this analysis is that taking labor rents into account does not alter any of the implications of the integration plan nor of the Fortress Europe possibility. Nonetheless, there are still important implications for some of the other special considerations.

---

30. Of course the standard welfare-enhancing effects of trade are still expected, so overall U.S.-European trade is beneficial to both parties. For the figures see Dickens (1992, pp. 36–37).

Between 1984 and 1989, the share of agriculture in U.S. trade with the EC fell by 6.7 percentage points.[31] The shadow cost of $1.00 of agricultural exports is about $1.02. On the other hand, the shadow cost of import-competing motor vehicles is 95 cents per dollar, and the shadow cost of import-competing electronics is 93 cents per dollar. If the United States were to succeed in pressing for an increase in its agricultural exports to Europe, and European industrial targeting were successful in creating a balanced increase in U.S. imports in transportation equipment and electronics, the U.S. loss of labor rents would be perhaps 8 percent of the value of the increase in trade, or about $600 million.[32] This is an amount large enough that it might not be completely offset by terms of trade effects; such a change could even reduce U.S. welfare.

Conclusions

Careful consideration of the many possible routes by which the integrated European market might affect earnings and employment in the United States yield the conclusion that the aggregate effects are likely to be so small as not to be noticed. Changes of capital flows will induce interest rate changes that are unlikely to reduce returns to labor by more than 1 percent in the short run or increase them by more than 1 percent over the next decade. Terms of trade effects are of an indeterminate sign and are unlikely to change the real value of U.S. labor incomes by more than 1 percent. Similarly the high-end estimates of the effects on employment, displacement, and the distribution of income are all infinitesimal. Adding an analysis of labor rents does not change any of these conclusions.

It is possible that special considerations may affect the fortunes of particular industries. U.S. banking firms may stand to benefit from the integrated market though the effect on the U.S. work force will be insignificant. The effects on the U.S. electronics industry are indeterminate as issues concerning public procurement and the extension or creation of protective laws are considered.

The EC's obvious intention to pursue an aggressive industrial and strategic trade policy at a Community-wide level raises concerns for U.S. high-technology and other high-wage industries. The long-run effects of these ventures could be considerable, particularly in light of the labor-rents considerations.

31. OECD (1990, various pages).
32. Dickens (1992, pp. 36–37).

The one area where a potentially large effect is possible is the U.S. macroeconomic response to a major trade war with the EC. Such an event could result in a 2.5 percent plunge in U.S. aggregate demand. The U.S. fiscal problems and the inflation induced by the increased price of EC imports could make it politically difficult to implement demand-management solutions to such a problem. Estimates of the micro-economic effects of a trade war are small.

The probability of a major dispute with the EC is increased by U.S. insistence that the EC open its market for agricultural products. Given the analysis of the labor-rent flows that such a change would induce, it seems foolhardy for the United States to persist in pressing the EC on the issue. The EC agricultural policy is a blessing in disguise; the U.S. should concentrate its diplomatic resources on ensuring fair treatment for U.S. high-wage exports.

References

Baldwin, Richard E., and Paul Krugman. 1988. "Industrial Policy and International Competition in Wide-Bodied Jet Aircraft." In Richard E. Baldwin, ed., *Trade Policy, Issues and Empirical Analysis*, conference report. University of Chicago Press.

Bhagwati, Jagdish N., and T. N. Srinivasan. 1983. *Lectures on International Trade*. MIT Press.

Cecchini, Paolo. 1988. *The European Challenge 1992: The Benefits of a Single Market*. Aldershot, U.K.: Wildwood House.

Cline, William R. 1989. *United States External Adjustment and the World Economy*. Washington: Institute for International Economics.

Congressional Budget Office. 1990. *How the Economic Transformations in Europe Will Affect the United States*.

Data Resources Incorporated. 1989. "How to Prepare for the Single European Market." DRI executive briefing. Lexington, Mass.

Davis, Steven J., and John C. Haltiwanger. 1989. "Gross Job Creation, Gross Job Destruction and Employment Reallocation." Stanford: Hoover Institution. January.

DeClercq, Willy. 1988. "1992: The Impact on the Outside World," speech delivered at the Europaeisches Forum, August 1988. Quoted in Michael Calingaert, *The 1992 Challenge from Europe: Development of the European Community's Internal Market*. National Planning Association.

Dickens, William T. 1989. "Does It Matter What We Trade? Trade and Industrial Policy When Labor Markets Don't Clear." *Industrial Relations Research Association Series, Proceedings of the Forty-Second Annual Meeting*. Atlanta.

———. 1992. "Good Jobs: Increasing Worker Productivity with Trade and Industrial Policies." University of California at Berkeley, Department of Economics.

———. Forthcoming. *The US Labor Market Effects of European Economic Integration: Policy Considerations*. Washington: National Commission for Employment Policy.

Dickens, William T., and Kevin Lang. 1989. "Why It Matters What We Trade: A Case for Active Policy." In Laura D'Andrea Tyson, William T. Dickens, and John Zysman, eds., *The Dynamics of Trade and Employment*. Ballinger.

———. Forthcoming. "Labor Market Segmentation Theory: Reconsidering the Evidence." In William Darity, ed., *Labor Economics: Problems in Analysis*. Kluwer Academic.

Emerson, Michael, and others. 1988. *The Economics of 1992: The E.C. Commission's Assessment of the Economic Effects of Completing the Internal Market*. Oxford University Press.

Freeman, Richard B., and Lawrence F. Katz. 1990. "Will EC 1992 Help or Hurt US Workers?" In Jorge F. Perez-Lopez, Gregory K. Schoepfle, and John Yochelson, eds., *E.C. 1992: Implications for U.S. Workers.* Washington: Center for Strategic and International Studies.

Hufbauer, Gary C., ed. 1990. *Europe 1992: An American Perspective.* Brookings.

Katz, Lawrence F., and Kevin M. Murphy. 1992. "Changes in Relative Wages, 1963–1987: Supply and Demand Factors." *Quarterly Journal of Economics* 107 (February): 35–78.

Katz, Lawrence F., and Lawrence H. Summers. 1989. "Industry Rents: Evidence and Implications." *Brookings Papers on Economic Activity: Microeconomics*: 209–76.

Leonard, Jonathan S. 1987. "In the Wrong Place at the Wrong Time: The Extent of Structural and Frictional Unemployment." In Kevin Lang and Jonathan S. Leonard, eds., *Unemployment and the Structure of Labor Markets.* Basil Blackwell. 141–163.

Leonard, Jonathan S., and Marc A. Van Audenrode. 1991. "Corporatism Run Amok: Job Stability and Industrial Policy in Belgium and the United States." University of California at Berkeley, Department of Business Administration. March.

Murphy, Kevin M., and Finis Welch. 1992. "The Structure of Wages." *Quarterly Journal of Economics* 107 (February): 285–326.

Organization for Economic Cooperation and Development. 1990. *Foreign Trade by Commodities*, series C. Paris.

Topel, Robert H. 1989. "Comment." *Brookings Papers on Economic Activity: Microeconomics*: 283–88.

Yannopoulos, George N. 1988. *Customs Unions and Trade Conflicts: The Enlargement of the European Community.* London: Routledge.

CHAPTER ELEVEN

European Labor Markets: The Eastern Dimension

Jasminka Sohinger and Daniel Rubinfeld

THE END OF the cold war and the sweeping political and economic changes in central and eastern Europe have fundamentally changed the relationship of the European Community (EC) to its international neighbors.[1] One economic segment of the EC that has been sensitive to these events and is likely to remain so is the labor market.

The severe political and economic disturbances in the reforming central and eastern Europe countries are having immediate and profound effects on their domestic labor markets. These changes are likely to exert additional supply pressures on the European labor market, especially as the prospects of eventual enlargement of the European Community to include its eastern neighbors come closer to reality. The overall outlook for the EC need not be gloomy, however. It is possible that access to a new source of relatively well educated and highly skilled labor can lead to higher productivity and a higher GDP for EC member countries.

This chapter is organized as follows. The first section puts post-1989 east-west European integration into perspective. The next section begins the analysis of central and eastern European labor markets by concentrating on the effects of the economic reforms. The following section examines the consequences of changes in the labor markets in central and eastern Europe for EC labor markets.

East-West Integration

Europe has once again become a focus of intense economic and political reshuffling. Major developments in the region are characterized not only

1. The present analysis considers the formerly socialist economies of central and eastern Europe, exclusive of the former Soviet Union and its former republics.

by the formation of a new economic superpower, the European Community in western Europe, but also by profound economic reforms and increasing political instability in the eastern half of the continent.

The European Community cannot be indifferent to the intense economic and political turmoil in central and eastern Europe; not only are the regions economically interdependent, but political and security issues are also involved. Although the European Community itself is still undergoing consolidation (it would have been easier had the revolutions of 1989 happened after the integration of 1992), its main political challenge as regards the East is to take the lead in the construction of a greater democratic Europe. The EC and the United States have opportunities in and responsibilities for the liberalization of the central and eastern European countries. The EC in particular cannot isolate itself from the macroeconomic effects resulting from the changing trade patterns and industrial structure in central and eastern Europe.[2]

The EC must be concerned with two matters regarding the reforms of these economies. The first is to secure the irreversibility of the process of transformation into market-oriented economies and pluralistic democracies. The second is to sustain and nurture these reforms. As many observers have recognized, the transformation of central and eastern Europe cannot be accomplished painlessly. In fact, decreases in output and employment are occurring in higher proportions than expected. The sharply deteriorating living conditions have created considerable internal political pressures. These troubled economic conditions make it difficult to reach the necessary social consensus for successful reform. Perhaps the aspiration of the peoples of the central and eastern European countries to "return to Europe" is the ultimate force holding the reform process together.

Recently, the EC has entertained requests for accession from Austria, Sweden, Finland, and Switzerland. (It turned down Turkey in 1987, and the applications of Cyprus and Malta are still pending.) It seems clear that the next wave of enlargement, after accommodating the richer countries of the European Free Trade Association (EFTA), will be the accession of the successfully reformed central and eastern European economies. In fact, the EC has set up Association Agreements and has established the European Bank for Reconstruction and Development (EBRD) to foster the transfer of economic resources.

2. According to Portes (1991, p. 31) for example, the EC "cannot afford, politically or economically, to permit failure in the democratic transformation of Eastern Europe."

In 1991 Association agreements were reached with Hungary, Czechoslovakia, and Poland and in 1993 with Bulgaria and Romania. The purpose is to help the new democracies become stable and pluralistic, to assist with their transformation into market economies, and to increase their security. The goal is to prepare the associate member countries to become full EC members by meeting specific targets: achieving pluralistic democracy, meeting the standards of the European Convention on Human Rights, establishing functioning market economies, and acquiring the legislative and administrative capability to implement and enforce the rules and legislation of the European Community.

The Association Agreements are bilateral—they abolish tariffs on most manufactured goods produced and give the associate members full and immediate access to most of the EC markets. However, the sectors in which the central and eastern European countries have the greatest competitive advantage, such as agriculture, textiles, steel, and coal, will be granted full market access only gradually. Conversely, the three new associate members will open up their markets to EC manufactured goods in stages over a period of four to five years.

Besides granting the new associate members concessions on market access, the Association Agreements also deal with such issues as the movement of workers and capital and economic, financial, and cultural cooperation. The extent to which the laws of the associated countries approximate EC law is recognized as a major precondition for their integration into the Community. More generally, establishing a set of legal and market institutions is considered crucial for the actual transition to a market economy. Once established, such institutions would provide for a degree of assurance that these countries' market orientation will become permanent.

The EBRD became operational in April 1991 as a new international institution of the post–cold war period. Conceived not simply as just another international governmental organization that finances development projects, its *raison d'être* is to actively support and oversee the transformation of the central and eastern European and the former Soviet Union economies to market-based democratic societies. Consequently, most EBRD loans are subject to explicit political conditions.

The forty governments involved in setting up the EBRD realized that developments in central and eastern Europe were promising but potentially dangerous; this left the West with some responsibility for security and stability throughout Europe. At the same time the western countries also realized that the central and eastern European labor force is literate and skilled and that its industry is potentially competitive. Finally, it was understood that political changes could not be sustained if economic dislocations became permanent.

The main focus of EBRD activities is the private sector (only 40 percent of the bank's funds can be used to support the public sector). Thus "using a public sector organization ... to pursue private sector development while maintaining a high credit rating when lending to risky ventures is the key challenge for the EBRD in the 1990s."[3] An additional task carried out by the EBRD in coordination with the World Bank and the International Monetary Fund (IMF) is to provide assistance in establishing new financial institutions (pension funds, mutual funds, stock exchanges, and so forth). This assistance and advice is an essential part of the aid program because of the limited capacity of the recipient countries to absorb capital. Another concern of the bank is environmental protection and restoration. This is of major importance not only to the central and eastern European countries, but because of industrial restructuring and migration, to their neighbors as well.

Economic Reforms and the Labor Markets

The implementation of economic reforms in central and eastern Europe has left virtually no segment of these economies unchanged. The changes were abrupt and monumental because eastern Europe had no experience with western-style factor markets and only slight experience with product markets (in a context of administratively distorted relative prices). The overview of labor markets that follows is, unfortunately, somewhat scanty because accurate and reliable labor statistics in the central and eastern European countries do not exist.

In the central and eastern European economies the very existence of labor markets was formerly negated on ideological grounds. In the traditional Marxist perspective, labor is not a commodity. Consequently it cannot be exchanged on the market. Everyone is free to work and has a right to do so. Firms (mostly large state-owned enterprises) cannot lay off workers except in disciplinary cases; as a result, there can be no official unemployment.

In practice, of course, there was considerable labor hoarding and hid-

3. Rollo (1991, p. 2).

den unemployment in state-owned enterprises. Before the introduction of economic reforms in Poland, labor hoarding was estimated at a minimum of 20 percent of total employment and possibly as much as one-third.[4] Most workers in central and eastern European countries were employed in the state sector, a typical characteristic of a command economy. In Poland at the end of 1989, for example, 63 percent of the workforce was employed in the state sector.[5]

Another distinctive feature of the labor markets before reforms was the relatively high participation rates of women. Figure 11-1 compares labor force participation rates by gender in central and eastern European countries in the late 1980s to those in selected OECD countries in 1988. The high female labor force participation rates typical of most of the central and eastern European countries were approached only by Sweden and to a lesser extent, the United Kingdom.[6] Particularly striking is Albania, where female labor participation rates actually surpassed male rates.[7]

By contrast, female and male average earnings in the late 1980s and early 1990s show no distinctive pattern. Although relative female earnings (as a percentage of male earnings) were higher on average in the EC, there were exceptions to the rule (figure 11-2). In fact, the highest relative female earnings were in the former Yugoslavia, and the lowest in the United Kingdom.

With respect to wage-setting in the centrally planned economies in general, rates were administratively regulated and were not determined in relation to the productivity levels. Wage differentials were relatively narrow, and the costs of labor were very low. Despite experiments with workers' participation in firms' management in the former Yugoslavia, Hungary, and Poland, no effective incentive scheme existed that actually prompted the workers to strive for higher productivity. The rigidities of the labor markets in the socialist economies resulted in tremendous inefficiencies because there was little worker incentive. A primary problem was the absence of a mechanism to close unprofitable firms or to encourage workers to move from relatively unprofitable firms to more profitable ones.[8]

4. Gora (1991, p. 151).
5. Gora (1991, p. 154).
6. Norway and Finland had rates that were similar to Sweden.
7. This is also true of Bulgaria, not shown here.
8. According to Vodopivec (1990), the system led to inefficient labor allocation, suppressed work incentives, and inherent wage drift. At the root of this syndrome was the lack of appropriate mechanisms to enforce the exit of firms or workers, resulting in massive employment subsidization.

Figure 11-1. *Labor Force Participation Rates in Europe, by Gender, Late 1980s*

Percent

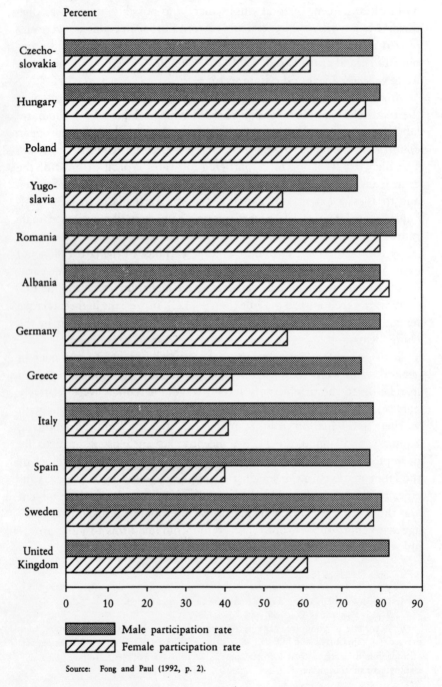

Source: Fong and Paul (1992, p. 2).

Figure 11-2. *Relative Female Average Earnings, Selected European Countries, Late 1980s*

Percent

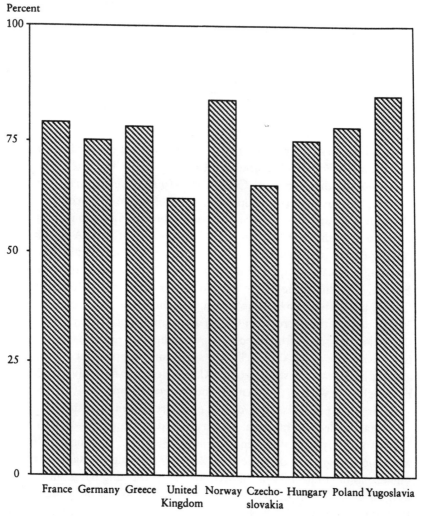

Source: Fong and Paul (1992, figure 1).

Labor market developments in central and eastern Europe have been influenced not only by the evolution of product and factor markets but by changes in macroeconomic policy. In fact, economic reforms started with macroeconomic stabilization measures, a prominent part of which was the anti-inflation program that produced significant labor market effects. In part because of this program and in part because of three other

Table 11-1. *Annual Percentage Change in GDP, Selected Eastern European Countries, 1989–91*

Country	1989–90	1990–91
Bulgaria	−13.6	−15.0
Czechoslovakia	−1.0	−16.0
Hungary	−4.0	−8.0
Poland	−11.6	−8.0
Romania	−7.9	−13.7

Sources: PlanEcon, Inc., *PlanEcon Report*, vol. 7 (October 10, 1991), p. 2; vol. 7 (November 8, 1991), p. 2; vol. 7 (December 30, 1991), p. 2; vol. 8 (February 28, 1992), p. 3; vol. 8 (November 13, 1992), p. 2.

external factors, all the reforming economies experienced severe decreases in GDP and substantial decreases in wages. The three other factors were the dissolution of CMEA (the Council for Mutual Economic Assistance—the eastern European bloc); the rise in oil prices following the Gulf War; and the changed position of the East German market after unification with West Germany. The dissolution of CMEA meant that trading had to occur with hard currency at world prices; it also led to an oil supply shock after the USSR stopped subsidized sales of oil to eastern Europe. The diminished supplies and higher prices of oil following the Gulf War affected eastern Europe's highly energy-intensive industry and contributed to the decrease in GDP. East Germany, for its part, had been the major exporter of high-technology engineering products and chemicals within the CMEA as well as a significant importer of central and eastern European consumer goods. Unification substantially reduced its high-technology exports to central and eastern Europe.

Table 11-1 provides some details of the recession in eastern Europe. The smallest decline in output was registered in Hungary—8 percent in 1990–91, following a 4 percent decline in 1989–90. (By contrast, the EC was enjoying growth of more than 2 percent during the same period.) The economic indicators in the second year of the "big bang" in Poland showed a decline in output of 8 to 10 percent following a decline of almost 12 percent in 1989–90. In Bulgaria the official figures reported a 15 percent drop in GDP in 1990–91, and in Czechoslovakia the decline accelerated from 1 percent in 1989–90 to 16 percent in 1990–91. The Romanian GDP decrease of 7.9 percent in 1990–91 intensified in 1991 to 13.7 percent. It is projected to decline another 15 percent in 1992.

In spite of the limited reliability of the data compiled for the central and eastern European economies there is ample evidence of large reductions in output. With the reductions these economies began to experience open unemployment, although some suggest that "unemployment did

Table 11-2. *Unemployment Rates in Four Eastern European Countries, by Month, 1990*

Percent

Month	Poland	Czechoslovakia	Hungary	Bulgaria
January	0.30	n.a.	0.60	n.a.
February	0.80	n.a.	n.a.	n.a.
March	1.50	0.07	n.a.	n.a.
April	1.90	0.08	n.a.	n.a.
May	2.40	0.10	n.a.	n.a.
June	3.10	0.14	n.a.	n.a.
July	3.80	0.21	n.a.	0.80
August	4.50	0.30	n.a.	0.80
September	5.00	0.42	n.a.	1.00
October	5.50	0.63	n.a.	1.20
November	5.90	0.74	1.70	1.50
December	6.10	0.85	n.a.	1.60

Sources: Gora (1991, p.157); Hars, Kovari, and Nagy (1991, p.169); Kapl, Sojka, and Tepper (1991, p. 203); Jones (1991, p. 217).
n.a. Not available.

not rise to anything like the levels that would surely have accompanied comparable falls in output in the West."[9] The unemployment rates for the same countries (with the exception of Romania for which no data were available) are shown in table 11-2.

Unemployment rose even more sharply after 1990. Poland's rate reached 10.4 percent in 1991 and more than 12 percent in 1992. In Czechoslovakia it rose from less than 1 percent in 1990 to 7.5 percent by the end of 1991. In Hungary the rate reached 10 percent in 1991. The rate of unemployment in Bulgaria was 8 percent in 1991.[10]

Although the absolute rates of unemployment do not seem very high by U.S. standards, they remain quite worrisome from a social perspective, especially because of continuing labor hoarding and hidden unemployment. Of primary concern is the lack of an adequate safety net or policy for adequately training workers. Labor compensation schemes, unemployment insurance, retraining programs, and so forth are only at the experimental stages, as are other macroeconomic policies that might ameliorate substantial unemployment.

Most of the restructuring and privatization efforts that followed macroeconomic stabilization were aimed at eliminating the inefficiencies in the vastly overgrown state-owned industries. The labor market effects of this economic restructuring have been serious; massive layoffs gener-

9. Standing and Sziracki (1991, p. 138).
10. *PlanEcon Reports* (1992).

ally occurred soon after the introduction of the reforms. Changes in the mix of jobs by skill level and by occupational sector are evident (due in part to new types of firms operating in the market).[11] The resulting high levels of structural unemployment are aggravated by the lack of labor market institutions to facilitate the quick transfer of workers from one employer to another.

The necessity for rapid adjustment poses several major problems related to the search for a feasible regulatory framework in health, workplace safety, and equal opportunity; an institutional structure to provide a social safety net; and a workable mode of wage determination. In all three the influence of the European Community's practices will be very significant. Thus, the Association Agreements provide a model regulatory framework for the central and eastern European countries. Regarding wage determination, the eastern European countries are also likely to emulate the EC model. Because wage rates are relatively low and not determined by the market, aggregate wages will have to increase as a share of all other sources of remuneration, and wage rates will have to be linked more closely to productivity. Wage differentials between sectors and skill levels can be expected to increase when these changes are made. This in turn raises the possibility that new gaps in income distribution will produce new social conflicts.

Specific problems emerge in connection with the institutional structure of labor markets. Labor market institutions and policies in western Europe developed over many years and are better suited to deal with such problems as frictional or cyclical unemployment, which occur in a near full-employment economy. In the central and eastern European countries the adjustments must, of necessity, be rapid. These adjustments are made especially difficult politically because of the possibility of ethnic segmentation if unemployment levels rise unevenly among different nationalities. Finally, the regional imbalances caused by the dismantling of heavy industry and the resulting massive layoffs create additional problems because they are often linked to increased ethnic and social tensions.[12] For example, the closings of obsolete factories in Czechoslovakia where the majority of workers happen to be Slovak is very likely to increase Slovak

11. For example, in Poland between 1980 and 1990, employment growth increased by 50.5 percent in health care and social welfare, by 15.4 percent in finance and insurance, and by 14.2 percent in public administration and justice. However, employment growth decreased by 12.1 percent in manufacturing and mining, by 18.3 percent in forestry, and by 20.6 percent in transport. See Gora (1991, table 1).

12. See Standing and Sziracki (1991).

antagonism toward the Czechs, and this will be amplified by social tensions that always accompany such measures.

One of the most important results of economic restructuring and privatization is the increasing number of small and medium-sized firms (at the expense of huge obsolete conglomerates). In addition, the number of workers in the private sector is increasing relative to those employed in the public sector, although the sharp decline in employment in the public sector so far has outweighed the growth of employment in the private sector.[13] This phenomenon is sometimes referred to as the sliding privatization of employment.

The most immediate consequence of both of these phenomena is the decrease in the overall rate of unionization. Under the old system, trade unions were organized at the national level and organized functionally as an extended form of Communist party rule. With the reforms, the role of trade unions is undergoing significant change, although it is not yet clear whether national general unions will be preserved in some form or whether the tendency toward industrial and crafts unions or company unions will prevail.

The number of trade unions that are independent of political parties is growing. This development has spawned pluralism—and conflict— among the rival union confederations.[14] On the national level, the trend in industrial relations seems to point toward collective bargaining as a new form of cooperative conflict management.

There has been a clear need in central and eastern Europe for a new model of industrial democracy and an institutional structure for settling industrial disputes. New tripartite structures involving government, employers, and trade unions representing employees have emerged in response. For example, in Bulgaria the National Council for the Coordination of Interests was established in 1990 as an independent agent of social change. These new institutions, which are actively involving unions in broader policymaking, are influenced by the European model, and there are strong tendencies to approximate it in the long run.

Successful reform of central and eastern European labor markets will mean increased labor mobility. Before reform, labor mobility was limited, in part because of the employment policies of state-owned enterprises and the shortage of capital and the regional concentrations of required infrastructure relating to housing, health care, education, and

13. Standing and Sziracki (1991, p. 142).
14. For the example of Bulgaria, see Jones (1991, p. 225).

Table 11-3. *Economic Growth, Employment Growth, and Unemployment Rates in the EC, 1985–89*

Percent

Indicator	1985	1986	1987	1988	1989
GDP growth	2.5	2.6	2.9	3.4	2.8
Employment growth	0.6	0.8	0.9	1.1	0.9
Unemployment rate	11.8	11.9	11.6	11.3	11.0

Source: Belous, Hartley, and McClenahan (1992, p. 118).

training. Voluntary labor mobility, a prerequisite of large-scale labor relocation, requires government policies for social protection and an adequate social safety net.

It is clear that the patterns of labor mobility within central and eastern European countries will involve movement from obsolete state enterprises to newer small and medium-sized private firms. Internationally, however, given the economic and political difficulties at home, these patterns will also entail increasing migratory pressures on the EC labor market.

Can Fortress Europe Isolate Itself?

Although economic activity has been on the rise in the EC, unemployment has not ceased to be a problem. Thus, as table 11-3 shows, GDP growth ranged from 2.5 to 3.4 percent in the latter half of the 1980s, while unemployment rates never fell below 11 percent. Not only are unemployment rates higher than the norm in the EC, there has been a comparatively low rate of employment growth.

It is worth noting that throughout the 1980s, EC labor force participation rates have been relatively low in comparison to both the United States and most of the central and eastern European countries. For example, the labor force participation rate was 65.8 percent in France, 54.7 percent in Spain, 67.2 percent in Germany, and 72.0 percent in the United Kingdom. By comparison, the comparable rate was 76 percent in the United States and Japan, 78.9 percent in Czechoslovakia, 78 percent in Poland, and 79.6 percent in Romania.[15]

Both the regional component and the gender characteristics of the European labor markets are very pronounced (table 11-4). The unemploy-

15. For the United States and Japan, see Belous, Hartley, and McClenahan (1992, p. 117). For the EC and central and eastern European countries, see Gelb and Grey (1991, p. 5).

Table 11-4. *Unemployment Rates and Female Employment Rates in the EC, by Country, Second Quarter, 1988*

Country	Unemployment rate as percentage of labor force	Female employment rate
Belgium	12.3	51.3
West Germany	8.1	51.8
Spain	20.5	37.5
France	10.8	55.8
Ireland	19.2	51.8
Italy	14.0	43.2
Netherlands	11.5	41.1
United Kingdom	10.6	62.0

Source: Belous, Hartley, and McClenahan (1992, p. 118).

ment rate varied from 8.1 percent in West Germany to 20.5 percent in Spain. The female employment rate also showed considerable regional differences. In Spain only one-third of the female population was employed; in West Germany 62 percent were. Comparing these figures with central and eastern Europe, where female labor participation has traditionally been high, it is reasonable to assume that any significant labor market interaction between the two would lead to increased female participation in the west European labor market as well.

Recent research has shown that the elimination of legal barriers to migration among EC countries has yet to produce substantial migratory flows.[16] In fact, the principal pattern of migration has always been from nonmember states to the more affluent EC countries. In fact, it has been estimated that by mid-1992 there were 8 million foreign nationals in the EC member states, 3.5 million of whom were in the labor force, a figure not including illegal immigrants or those seeking political asylum.[17] However, the most significant impact for European labor markets is yet to come, to arise either as the EC is enlarged or if serious, prolonged political and economic trouble persists in the central and eastern European countries.

The most urgent problems for the European labor market started with the fall of the Berlin Wall in 1989 and the economic crisis and transition in central and eastern Europe. The EC's failure to respond adequately and quickly to its first serious foreign policy challenge—in the former Yugoslavia—has greatly aggravated the preexisting problem of a con-

16. Molle and van Mourik (1988); Straubhaar (1988).
17. "Standing Committee on Employment Discusses Migrant Workers," *European Industrial Relations Review,* 221 (June 1992), p. 3.

siderable influx of migrants from central and eastern Europe across its borders. The political instability within the former Yugoslavia escalated into outright war, creating the worst European refugee crisis since World War II.

Given the geographical proximity as well as the historical and cultural ties with all the central and eastern European countries, such shocks are bound to have considerable effects throughout Europe, in particular on the European labor markets. The United Nations High Commission for Refugees has estimated that in July 1992 there were more than 2 million persons displaced because of the fighting in Croatia and Bosnia-Herzegovina. Most had stayed in Croatia, but 425,000 refugees (with the number still increasing) had crossed the borders into western Europe.

Some European countries have shown greater concern for the refugees. Germany has accepted more than 200,000, Austria and Hungary have taken in more than 50,000 each, Sweden nearly 45,000, and Switzerland about 17,500. Public pressure has moved the Luxembourg government to express its willingness to accept more refugees, and Denmark is ready to accept 1,000 more in addition to the 1,600 already there. However, according to the UN commission's list of July 29, 1992, France and Britain had accepted fewer than 1,200 refugees each, Belgium and Finland fewer than 1,000, Spain only 120, and Greece only 7.[18] Substantial burdens have continued to befall Croatia, which is coping with a large and still increasing number of refugees from Bosnia, despite its having suffered widespread destruction during the war on its territory.

With no stable political settlement in sight and with no homes to return to, many temporary political refugees will seek asylum and try to find jobs. Experience has shown that not all rejected asylum-seekers leave western Europe, even if they are not granted asylum. Some are officially tolerated for humanitarian reasons. Between 1983 and 1990, out of the 1.6 million asylum-seekers registered in western Europe, 640,000, or 40 percent, fell into this combined category of recognized or tolerated refugees.[19]

These statistics (as well as the data on unemployment rates and the slow growth of employment in the EC) suggest that the costs of the false belief in a Fortress Europe are likely to be very high. The all-permeating labor markets on the continent of Europe, which are very sensitive and are the first to register major shocks in an economy, will act as a conduc-

18. Kinzer (1992, p. A4).
19. Bohning (1991, p. 447).

tor transmitting shocks from one area into another. The awareness of such delicate interdependence places even greater responsibility on future policymaking in the EC.

Conclusion

The implementation of economic reforms in central and eastern Europe led initially to declines in real GDP and rapid increases in unemployment. Fortunately, labor market restructuring and privatization efforts aimed at eliminating inefficiencies and encouraging growth are well under way. A number of needs must be met if these adjustments are to be successful. Foremost among them are coherent health and workplace safety regulations, a regulatory structure that guarantees equal opportunity, and an institutional structure that offers a social safety net.

The reforms in central and eastern Europe pose important questions for the European Community. The EC has, to this point, failed to respond to the challenge resulting from the refugee problem created by the war in the former Yugoslavia. It is essential that the EC develop a coherent plan to deal with this and related labor migration issues in the future. There are risks for the EC if the additional labor supply exerts downward pressure on an unsteady economy, but there is a prospect of benefits as well given the numbers of relatively well educated and highly skilled workers in the labor pools of the central and eastern European countries.

References

Belous, Richard S., Rebecca S. Hartley, and Kelly L. McClenahan, eds. 1992. *European and American Labor Markets: Different Models and Different Results*. Washington: National Planning Association.

Bohning, W. R. 1991. "Integration and Immigration in Western Europe." *International Labour Review* 130 (4): 447.

Fong, Monica, and Gillian Paul. 1992. "Women's Employment in Central and Eastern Europe: The Gender Factor." *Transition: The Newsletter about Reforming Economies* 3 (June): 1–3.

Gelb, Alan H., and Cheryl W. Grey. 1991. *The Transformation of Economies in Central and Eastern Europe: Issues, Progress, and Prospects*. Washington:World Bank, 1991.

Gora, Marek. 1991. "Shock Therapy for the Polish Economy." *International Labour Review* 138 (2): 145–163.

Hars, Anes, Gyorgy Kovari, and Guyla Nagy. 1991. "Hungary Faces Unemployment." *International Labour Review* 130 (2): 169.

Jones, Derek C. 1991. "The Bulgarian Labour Market in Transition." *International Labour Review* 130 (2): 217.

Kapl, Martin, Milan Sojka, and Tomas Tepper. 1991. "Unemployment and Market-Oriented Reform in Czechoslovakia." *International Labour Review* 130 (2): 199–210.

Kinzer, Stephen. 1992. "Germany Chides Europe about Balkan Refugees." *New York Times* (July 29): A4.

Molle, Willem, and Aad van Mourik. 1988. "International Movements of Labor under Conditions of Economic Integration: The Case of Western Europe." *Journal of Common Market Studies* 26 (March).

Portes, Richard. 1991. "The European Community and Eastern Europe after 1992." In Tommaso Padoa-Scioppa, ed., *Europe 1992: Three Essays*, Essays in International Finance 182 (May): 31–43.

Rollo, J. M. C. 1991. "Preface." In Paul A. Menkveld, *Origin and Role of the European Bank for Reconstruction and Development*. London: Graham and Trotman.

Standing, Guy, and G. Sziracki. 1991. "Labour Market Issues in Eastern Europe's Transition." *International Labour Review* 130 (2): 137–44.

Straubhaar, Thomas. 1988. "International Labor Migration within a Common Market: Some Aspects of EC Experience." *Journal of Common Market Studies* 27 (September).

Vodopivec, Milan. 1990. "The Labor Market and the Transition of Socialist Economies," working paper 561. World Bank.

Index